THE MERCHANT OF VENICE

The RSC Shakespeare

Edited by Jonathan Bate and Eric Rasmussen

Chief Associate Editors: Héloïse Sénéchal and Jan Sewell

Associate Editors: Trey Jansen, Eleanor Lowe, Lucy Munro,
Dee Anna Phares

The Merchant of Venice

Textual editing: Eric Rasmussen

Introduction and Shakespeare's Career in the Theater: Jonathan Bate

Commentary: Eleanor Lowe and Héloïse Sénéchal

Scene-by-Scene Analysis: Esme Miskimmin

In Performance: Karin Brown (RSC stagings), Peter Kirwan (overview)

The Director's Cut and Playing Shylock (interviews by Jonathan Bate
and Kevin Wright):
David Thacker, Darko Tresnjak; Antony Sher, Henry Goodman

The RSC Shakespeare

William Shakespeare

THE MERCHANT OF VENICE

Edited by Jonathan Bate and Eric Rasmussen

Introduction by Jonathan Bate

The Modern Library
New York

CONTENTS

CONTENTS

INTRODUCTION

"WHICH IS THE MERCHANT HERE?"

In the summer of 1598, Shakespeare's acting company, the Lord Chamberlain's Men, registered their right to allow or disallow the printing of "a book of the Merchant of Venice or otherwise called the Jew of Venice." They seem to have been a little bit uncertain as to what they should call their new play. Or perhaps they were anxious to forestall any unauthorized publisher from producing a volume called "The Jew of Venice" and passing it off as their play. Christopher Marlowe's comi-tragic farce *The Jew of Malta* had been one of the biggest box-office hits of the age, so an echo of its title would have been an attractive proposition.

Fourteen comedies were collected by Shakespeare's fellow actors in the First Folio of his complete plays, published after his death. The majority of them had titles evocative of an idea (*All's Well That Ends Well*, *Love's Labour's Lost*, *Much Ado About Nothing*) or a time of year (*Twelfth Night*, *A Midsummer Night's Dream*, *The Winter's Tale*). Two of them indicate a group of characters in a particular place: gentlemen of Verona in one case, merry wives of Windsor in the other. One suggests a character type: *The Taming of the Shrew*. In the light of these patterns, it would have been reasonable to name the comedy registered in 1598 after an idea—Bassanio's successful quest for Portia is a case of "Love's Labour's Won," Portia's judgment on Shylock metes out "Measure for Measure." It would also have been reasonable to indicate a group of characters in a particular place: "The Merchants of Venice" (Bassanio, Lorenzo, Gratiano, Salerio, and Solanio are all merchants of one kind or another). Or it would have been possible to suggest a character type: "The Taming of the Jew."

In 1600 the play was published with a title page intended to whet the prospective reader's appetite: *The most excellent History of the Merchant of Venice. With the extreme cruelty of Shylock the Jew towards the said Merchant, in cutting a just pound of his flesh, and the obtaining of*

Portia by the choice of three chests. The character of Shylock and the courtship of Portia by Bassanio were clearly considered to be the play's principal selling points, and yet it is "the merchant," Antonio, who gets the top line of the title to himself, a unique distinction in the Folio corpus of Shakespearean comedy (his only rival in this regard is "the shrew" in her play, but "the taming" implicitly gives equal weight to her antagonist, the tamer). Given that Antonio has this unique distinction, one would have expected him to be the central focus of the action. Yet in no other Shakespearean play does the titular character have such a small role: Portia's is much the largest part, followed by Shylock and then Bassanio. Antonio is no more prominent in the dialogue than his friends Gratiano and Lorenzo. Ask a class of students "Who *is* the merchant of Venice?" and they will hesitate a moment—as they will not when asked who is the Prince of Denmark or the Moor of Venice.

The part almost seems to be deliberately underwritten. "In sooth I know not why I am so sad," says Antonio in the very first line of the play. His friends suggest some possible reasons: he is worried about his merchandise, or perhaps he is in love. Antonio denies both, proposing instead that to play the melancholy man is simply his given role in the theater of the world. Intriguingly, Shakespeare gives the name "Antonio" to discontented characters in two other plays. One is Sebastian's nautical companion in *Twelfth Night*, who keeps company with his friend day and night, even risks his own life for him, only to be ignored when Sebastian finds the love of a good woman. The other is Prospero's usurping brother in *The Tempest*, who has no wife or child of his own and who is again marginalized at the end of the play.

Some productions have explored the sense of exclusion associated with the Antonio figures by suggesting that they are made melancholy by unrequited homoerotic desire. Probably the first critic to identify this possibility as a hidden key to *The Merchant of Venice* was the (homosexual) poet W. H. Auden. In a dazzling essay called "Brothers and Others" (included in his volume of criticism *The Dyer's Hand*, 1962), Auden deftly identified Antonio as "a man whose emotional life, though his conduct may be chaste, is concentrated upon a member of his own sex." Auden wondered if Antonio's feelings for Bassanio were somewhat akin to those suggested by the closing couplet of Shakespeare's twentieth sonnet, addressed to a beautiful young man: "But since she [Nature] pricked thee out for women's pleasure, / Mine be thy love, and my love's use their treasure." The idea that the love of man for man may have an unrivaled spiritual intensity, whereas the congress of man and woman is bound up with breeding and property, has a long history.

It is Antonio rather than Bassanio, Auden suggests, who embodies the words on Portia's leaden casket: "'Who chooseth me must give and hazard all he hath.'" Antonio is prepared to give and hazard his own flesh as bond in the deal with Shylock that will provide Bassanio with the financial capital he needs in order to speculate on the marriage market. In Auden's view, this creates a strange correspondence between the merchant and the Jew: "Shylock, however unintentionally, did, in fact, hazard all for the sake of destroying the enemy he hated; and Antonio, however unthinkingly he signed the bond, hazarded all to secure the happiness of the man he loved." By setting Antonio's life as a forfeit, Antonio and Shylock enter into a bond that places them outside the normative rule of law that regulates society. Auden speculatively notes the "association of sodomy with usury" that can be traced back to Dante's *Inferno*.

Whether or not it is appropriate to invoke the idea of sexual transgression, Shakespeare often returned to a triangular structure of relationships in which close male friendship is placed at odds with desire for a woman. The pattern recurs not only in several of the plays but also as the implied narrative of the Sonnets. *The Merchant of Venice* begins with Bassanio seeking to borrow from his friend in order to finance the pursuit of a wealthy lover. He sets himself up as a figure from classical mythology: Jason in pursuit of the Golden Fleece. The analogy establishes Gratiano and Lorenzo as fellow Argonauts. Jason was renowned for being clever and brave, but also selfish and materialistic. His pattern of behavior was to gain the assistance of a woman—Ariadne, Medea—in realizing his ambitions, to become her lover and then to desert her and move on to a new adventure. With Jason as his role model, Bassanio has the potential to join the company of those other lovers in Shakespearean comedy—Claudio in *Much Ado About Nothing*, Bertram in *All's Well That Ends Well*—who are not worthy of the women they obtain.

To make such comparisons is to see that *The Merchant of Venice* is one of Shakespeare's darker comedies. The blurring of perspectives between the romantic and the sinister is especially apparent in the beautiful but ironic love-duet of Lorenzo and Jessica at the beginning of the final act. They compare themselves to some oft-sung partners from the world of classical mythology. But what kind of exemplary figures are these? Cressida, who was unfaithful to Troilus; Medea the poisoner; Thisbe, whose tragical fate, though comically represented in the Mechanicals' play in *A Midsummer Night's Dream*, was identical to Juliet's; and Dido, whom Aeneas deserted in his quest for imperial glory. They are all figures in the pantheon of tragedy, not comedy.

The cleverness that Bassanio shares with the mythological figure of Jason is apparent from his choice of casket. Portia's late father has devised a simple test to find her the right husband: those suitors who choose the golden or silver caskets are clearly motivated by desire for wealth and must therefore want to marry her for her money. The man who chooses lead obviously does not care about cash, so he is likely to love Portia for herself alone. Bassanio, however, recognizes that appearances are not to be trusted. Venice, sixteenth-century Europe's preeminent city of commercial exchange and conspicuous consumption, has taught him that credit allows a man to display himself above his means. He does not want to look like a fortune hunter when wooing Portia, so he borrows from Antonio in order to dress like a wealthy man: "By something showing a more swelling port / Than my faint means would grant continuance." He chooses the lead casket because he knows from his own example that "outward shows" may be least themselves and that the world is easily deceived "with ornament." Gold, he reasons, is for greedy Midas, so he spurns it—this is what he imagines Portia wants to hear. He is, of course, assisted by the hint she drops for his benefit; whereas Morocco and Aragon had to make their choice in silence, Bassanio's is heralded by a song that warns against trusting what appears to "the eyes." And yet the fact remains that Bassanio is driven by the quest for a wealthy spouse. Antonio is the one who really cares about love more than money, about the "bond" of friendship more than the legal and financial bond, about what is "dear" to his heart more than what is "dear" in the sense of expensive. For Shakespeare's audience, the words "merchant" and "Venice" were both synonymous with the pursuit of money, but paradoxically, Antonio is, of all the characters in the play, the one who is least bound to material possessions.

"IN BELMONT IS A LADY RICHLY LEFT"

Shortly after the Second World War, the Canadian literary critic Northrop Frye published a short essay that inaugurated the modern understanding that Shakespeare's comedies, for all their lightness and play, are serious works of art, every bit as worthy of close attention as his tragedies. Entitled "The Argument of Comedy," it proposed that the essential structure of Shakespearean comedy was ultimately derived from the "new comedy" of ancient Greece, which was mediated to the Renaissance via its Roman exponents Plautus and Terence. The "new comedy" pattern, described by Frye as "a comic Oedipus situation," turned on "the successful effort of a young man to outwit an opponent and possess the girl of his choice." The girl's father, or some other authority figure of the older generation, resists the match, but is outflanked, often thanks to an ingenious scheme devised by a clever servant, perhaps involving disguise or flight (or both). Frye, writing during Hollywood's golden age, saw an unbroken line from the classics to Shakespeare to modern romantic comedy: "The average movie of today is a rigidly conventionalized New Comedy proceeding toward an act which, like death in Greek tragedy, takes place offstage, and is symbolized by the final embrace."

The union of the lovers brings "a renewed sense of social integration," expressed by some kind of festival at the climax of the play—a marriage, a dance, or a feast. All right-thinking people come over to the side of the lovers, but there are others "who are in some kind of mental bondage, who are helplessly driven by ruling passions, neurotic compulsions, social rituals, and selfishness." Malvolio in *Twelfth Night*, Don John in *Much Ado About Nothing*, Jaques in *As You Like It*, Shylock in *The Merchant of Venice*: Shakespearean comedy frequently includes a party pooper, a figure who refuses to be assimilated into the harmony.

Frye's "The Argument of Comedy" pinpoints a pervasive structure: "the action of the comedy begins in a world represented as a normal world, moves into the green world, goes into a metamorphosis there in which the comic resolution is achieved, and returns to the normal world." But for Shakespeare, the green world, the forest and its fairies, is no less real than the court. Frye, again, sums it up brilliantly:

> This world of fairies, dreams, disembodied souls, and pastoral lovers may not be a "real" world, but, if not, there is something equally illusory in the stumbling and blinded follies of the "normal" world, of Theseus' Athens with its idiotic marriage law, of Duke Frederick and his melancholy tyranny [in *As You Like It*], of Leontes and his mad jealousy [in *The Winter's Tale*], of the Court Party with their plots and intrigues. The famous speech of Prospero about the dream nature of reality applies equally to Milan and the enchanted island. We spend our lives partly in a waking world we call normal and partly in a dream world which we create out of our own desires. Shakespeare endows both worlds with equal imaginative power, brings them opposite one another, and makes each world seem unreal when seen by the light of the other.*

The Merchant of Venice offers an exceptionally interesting set of variations on this pattern. The "new comedy" pattern of the lover getting his girl against the will of her father is there in the Lorenzo and Jessica plot. There is a (not so clever) servant in the form of Lancelet Gobbo. And there is a striking structural movement between two worlds. However, instead of the usual court or paternal household, the normative world, represented by Venice, is that of money and commercial exchange. Portia's rural estate in "Belmont," which means "beautiful mountain," stands in for the "green" world of wood or forest or pastoral community. Productions often portray it as an Arcadian realm of ease, integrity, and self-discovery that stands in contrast to the hard-nosed commerce of the duplicitous city. But

---

* "The Argument of Comedy" originally appeared in *English Institute Essays 1948*, ed. D. A. Robertson (1949), and has often been reprinted in critical anthologies. Frye himself adapted it for inclusion in his classic study, *Anatomy of Criticism* (1957).

although Belmont has an aura of magic and of music, it is not really a dream world.

Portia has been attracted to Bassanio for some time: he has previously visited Belmont in the guise of "a scholar and a soldier" in the retinue of another suitor. But it is when he reasons against gold that love takes her over, banishing all other emotions. She responds with a beautifully articulated self-revelation: ignore my riches, virtues, beauty, status, she says: "the full sum of me / Is sum of nothing, which to term in gross / Is an unlessoned girl, unschooled, unpractisèd." Yet even in rejecting the notion that people should be measured by the size of their bank balances, she cannot avoid using the language of money that suffuses the whole play ("sum," "gross"). The lesson of Belmont is actually a cynical one: choose wealth and you won't get it, appear to reject it and it will be yours. The Prince of Morocco, who takes things at face value, is roundly rejected. It will not be the last time that Shakespeare pits an honest Moor against a world of Italian intrigue.

For all their fine words, both Bassanio and Portia are engaged in "practice," a word that the Elizabethans associated with the figure of Machiavelli, archetypal Italianate schemer for self-advancement. Bassanio *is* the gold-digger he pretends not to be, while Portia has no intention of letting any man become "her lord, her governor, her king" in the way that she says she will. At the end of her submission speech, she gives Bassanio the ring (symbol of both wealth and marital union) that will later be the device whereby she tricks him and thus establishes her position as the dominant partner in the relationship. She may speak about giving him all her property—which is what marriage meant according to the law of the time—but when she returns from Venice to Belmont at the end of the play she continues to speak of "*my* house" and the light "burning in *my* hall."

As for Portia's claim that she is "unlessoned" and "unschooled," this is wholly belied by her bravura performance in the cross-dressed role of Balthasar, interpreting the laws of Venice with forensic skill that reduces the duke and his magnificoes to amazement. On leaving Belmont, she says that she and Nerissa will remain in a nunnery, the ultimate place of female confinement, until Bassanio's financial difficulties are resolved. She actually goes to the public arena of the

Venetian court, moving from passive (the woman wooed) to active (the problem solver). In the robes of a lawyer instead of those of a nun, she excels in the art of debate, deploying a rhetorical art calculated to delight Queen Elizabeth, who loved nothing more than to outmaneuver courtiers, diplomats, and suitors in the finer points of jurisprudence and theology.

"The quality of mercy is not strained": the quality of Portia's argument (and Shakespeare's writing) unfolds from the several meanings of "strained." Mercy is not constrained or forced, it must be freely given; nor is it partial or selective—it is a pure distillation like "the gentle rain from heaven," not the kind of liquid from which impure particles can be strained out. As in *Measure for Measure*, Shakespeare explores the tension between justice and mercy, here interpreted in terms of the opposition between the Old Testament Jewish law of "an eye for an eye" and Christ's New Testament covenant of forgiveness. When Shylock refuses to show mercy and stands by the old covenant, Portia's art is to throw his legal literalism back in his face: the corollary of his demand for an exact pound of flesh is that he should not spill a drop of Venetian blood. But if the quality of mercy is not strained, then neither should be that of conversion: a bitter taste is left when Shylock is constrained to become a Christian.

". . . AND WHICH THE JEW?"

Commerce, with which Venice was synonymous, depends on borrowing to raise capital. Christianity, however, disapproved of usury, the lending of money with interest. The Jewish moneylender was early modern Europe's way out of this impasse. Venice was famous for its ghetto in which the Jews were constrained to live, even as they oiled the wheels of the city's economy. Shakespeare does not mention the ghetto, but he reveals a clear understanding of how the system worked when Shylock refuses Antonio's invitation to dinner: "I will buy with you, sell with you, talk with you, walk with you, and so following, but I will not eat with you, drink with you, nor pray with you." There is sociability and commerce between different ethnic and religious groups, but spiritual practices and customs are kept distinct. Shylock will not go to dinner because his religion prevents him from eating pork, but ultimately he regards questions of business as more important than those of faith: he hates Antonio "for he is a Christian, / *But more*, for that in low simplicity / He lends out money gratis and brings down / The rate of usance here with us in Venice."

The historical reality in the age of Shakespeare was that Christians did lend money to each other with interest, while Judaic law as well as Christian frowned upon extortion. What one person regards as immoral exploitation another may regard as legitimate business practice. Shylock makes exactly this point when referring to "my bargains and my well-won thrift, / Which he [Antonio] calls interest." There are Christian usurers in other plays of the time. Besides, Shylock does *not* charge interest on the three thousand ducats he lends Antonio: instead, he takes out a bond, albeit of a rather unusual kind, as his insurance policy. One of the play's key puns, alongside those on terms that are both commercial and emotional such as "dear" and "bond," is "rate," which in the dialogue between Bassanio and Shylock about Antonio refers first to the question of interest rates and then to berating in the sense of abuse. The berating of Jew by Christian, and vice versa, is a screen for the real issue, which is the question of who has money and hence power (including the power to win a wealthy, clever, and beautiful wife).

We should therefore be wary of crude generalizations about the anti-Semitism of the play or of the age. It is often said that the original stage Shylock would have had a wig of red hair and a long bottle-like nose, making him into a stereotypical Jew. He was certainly represented thus when the play was revived after the theaters reopened following the Restoration of the monarchy in 1660, but there is no evidence that this is how he looked in Shakespeare's own theater. Portia's line on arriving in the courtroom, "Which is the merchant here, and which the Jew?," suggests that in terms of superficial appearance Antonio and Shylock are not readily distinguishable. It is not easily compatible with a caricature Jew. Nor does the dialogue at any point allude to the anti-Semitic propaganda that has defiled the centuries. There are no allusions to the story of Hugh of Lincoln, to poisoning wells, desecrating the host, ritual murder, crucified children. Shylock speaks of his "sacred nation," but no one replies with the old anti-Semitic accusation that the Jews are to be hated because they murdered Christ. There are, then, different degrees of prejudice in the play, just as there were different degrees of respect and disrespect for Jews in Shakespeare's Europe. Some, but not all, of the Christians in the play spit upon Shylock simply because he is a Jew. They are the same Christians who don't spend much time going to church, giving money to the poor, or turning the other cheek.

Barabas, the Jew of Malta in the play written by Marlowe a few years before, answers to the stereotype of the Jew in love with his moneybags (though he does also love his daughter), whereas Shylock famously appeals to a common humanity that extends across the ethnic divide:

> He hath disgraced me, and hindered me half a million, laughed at my losses, mocked at my gains, scorned my nation, thwarted my bargains, cooled my friends, heated mine enemies, and what's the reason? I am a Jew. Hath not a Jew eyes? Hath not a Jew hands, organs, dimensions, senses, affections, passions? Fed with the same food, hurt with the same weapons, subject to the same diseases, healed by the same means, warmed and cooled by the same winter and summer, as a Christian is? If you prick us, do we not bleed? If you tickle us, do we not laugh? If you poison us, do we not die?

In Elizabethan England the test for a witch was the pricking of her thumb: if it did not bleed, the woman was in league with the devil. Shylock's "If you prick us, do we not bleed" is a way of saying "do not demonize the Jews—we are not like witches." "The villainy you teach me I will execute," he continues: if you do demonize me, then I will behave diabolically. The alien, the oppressed minority, sees no alternative but to fight back: "And if you wrong us, shall we not revenge?" This is the point of parting between the Jewish law of "an eye for an eye" and the Christian notion of turning the other cheek and showing the quality of mercy. The consequence of Shylock's insistence on the law of revenge, his failure to show mercy when

Portia gives him the opportunity to do so, is his forced conversion. This sticks in the throat of the modern audience because it shows a lack of respect for religious difference, but for most of Shakespeare's original audience it would have seemed like an act of mercy. Despite his willingness to murder Antonio, he is still given the opportunity of salvation.

The representation of Shylock as monstrous villain has played a part in the appalling history of European anti-Semitism. But such a representation necessarily occludes the subtler moments of Shakespeare's characterization. A ring is not only the device whereby Portia and Nerissa assert their moral and verbal superiority over their husbands, but also the means by which Shylock is humanized:

> TUBAL   One of them showed me a ring that he had of your daughter for a monkey.
>
> SHYLOCK   Out upon her! Thou torturest me, Tubal. It was my turquoise, I had it of Leah when I was a bachelor. I would not have given it for a wilderness of monkeys.

The role of Shylock has been a gift to great actors down the ages because it gives them the opportunity not only to rage and to be outrageous, but also to turn the mood in an instant, to be suddenly quiet and hurt and sorrowful. When Shylock gleefully whets his knife in the trial scene, he presents the very image of a torturer. But he is tortured himself, simply through the memory of a girl called Leah whom he loved and married, and who bore his daughter (who has deserted both him and his faith) and who died and of whom all that remained was a ring that he would not have given for a wilderness of monkeys.

ABOUT THE TEXT

Shakespeare endures through history. He illuminates later times as well as his own. He helps us to understand the human condition. But he cannot do this without a good text of the plays. Without editions there would be no Shakespeare. That is why every twenty years or so throughout the last three centuries there has been a major new edition of his complete works. One aspect of editing is the process of keeping the texts up to date—modernizing the spelling, punctuation, and typography (though not, of course, the actual words), providing explanatory notes in the light of changing educational practices (a generation ago, most of Shakespeare's classical and biblical allusions could be assumed to be generally understood, but now they can't).

Because Shakespeare did not personally oversee the publication of his plays, with some plays there are major editorial difficulties. Decisions have to be made as to the relative authority of the early printed editions, the pocket format "quartos" published in Shakespeare's lifetime and the elaborately produced "First Folio" text of 1623, the original "Complete Works" prepared for the press after his death by Shakespeare's fellow actors, the people who knew the plays better than anyone else.

The Merchant of Venice is one of three comedies where the Folio text was printed from a marked-up copy of a First Quarto (the others are *Love's Labour's Lost* and *Much Ado About Nothing*). The standard procedure for the modern editor is to use the First Quarto as the copy text but to import stage directions, act divisions, and some corrections from Folio. Our Folio-led policy means that we follow the reverse procedure, using Folio as copy text, but deploying the First Quarto as a "control text" that offers assistance in the correction and identification of compositors' errors. Differences are for the most part minor.

The following notes highlight various aspects of the editorial process and indicate conventions used in the text of this edition:

Lists of Parts are supplied in the First Folio for only six plays, not including *The Merchant of Venice*, so the list here is editorially supplied. Capitals indicate that part of the name which is used for speech headings in the script (thus "Prince of ARAGON, suitor to Portia").

Locations are provided by the Folio for only two plays, of which *The Merchant of Venice* is not one. Eighteenth-century editors, working in an age of elaborately realistic stage sets, were the first to provide detailed locations ("another part of the city"). Given that Shakespeare wrote for a bare stage and often an imprecise sense of place, we have relegated locations to the explanatory notes at the foot of the page, where they are given at the beginning of each scene where the imaginary location is different from the one before. In the case of *The Merchant of Venice*, the action is divided between Venice and Portia's country estate of Belmont.

Act and Scene Divisions were provided in the Folio in a much more thoroughgoing way than in the Quartos. Sometimes, however, they were erroneous or omitted; corrections and additions supplied by editorial tradition are indicated by square brackets. Five-act division is based on a classical model, and act breaks provided the opportunity to replace the candles in the indoor Blackfriars playhouse which the King's Men used after 1608, but Shakespeare did not necessarily think in terms of a five-part structure of dramatic composition. The Folio convention is that a scene ends when the stage is empty. Nowadays, partly under the influence of film, we tend to consider a scene to be a dramatic unit that ends with either a change of imaginary location or a significant passage of time within the narrative. Shakespeare's fluidity of composition accords well with this convention, so in addition to act and scene numbers we provide a *running scene* count in the right margin at the beginning of each new scene, in the typeface used for editorial directions. Where there is a scene break caused by a momentary bare stage, but the location does not change and extra time does not pass, we use the convention *running scene continues*. There is inevitably a degree of editorial judgment in making such calls, but the system is very valuable in suggesting the pace of the plays.

Speakers' Names are often inconsistent in Folio. We have regularized speech headings, but retained an element of deliberate inconsistency in entry directions, in order to give the flavor of Folio. Thus LANCELET is always so-called in his speech headings, but is "*Clown*" in entry directions.

Verse is indicated by lines that do not run to the right margin and by capitalization of each line. The Folio printers sometimes set verse as prose, and vice versa (either out of misunderstanding or for reasons of space). We have silently corrected in such cases, although in some instances there is ambiguity, in which case we have leaned toward the preservation of Folio layout. Folio sometimes uses contraction ("turnd" rather than "turned") to indicate whether or not the final "-ed" of a past participle is sounded, an area where there is variation for the sake of the five-beat iambic pentameter rhythm. We use the convention of a grave accent to indicate sounding (thus "turnèd" would be two syllables), but would urge actors not to overstress. In cases where one speaker ends with a verse half line and the next begins with the other half of the pentameter, editors since the late eighteenth century have indented the second line. We have abandoned this convention, since the Folio does not use it, nor did actors' cues in the Shakespearean theater. An exception is made when the second speaker actively interrupts or completes the first speaker's sentence.

Spelling is modernized, but older forms are very occasionally maintained where necessary for rhythm or aural effect.

Punctuation in Shakespeare's time was as much rhetorical as grammatical. "Colon" was originally a term for a unit of thought in an argument. The semicolon was a new unit of punctuation (some of the Quartos lack them altogether). We have modernized punctuation throughout, but have given more weight to Folio punctuation than many editors, since, though not Shakespearean, it reflects the usage of his period. In particular, we have used the colon far more than many editors: it is exceptionally useful as a way of indicating how many Shakespearean speeches unfold clause by clause in a developing argument that gives the illusion of enacting the process of thinking in the moment. We have also kept in mind the origin of punctuation in classical times as a way of assisting the actor and orator: the comma suggests the briefest of pauses for breath, the colon a middling one, and a full stop or period a longer pause. Semi-colons, by contrast, belong to an era of punctuation that was only just coming in during Shakespeare's time and that is coming to an end now: we have accordingly only used them where they occur in our copy texts (and not always then). Dashes are sometimes used for parenthetical interjections where the Folio has brackets. They are also used for interruptions and changes in train of thought. Where a change of addressee occurs within a speech, we have used a dash preceded by a period (or occasionally another form of punctuation). Often the identity of the respective addressees is obvious from the context. When it is not, this has been indicated in a marginal stage direction.

Entrances and Exits are fairly thorough in Folio, which has accordingly been followed as faithfully as possible. Where characters are omitted or corrections are necessary, this is indicated by square brackets (e.g. "[*and Attendants*]"). *Exit* is sometimes silently normal-ized to *Exeunt* and *Manet* anglicized to "remains." We trust Folio positioning of entrances and exits to a greater degree than most edi-tors.

Editorial Stage Directions such as stage business, asides, indica-tions of addressee and of characters' position on the gallery stage are only used sparingly in Folio. Other editions mingle directions of this kind with original Folio and Quarto directions, sometimes mark-ing them by means of square brackets. We have sought to distin-guish what could be described as *directorial* interventions of this kind from Folio-style directions (either original or supplied) by placing them in the right margin in a different typeface. There is a degree of subjectivity about which directions are of which kind, but the proce-dure is intended as a reminder to the reader and the actor that Shakespearean stage directions are often dependent upon editorial inference alone and are not set in stone. We also depart from editorial tradition in sometimes admitting uncertainty and thus printing permissive stage directions, such as an *Aside?* (often a line may be equally effective as an aside or as a direct address—it is for each production or reading to make its own decision) or a *may exit* or a piece of business placed between arrows to indicate that it may occur at various different moments within a scene.

Line Numbers in the left margin are editorial, for reference and to key the explanatory and textual notes.

Explanatory Notes at the foot of each page explain allusions and gloss obsolete and difficult words, confusing phraseology, occasional major textual cruces, and so on. Particular attention is given to nonstandard usage, bawdy innuendo, and technical terms (e.g. legal and military language). Where more than one sense is given, commas indicate shades of related meaning, slashes alternative or double meanings.

Textual Notes at the end of the play indicate major departures from the Folio. They take the following form: the reading of our text is given in bold and its source given after an equals sign, with "Q" indicating a Quarto reading, Q2 a reading from the Second Quarto of 1619, "F2" a reading from the Second Folio of 1632, and "Ed" one that derives from the subsequent editorial tradition. The rejected Folio ("F") reading is then given. Thus for Act 2 Scene 9 line 45: **"peasantry** = Q. F = pleasantry" means that the Folio text's "pleasantry" has been rejected in favor of the Quarto reading "peasantry," which seems to make better sense of the line.

KEY FACTS

MAJOR PARTS: *(with percentage of lines/number of speeches/scenes on stage)* Portia (22%/117/9), Shylock (13%/79/5), Bassanio (13%/73/6), Gratiano (7%/58/7), Lorenzo (7%/47/7), Antonio (7%/47/6), Lancelet Gobbo (6%/44/6), Salerio (5%/31/7), Morocco (4%/7/2), Nerissa (3%/36/7), Jessica (3%/26/7), Solanio (2%/20/5), Duke (2%/18/1), Aragon (2%/4/1), Old Gobbo (1%/19/1).

LINGUISTIC MEDIUM: 80% verse, 20% prose.

DATE: Registered for publication July 1598 and mentioned in Francis Meres' 1598 list of Shakespeare's comedies; reference to a ship called the *Andrew* suggests late 1596 or early 1597, when the Spanish vessel *St. Andrew*, which had been captured at Cadiz after running aground, was much in the news.

SOURCES: There are many ancient and medieval folk variations on the motif of a body part demanded as surety for a bond. The setting of the story in Venice, the pursuit of "the lady of Belmonte" as the reason the hero needs the money, the bond being made by a friend rather than the hero himself, the identification of the moneylender as a Jew, and the lady disguising herself as a male lawyer, coming to Venice and arguing that the bond does not allow for the shedding of blood all come from a tale in Ser Giovanni Fiorentino's collection *Il Pecorone* ("The Dunce," in Italian, published 1558—no English translation). A lost English play of the 1570s called *The Jew* may have been an intervening source. The character of Shylock and the elopement of his daughter with a Christian are strongly shaped by Christopher Marlowe's highly successful play *The Jew of Malta* (c.1590). The choice between three caskets as a device to identify a worthy marriage partner is another ancient motif; the closest surviving precedent is a story in the medieval *Gesta Romanorum* (translated by Richard Robinson, 1577, revised 1595 with use of the rare word "insculpt," which is echoed in Morocco's speech).

TEXT: Quarto 1600: a good quality text, apparently set from a fair copy of the dramatist's manuscript; reprinted 1619, with some errors and some corrections. Folio text was set from a copy of the first Quarto, making some corrections, introducing some errors, and apparently drawing on a theatrical manuscript for stage directions, including music cues. We follow Folio where it corrects or modernizes Quarto, but restore Quarto where Folio changes appear to be printers' errors. The only serious textual problem concerns the Venetian gentlemen known in the theatrical profession as the "Salads." They are initially identified in entry directions and speech headings as "Salarino" and "Solanio" (variously abbreviated, most commonly to "Sal." and "Sol."), but never named in the dialogue, so are unidentified from the point of view of a theater audience. Folio reverses their speech headings at the beginning of the opening scene, probably erroneously. In Act 3 Scene 2 "Salerio" arrives in Belmont as "a messenger from Venice"; he is named in the dialogue, so identifiable to the audience. Is this a third character, a composite of the first two, or—more probably—has Shakespeare forgotten that he began with "Salarino"? In the following scene, Quarto has "Salerio" back in Venice with Antonio and Shylock, which must be an error—he has only just exited from Belmont with Bassanio. Folio intelligently corrects the Act 3 Scene 3 entry direction to "Solanio." In Act 4 Scene 1, "Salerio" has returned with Bassanio. Some editions and productions have retained Salarino, Solanio, and Salerio, but it seems more likely that Salarino and Salerio are intended to be the same character: we have followed this assumption.

THE MERCHANT OF VENICE

LIST OF PARTS

ANTONIO, a merchant of Venice

BASSANIO, his friend, suitor to Portia

LORENZO, friend of Antonio and Bassanio, in love with Jessica

GRATIANO, friend of Antonio and Bassanio

SALERIO ⎱ friends of Antonio and
SOLANIO ⎰ Bassanio

LEONARDO, servant to Bassanio

PORTIA, an heiress

NERISSA, her gentlewoman-in-waiting

BALTHASAR, servant to Portia

STEPHANO, servant to Portia

Prince of ARAGON, suitor to Portia

Prince of MOROCCO, suitor to Portia

SHYLOCK, a Jew of Venice

JESSICA, his daughter

TUBAL, a Jew, Shylock's friend

LANCELET GOBBO, the clown, servant to Shylock and later Bassanio

OLD GOBBO, Lancelet's father

DUKE of Venice

Magnificoes of Venice

A Jailer, Attendants and Servants

Act 1 [Scene 1]

Enter Antonio, Salerio and Solanio

ANTONIO   In sooth I know not why I am so sad.
It wearies me, you say it wearies you;
But how I caught it, found it, or came by it,
What stuff 'tis made of, whereof it is born,
5   I am to learn:
And such a want-wit sadness makes of me
That I have much ado to know myself.

SALERIO   Your mind is tossing on the ocean,
There where your argosies with portly sail
10   Like signiors and rich burghers on the flood,
Or as it were the pageants of the sea,
Do overpeer the petty traffickers
That curtsy to them, do them reverence,
As they fly by them with their woven wings.

15   SOLANIO   Believe me, sir, had I such venture forth,
The better part of my affections would
Be with my hopes abroad. I should be still
Plucking the grass to know where sits the wind,
Peering in maps for ports and piers and roads,
20   And every object that might make me fear
Misfortune to my ventures out of doubt
Would make me sad.

SALERIO   My wind cooling my broth
Would blow me to an ague, when I thought
25   What harm a wind too great might do at sea.

1.1 *Location: Venice* **1 sooth** truth **4 stuff** substance **whereof . . . born** i.e. what is
its cause **5 to learn** yet to discover **6 want-wit** senseless idiot **7 ado** trouble **8 tossing
on** troubled/preoccupied with **9 argosies** large merchant ships **portly** stately, majestic
sail sails/(act of) sailing **10 signiors** sirs/gentlemen **burghers** citizens **flood** sea
11 pageants spectacles, shows **12 overpeer** look down upon **petty traffickers** inferior
merchant ships **13 curtsy** bow or curtsy, perhaps suggested by the bobbing of the smaller
ships in the argosies' wake **do them reverence** pay them respect **14 fly** speed **woven
wings** material sails (also suggestive of the wings of a **fly**) **15 venture** risky business
enterprise **forth** away from home, i.e. on the seas **16 better part** greater half **affections**
emotions/thoughts **17 hopes** expectations, prospects **still** constantly **18 where sits** i.e.
which way blows **19 roads** harbors **24 ague** fever, shaking

I should not see the sandy hour-glass run,
But I should think of shallows and of flats,
And see my wealthy *Andrew* docked in sand,
Vailing her high top lower than her ribs

30　To kiss her burial; should I go to church
And see the holy edifice of stone,
And not bethink me straight of dang'rous rocks,
Which touching but my gentle vessel's side,
Would scatter all her spices on the stream,

35　Enrobe the roaring waters with my silks,
And in a word, but even now worth this,
And now worth nothing? Shall I have the thought
To think on this, and shall I lack the thought
That such a thing bechanced would make me sad?

40　But tell not me, I know, Antonio
Is sad to think upon his merchandise.

ANTONIO　Believe me, no. I thank my fortune for it,
My ventures are not in one bottom trusted,
Nor to one place; nor is my whole estate

45　Upon the fortune of this present year:
Therefore my merchandise makes me not sad.

SALERIO　Why, then you are in love.

ANTONIO　Fie, fie!

SOLANIO　Not in love neither: then let us say you are sad

50　Because you are not merry; and 'twere as easy
For you to laugh and leap, and say you are merry
Because you are not sad. Now, by two-headed Janus,
Nature hath framed strange fellows in her time:
Some that will evermore peep through their eyes

---

26 should i.e. could　**27 flats** sandbanks　**28** *Andrew* name of a ship　**29 Vailing** lowering (in submission)　**high top** top section of the mast　**ribs** i.e. body of the ship　**30 burial** burial place　**should I** was I able to　**32 bethink me straight** think immediately　**33 but** merely　**gentle** noble/harmless　**34 stream** current　**35 waters . . . silks** may play on idea of "watered silk," a relatively new fabric　**36 even** just　**this** this much (i.e. the value of the cargo)　**39 bechanced** having happened　**43 bottom** ship's bottom, hold　**44 estate** fortunes/circumstances　**45 Upon** dependent on/risked upon　**fortune** chance, fate　**48 Fie** expression of impatience or disgust　**52 Janus** Roman god with two faces　**53 framed** formed　**54 peep** peer through eyes half-closed in laughter

55   And laugh like parrots at a bagpiper,
      And other of such vinegar aspect
      That they'll not show their teeth in way of smile,
      Though Nestor swear the jest be laughable.

Enter Bassanio, Lorenzo and Gratiano

SOLANIO   Here comes Bassanio, your most noble kinsman,
60   Gratiano and Lorenzo. Fare ye well,
      We leave you now with better company.

SALERIO   I would have stayed till I had made you merry,
      If worthier friends had not prevented me.

ANTONIO   Your worth is very dear in my regard.
65   I take it your own business calls on you,
      And you embrace th'occasion to depart.

SALERIO   Good morrow, my good lords.

BASSANIO   Good signiors both, when shall we laugh? Say, when?
      You grow exceeding strange. Must it be so?
70   SALERIO   We'll make our leisures to attend on yours.

Exeunt Salerio and Solanio

LORENZO   My lord Bassanio, since you have found Antonio,
      We two will leave you, but at dinnertime
      I pray you have in mind where we must meet.

BASSANIO   I will not fail you.

75   GRATIANO   You look not well, Signior Antonio.
      You have too much respect upon the world:
      They lose it that do buy it with much care.
      Believe me, you are marvellously changed.

ANTONIO   I hold the world but as the world, Gratiano,
80   A stage where every man must play a part,
      And mine a sad one.

---

55 bagpiper bagpipes were thought to sound melancholic   **56 other** others   **vinegar aspect** sour expression   **58 Though** even if   **Nestor** Trojan leader, noted for his wisdom and gravity   *Gratiano* according to a contemporary Italian dictionary, a name given to a foolish or clownish character in a play   **63 prevented** forestalled   **64 dear** valuable   **regard** consideration   **66 embrace** welcome   **th'occasion** the opportunity   **68 laugh** i.e. meet for some fun   **69 strange** distant/unfamiliar   **70 leisures . . . yours** spare time accommodate yours, i.e. ensure we are available when you are   **73 have in mind** i.e. think about   **76 respect . . . world** concern for worldly affairs/business   **77 it** enjoyment (especially of material wealth)   **buy . . . care** i.e. worry so much about it   **78 marvellously** extremely   **79 hold** consider, view

GRATIANO   Let me play the fool:
With mirth and laughter let old wrinkles come,
And let my liver rather heat with wine
85   Than my heart cool with mortifying groans.
Why should a man whose blood is warm within,
Sit like his grandsire cut in alabaster?
Sleep when he wakes and creep into the jaundices
By being peevish? I tell thee what, Antonio—
90   I love thee, and it is my love that speaks—
There are a sort of men whose visages
Do cream and mantle like a standing pond,
And do a wilful stillness entertain,
With purpose to be dressed in an opinion
95   Of wisdom, gravity, profound conceit,
As who should say, 'I am, sir, an oracle,
And when I ope my lips, let no dog bark!'
O my Antonio, I do know of these
That therefore only are reputed wise
100   For saying nothing; when I am very sure
If they should speak, would almost damn those ears
Which, hearing them, would call their brothers fools.
I'll tell thee more of this another time.
But fish not with this melancholy bait
105   For this fool gudgeon, this opinion.
Come, good Lorenzo. Fare ye well awhile,
I'll end my exhortation after dinner.

---

83 old your former/plentiful/familiar, "good old" (puns on the sense of "elderly")   **84 liver** thought to be the seat of the passions   **85 heart . . . groans** groans were believed to drain blood from the heart   **mortifying** penitential/deadly   **87 grandsire** grandfather   **cut in alabaster** i.e. a statue on a tomb   **88 creep . . . jaundices** become yellow from an excess of yellow bile or choler   **89 peevish** irritable, morose   **91 visages** faces   **92 cream and mantle** become covered in a layer of scum (i.e. are calm/expressionless)   **standing** still/stagnant   **93 wilful** deliberate   **stillness** restraint/quietness   **entertain** maintain   **94 dressed . . . opinion** invested with a reputation   **95 conceit** understanding   **96 As . . . say** as if to say   **97 ope** open   **101 damn . . . fools** condemn the hearers for obliging them to call the speakers fools (according to the Bible a damnable offense)   **104 melancholy bait** i.e. silence used to fool people into assuming you are wise   **105 fool** foolish   **gudgeon** proverbially gullible fish   **107 exhortation** earnest speech/entreaty

LORENZO   Well, we will leave you then till dinnertime. *To Antonio*
I must be one of these same dumb wise men,   *and Bassanio*
110   For Gratiano never lets me speak.

GRATIANO   Well, keep me company but two years more,
Thou shalt not know the sound of thine own tongue.

ANTONIO   Fare you well, I'll grow a talker for this gear.

GRATIANO   Thanks, i'faith, for silence is only commendable
115   In a neat's tongue dried and a maid not vendible.

Exit [Gratiano with Lorenzo]

ANTONIO   Is that anything now?

BASSANIO   Gratiano speaks an infinite deal of nothing, more
than any man in all Venice. His reasons are two grains of
wheat hid in two bushels of chaff: you shall seek all day ere
120   you find them, and when you have them, they are not worth
the search.

ANTONIO   Well, tell me now, what lady is the same
To whom you swore a secret pilgrimage
That you today promised to tell me of?

125   BASSANIO   'Tis not unknown to you, Antonio,
How much I have disabled mine estate
By something showing a more swelling port
Than my faint means would grant continuance.
Nor do I now make moan to be abridged
130   From such a noble rate, but my chief care
Is to come fairly off from the great debts
Wherein my time something too prodigal
Hath left me gaged. To you, Antonio,
I owe the most in money and in love,
135   And from your love I have a warranty

---

109 dumb silent   **113 grow** become   **for this gear** as a result of this talk/on account of this
matter   **115 neat's tongue dried** cured ox tongue   **vendible** saleable/sought-after (for
marriage)   **116 Is . . . now?** Did that (talk) mean anything?   **118 reasons** reasonings,
opinions   **119 ere** before   **122 same** i.e. one   **126 disabled** devalued   **127 something**
somewhat   **swelling port** extravagant lifestyle   **128 faint** inadequate   **grant continuance**
allow maintenance (of)   **129 make moan** complain   **abridged** deprived   **130 noble rate**
high style of living   **care** concern   **131 come . . . from** i.e. repay   **132 time** (young)
age/time spent   **prodigal** excessive, lavish   **133 gaged** pledged/entangled   **135 warranty**
authorization

To unburden all my plots and purposes
How to get clear of all the debts I owe.

ANTONIO   I pray you good Bassanio, let me know it,
And if it stand as you yourself still do,

140   Within the eye of honour, be assured
My purse, my person, my extremest means,
Lie all unlocked to your occasions.

BASSANIO   In my schooldays, when I had lost one shaft,
I shot his fellow of the selfsame flight

145   The selfsame way with more advisèd watch
To find the other forth, and by adventuring both
I oft found both. I urge this childhood proof
Because what follows is pure innocence.
I owe you much and, like a wilful youth,

150   That which I owe is lost. But if you please
To shoot another arrow that self way
Which you did shoot the first, I do not doubt,
As I will watch the aim, or to find both,
Or bring your latter hazard back again,

155   And thankfully rest debtor for the first.

ANTONIO   You know me well, and herein spend but time
To wind about my love with circumstance,
And out of doubt you do me now more wrong
In making question of my uttermost

160   Than if you had made waste of all I have.
Then do but say to me what I should do
That in your knowledge may by me be done,
And I am pressed unto it: therefore speak.

---

136 unburden reveal   140 Within . . . honour i.e. honorable   142 occasions needs
143 shaft arrow   144 his . . . flight the same type of arrow   145 advisèd careful   146 forth
out   adventuring risking   147 urge bring forward   proof test/example   148 innocence
sincerity   151 self same   153 or either   154 hazard i.e. that which was risked subsequently
155 rest remain   156 spend but only waste   157 wind . . . circumstance ingratiate yourself
by speaking in an elaborate, roundabout way   158 out of without   159 making . . .
uttermost questioning my offer of all the help I can give   160 made waste spent/wasted
161 but only   163 pressed enlisted

BASSANIO   In Belmont is a lady richly left,
165   And she is fair and, fairer than that word,
Of wondrous virtues. Sometimes from her eyes
I did receive fair speechless messages.
Her name is Portia, nothing undervalued
To Cato's daughter, Brutus' Portia.
170   Nor is the wide world ignorant of her worth,
For the four winds blow in from every coast
Renownèd suitors, and her sunny locks
Hang on her temples like a golden fleece,
Which makes her seat of Belmont Colchos' strand,
175   And many Jasons come in quest of her.
O my Antonio, had I but the means
To hold a rival place with one of them,
I have a mind presages me such thrift,
That I should questionless be fortunate.
180   ANTONIO   Thou know'st that all my fortunes are at sea,
Neither have I money, nor commodity
To raise a present sum: therefore go forth.
Try what my credit can in Venice do,
That shall be racked, even to the uttermost,
185   To furnish thee to Belmont, to fair Portia.
Go presently inquire, and so will I,
Where money is, and I no question make
To have it of my trust or for my sake.   *Exeunt*

---

164 richly left with a large inheritance (left by her father)   **166 Sometimes** formerly, at one
time   **168 nothing undervalued To** worth no less than   **169 Cato** Roman politician of the
second century BC   **Brutus** Roman politician of the first century BC, married to **Portia**
173 golden fleece in Greek mythology the valued prize sought for by **Jason**   **174 seat** rural
estate   **strand** the shore of **Colchos** (Colchis), where the fleece was found   **178 presages**
that predicts   **thrift** profit/advantage   **179 questionless** without question   **181 commodity**
goods   **182 present** immediate, ready   **183 Try** find out   **184 racked** stretched
185 furnish thee equip you to go   **186 presently** at once (to)   **188 of my trust** on my credit
as a merchant   **sake** i.e. friendship's sake

[Act 1 Scene 2]   *running scene 2*

Enter Portia with her waiting woman, Nerissa

PORTIA   By my troth, Nerissa, my little body is aweary of this
great world.

NERISSA   You would be, sweet madam, if your miseries were
in the same abundance as your good fortunes are, and yet,
5   for aught I see, they are as sick that surfeit with too much, as
they that starve with nothing; it is no small happiness,
therefore, to be seated in the mean. Superfluity comes sooner
by white hairs, but competency lives longer.

PORTIA   Good sentences and well pronounced.

10   NERISSA   They would be better if well followed.

PORTIA   If to do were as easy as to know what were good to
do, chapels had been churches and poor men's cottages
princes' palaces. It is a good divine that follows his own
instructions; I can easier teach twenty what were good to be
15   done than be one of the twenty to follow mine own teaching.
The brain may devise laws for the blood, but a hot temper
leaps o'er a cold decree—such a hare is madness the youth,
to skip o'er the meshes of good counsel the cripple; but this
reason is not in fashion to choose me a husband. O me, the
20   word 'choose!' I may neither choose whom I would, nor
refuse whom I dislike, so is the will of a living daughter
curbed by the will of a dead father. Is it not hard, Nerissa,
that I cannot choose one nor refuse none?

NERISSA   Your father was ever virtuous, and holy men at
25   their death have good inspirations: therefore the lottery that
he hath devised in these three chests of gold, silver and lead,

---

1.2   *Location: Belmont   waiting woman* companion and confidante; she is a genteel
character, not a servant   **1 troth** faith   **3 would be** would have real reason to be (weary)
5 aught anything   **surfeit** feed to excess   **7 mean** middle   **Superfluity** overindulgence
comes sooner by sooner gains   **8 competency** sufficiency/modest means   **9 sentences**
maxims   **pronounced** delivered   **13 divine** clergyman   **16 blood** passions (i.e. not reason)
hot temper passionate, impulsive temperament   **17 cold decree** i.e. sensible advice
18 meshes nets, traps   **19 in fashion** the (right) way   **20 would** want   **21 will** desire
22 will testament/inclination   **25 lottery** game of chance

whereof who chooses his meaning chooses you, will no
doubt never be chosen by any rightly but one who you shall
rightly love. But what warmth is there in your affection
30   towards any of these princely suitors that are already come?

PORTIA   I pray thee overname them, and as thou namest
them, I will describe them, and according to my description
level at my affection.

NERISSA   First, there is the Neapolitan prince.

35   PORTIA   Ay, that's a colt indeed, for he doth nothing but talk
of his horse, and he makes it a great appropriation to his
own good parts that he can shoe him himself. I am much
afraid my lady his mother played false with a smith.

NERISSA   Then is there the County Palatine.

40   PORTIA   He doth nothing but frown, as who should say, 'An
you will not have me, choose.' He hears merry tales and
smiles not. I fear he will prove the weeping philosopher when
he grows old, being so full of unmannerly sadness in his
youth. I had rather to be married to a death's-head with a
45   bone in his mouth than to either of these. God defend me
from these two!

NERISSA   How say you by the French lord, Monsieur Le Bon?

PORTIA   God made him, and therefore let him pass for a
man. In truth, I know it is a sin to be a mocker, but he! Why,
50   he hath a horse better than the Neapolitan's, a better bad
habit of frowning than the Count Palatine. He is every man
in no man. If a throstle sing, he falls straight a capering, he
will fence with his own shadow. If I should marry him, I
should marry twenty husbands. If he would despise me, I

27 who whoever   his meaning i.e. the chest he intended   28 rightly correctly (sense
then shifts to "truly")   31 overname list   33 level at point to/guess at   34 Neapolitan
inhabitants of Naples were famed for their horsemanship   35 colt foolish/lustful youth (puns
on the sense of "young horse")   36 appropriation addition/special feature   37 parts abilities
38 played false was unfaithful   smith blacksmith   39 County Count   Palatine possessing
royal privileges over his region   40 who if one   An if   41 choose i.e. do as you like
42 prove prove to be   weeping philosopher Heraclitus of Ephesus, a reclusive and melancholy
philosopher of 500 BC   43 unmannerly impolite/immoderate   sadness gravity/melancholy
44 death's-head skull   47 How what   by about   Le Bon the good (French)   50 better bad
i.e. worse   51 He . . . man he copies characteristics of everyone else but lacks his own identity
52 throstle thrush   straight straightaway   a capering to dancing

55   would forgive him, for if he love me to madness, I should
        never requite him.

NERISSA   What say you then to Falconbridge, the young
        baron of England?

PORTIA   You know I say nothing to him, for he understands
60   not me, nor I him: he hath neither Latin, French, nor Italian,
        and you will come into the court and swear that I have a
        poor pennyworth in the English. He is a proper man's
        picture, but alas, who can converse with a dumb show? How
        oddly he is suited. I think he bought his doublet in Italy, his
65   round hose in France, his bonnet in Germany, and his
        behaviour everywhere.

NERISSA   What think you of the other lord, his neighbour?

PORTIA   That he hath a neighbourly charity in him, for he
        borrowed a box of the ear of the Englishman and swore he
70   would pay him again when he was able. I think the
        Frenchman became his surety and sealed under for another.

NERISSA   How like you the young German, the Duke of
        Saxony's nephew?

PORTIA   Very vilely in the morning when he is sober, and
75   most vilely in the afternoon when he is drunk: when he is
        best, he is a little worse than a man, and when he is worst, he
        is little better than a beast. An the worst fall that ever fell, I
        hope I shall make shift to go without him.

NERISSA   If he should offer to choose, and choose the right
80   casket, you should refuse to perform your father's will, if you
        should refuse to accept him.

PORTIA   Therefore, for fear of the worst, I pray thee set a
        deep glass of Rhenish wine on the contrary casket, for if the

---

55 if even if   59 say i.e. speak (puns on Nerissa's meaning, "think about")   61 come . . .
swear i.e. testify   62 poor . . . the i.e. very little   proper man's picture the image of an
attractive man   63 dumb show mime   64 suited dressed   doublet close-fitting jacket
65 round hose short breeches, puffed out at the hips   bonnet hat   69 borrowed received
71 surety guarantor   sealed under pledged (literally, set his seal)   another i.e. a further box
of the ear   73 Saxony former principality of Germany   77 beast may pun on best   An if
fall befall, happen   78 make shift arrange, manage   80 you should you would   83 Rhenish
wine German white wine   contrary incorrect   if even if

devil be within, and that temptation without, I know he will
85   choose it. I will do anything, Nerissa, ere I will be married to
a sponge.

NERISSA   You need not fear, lady, the having any of these
lords. They have acquainted me with their determinations,
which is indeed to return to their home, and to trouble you
90   with no more suit, unless you may be won by some other sort
than your father's imposition, depending on the caskets.

PORTIA   If I live to be as old as Sibylla, I will die as chaste as
Diana, unless I be obtained by the manner of my father's
will. I am glad this parcel of wooers are so reasonable, for
95   there is not one among them but I dote on his very absence,
and I wish them a fair departure.

NERISSA   Do you not remember, lady, in your father's time, a
Venetian, a scholar and a soldier, that came hither in
company of the Marquis of Montferrat?

100   PORTIA   Yes, yes, it was Bassanio, as I think, so was he called.

NERISSA   True, madam. He, of all the men that ever my
foolish eyes looked upon, was the best deserving a fair lady.

PORTIA   I remember him well, and I remember him worthy
of thy praise.

Enter a Servingman

105   SERVANT   The four strangers seek you, madam, to take their
leave. And there is a forerunner come from a fifth, the Prince
of Morocco, who brings word the prince his master will be
here tonight.

PORTIA   If I could bid the fifth welcome with so good heart as
110   I can bid the other four farewell, I should be glad of his
approach. If he have the condition of a saint and the
complexion of a devil, I had rather he should shrive me than

---

84 **without** on the outside   86 **sponge** i.e. excessive drinker   88 **determinations** resolutions
90 **suit** courtship   **sort** way   91 **imposition** command   92 **Sibylla** Cumaean prophetess
whom Apollo granted as many years of life as there were grains in her handful of sand
93 **Diana** Roman goddess of chastity   94 **parcel** company   99 **Montferrat** Italian dukedom
102 **foolish** inexperienced   105 **four strangers** foreign suitors (in fact, six have been
mentioned)   106 **forerunner** messenger   111 **condition** disposition   112 **complexion** . . .
devil traditionally black   **shrive me** hear my confession, absolve me

wive me. Come, Nerissa.—Sirrah, go before; whiles   *To the*
we shut the gate upon one wooer, another knocks   *Servingman*
115   at the door.   *Exeunt*

[Act 1 Scene 3]   *running scene 3*

Enter Bassanio with Shylock the Jew

SHYLOCK   Three thousand ducats, well.

BASSANIO   Ay, sir, for three months.

SHYLOCK   For three months, well.

BASSANIO   For the which, as I told you, Antonio shall be
5   bound.

SHYLOCK   Antonio shall become bound, well.

BASSANIO   May you stead me? Will you pleasure me? Shall I
know your answer?

SHYLOCK   Three thousand ducats for three months and
10   Antonio bound.

BASSANIO   Your answer to that.

SHYLOCK   Antonio is a good man.

BASSANIO   Have you heard any imputation to the contrary?

SHYLOCK   Ho, no, no, no, no! My meaning in saying he is a
15   good man is to have you understand me that he is sufficient.
Yet his means are in supposition: he hath an argosy bound to
Tripolis, another to the Indies, I understand moreover, upon
the Rialto, he hath a third at Mexico, a fourth for England,
and other ventures he hath squandered abroad. But ships are
20   but boards, sailors but men. There be land-rats and water-
rats, water-thieves and land-thieves—I mean pirates—and
then there is the peril of waters, winds and rocks. The man is,

---

113 **wive** marry   **Sirrah** sir (used to an inferior)   **1.3** *Location: Venice*   **Shylock**
perhaps from the Hebrew *Shallach* ("cormorant"), or from "Shiloh" (Genesis 49:10, although
the word means "messiah"); possible connotations of wary secrecy and hoarding (shy lock)
1 **ducats** gold coins   5 **bound** bound in obligation to repay   7 **stead** assist   **pleasure** oblige
13 **imputation** accusation   15 **sufficient** of adequate means   16 **supposition** uncertainty
17 **Tripolis** Tripoli, North African port (now in Libya)   **Indies** East Indies   18 **Rialto**
merchants' exchange in Venice; also bridge over the Grand Canal   19 **squandered**
scattered/sent recklessly   21 **pirates** puns on **rats**

notwithstanding, sufficient. Three thousand ducats. I think I
may take his bond.

25 BASSANIO   Be assured you may.

SHYLOCK   I will be assured I may. And that I may be assured, I
will bethink me. May I speak with Antonio?

BASSANIO   If it please you to dine with us.

SHYLOCK   Yes, to smell pork, to eat of the habitation which
30   your prophet the Nazarite conjured the devil into. I will buy
with you, sell with you, talk with you, walk with you, and so
following, but I will not eat with you, drink with you, nor
pray with you. What news on the Rialto? Who is he comes
here?

Enter Antonio

35 BASSANIO   This is Signior Antonio.

SHYLOCK   How like a fawning publican he looks!   *Aside*
I hate him for he is a Christian,
But more, for that in low simplicity
He lends out money gratis and brings down
40   The rate of usance here with us in Venice.
If I can catch him once upon the hip,
I will feed fat the ancient grudge I bear him.
He hates our sacred nation, and he rails—
Even there where merchants most do congregate—
45   On me, my bargains and my well-won thrift,
Which he calls interest. Cursèd be my tribe,
If I forgive him!

BASSANIO   Shylock, do you hear?

SHYLOCK   I am debating of my present store,
50   And by the near guess of my memory,

---

23 **notwithstanding** nevertheless   26 **assured** shifts sense to "guaranteed against risks"
27 **bethink me** consider it   29 **habitation** i.e. the body of a pig   30 **Nazarite** someone from
Nazareth, i.e. Jesus   32 **following** forth   36 **publican** tax collector   38 **low simplicity**
humble naïveté/foolishness   39 **gratis** for nothing (i.e. without charging interest)
40 **usance** lending money at interest   41 **upon the hip** at a disadvantage (wrestling term)
42 **fat** until fat   43 **our sacred nation** i.e. the Jewish people   **rails** rants/is abusive (about)
44 **there . . . congregate** i.e. on the Rialto   45 **thrift** profit   46 **tribe** i.e. one of the twelve
tribes of Israel, from which all Jews were descended   49 **debating . . . store** considering my
supply of ready money

I cannot instantly raise up the gross
Of full three thousand ducats. What of that?
Tubal, a wealthy Hebrew of my tribe,
Will furnish me; but soft! How many months

55 Do you desire?—Rest you fair, good signior.   *To Antonio*
Your worship was the last man in our mouths.

ANTONIO   Shylock, albeit I neither lend nor borrow
By taking nor by giving of excess,
Yet to supply the ripe wants of my friend,

60 I'll break a custom.—Is he yet possessed   *To Bassanio*
How much ye would?

SHYLOCK   Ay, ay, three thousand ducats.

ANTONIO   And for three months.

SHYLOCK   I had forgot—three months—you told me so.

65 Well then, your bond. And let me see, but hear you,
Methoughts you said you neither lend nor borrow
Upon advantage.

ANTONIO   I do never use it.

SHYLOCK   When Jacob grazed his uncle Laban's sheep—

70 This Jacob from our holy Abram was,
As his wise mother wrought in his behalf,
The third possessor; ay, he was the third—

ANTONIO   And what of him? Did he take interest?

SHYLOCK   No, not take interest, not, as you would say,

75 Directly interest. Mark what Jacob did:
When Laban and himself were compromised
That all the eanlings which were streaked and pied
Should fall as Jacob's hire, the ewes, being rank,

---

51 gross total   **53 Tubal** name found in Genesis 10:2   **54 furnish** supply   **soft** wait a
moment   **55 Rest you fair** form of greeting ("may you remain well")   **56 Your . . . mouths**
i.e. we were just talking about you   **58 excess** i.e. interest   **59 ripe wants** pressing needs
60 possessed notified of   **61 would** want   **65 bond** contract/pledge   **67 advantage** interest
68 use employ (puns on the sense of "interest")   **69 Jacob . . . sheep** with his mother's help,
Jacob tricked his father into making him heir; fleeing his brother Esau's wrath, he went to work
for his **uncle Laban** (Genesis 27 and 30)   **70 from** descended from   **Abram** Abraham
71 wrought brought about, arranged   **72 third possessor** i.e. of the birthright (after
Abraham and Isaac)   **75 Mark** pay attention to   **76 were compromised** had reached
agreement   **77 eanlings** newborn lambs   **pied** spotted with another color   **78 fall as**
become   **hire** wages   **rank** lustful/in heat

In end of autumn turnèd to the rams,
80 And, when the work of generation was
    Between these woolly breeders in the act,
    The skilful shepherd peeled me certain wands,
    And in the doing of the deed of kind,
    He stuck them up before the fulsome ewes,
85 Who then conceiving, did in eaning time
    Fall parti-coloured lambs, and those were Jacob's.
    This was a way to thrive, and he was blest:
    And thrift is blessing, if men steal it not.

ANTONIO   This was a venture, sir, that Jacob served for,
90 A thing not in his power to bring to pass,
    But swayed and fashioned by the hand of heaven.
    Was this inserted to make interest good?
    Or is your gold and silver ewes and rams?

SHYLOCK   I cannot tell, I make it breed as fast.
95 But note me, signior—

ANTONIO   Mark you this, Bassanio,
    The devil can cite Scripture for his purpose.
    An evil soul producing holy witness
    Is like a villain with a smiling cheek,
100 A goodly apple rotten at the heart.
    O, what a goodly outside falsehood hath!

SHYLOCK   Three thousand ducats, 'tis a good round sum.
    Three months from twelve, then let me see, the rate—

ANTONIO   Well, Shylock, shall we be beholding to you?

105 SHYLOCK   Signior Antonio, many a time and oft
    In the Rialto you have rated me
    About my moneys and my usances.
    Still have I borne it with a patient shrug,

---

80 generation procreation   **82 peeled . . . wands** stripped the bark off particular sticks
83 in . . . kind while the sheep were engaged in their natural act (i.e. breeding)   **84 stuck . . .
ewes** refers to the idea that what the mother sees during conception influences the appearance
of the offspring   **fulsome** lustful   **85 eaning** lambing   **86 Fall** drop, give birth to   **87 thrive**
profit   **89 venture** enterprise   **served** served God   **91 fashioned** arranged, created
92 inserted introduced, brought up   **good** i.e. justifiable   **100 goodly** wholesome-looking
104 beholding indebted   **106 rated** berated, reproached (puns on **rate**)

For sufferance is the badge of all our tribe.
110   You call me misbeliever, cut-throat dog,
And spit upon my Jewish gaberdine,
And all for use of that which is mine own.
Well then, it now appears you need my help.
Go to, then. You come to me and you say
115   'Shylock, we would have moneys'—you say so,
You that did void your rheum upon my beard,
And foot me as you spurn a stranger cur
Over your threshold. Moneys is your suit.
What should I say to you? Should I not say,
120   'Hath a dog money? Is it possible
A cur should lend three thousand ducats?' Or
Shall I bend low and in a bondman's key,
With bated breath and whisp'ring humbleness,
Say this: 'Fair sir, you spat on me on Wednesday last;
125   You spurned me such a day; another time
You called me dog, and for these courtesies
I'll lend you thus much moneys'?

ANTONIO   I am as like to call thee so again,
To spit on thee again, to spurn thee too.
130   If thou wilt lend this money, lend it not
As to thy friends, for when did friendship take
A breed of barren metal of his friend?
But lend it rather to thine enemy,
Who, if he break, thou mayst with better face
135   Exact the penalties.

SHYLOCK   Why, look you how you storm!
I would be friends with you and have your love,
Forget the shames that you have stained me with,
Supply your present wants and take no doit

---

109 **sufferance** endurance   111 **gaberdine** loose cloak or coat   112 **use** employment (puns
on sense of "financial interest")   114 **Go to** expression of impatient dismissal   116 **void**
discharge, empty   **rheum** spittle   117 **foot** kick   **spurn** despise/reject/strike   **stranger cur**
unknown dog   118 **suit** request   122 **bondman's key** serf's tone   123 **bated** subdued
128 **like** likely   132 **A . . . metal** an unnatural increase of money—i.e. interest   **barren**
unable to reproduce naturally   **of** from   134 **break** i.e. fail to repay the sum   **better** more
willing   139 **doit** small coin (i.e. tiny amount)

140   Of usance for my moneys, and you'll not hear me:
       This is kind I offer.

       BASSANIO   This were kindness.

       SHYLOCK   This kindness will I show:
       Go with me to a notary, seal me there
145   Your single bond, and in a merry sport
       If you repay me not on such a day,
       In such a place, such sum or sums as are
       Expressed in the condition, let the forfeit
       Be nominated for an equal pound
150   Of your fair flesh, to be cut off and taken
       In what part of your body it pleaseth me.

       ANTONIO   Content, in faith, I'll seal to such a bond
       And say there is much kindness in the Jew.

       BASSANIO   You shall not seal to such a bond for me.
155   I'll rather dwell in my necessity.

       ANTONIO   Why, fear not, man, I will not forfeit it.
       Within these two months—that's a month before
       This bond expires—I do expect return
       Of thrice three times the value of this bond.

160   SHYLOCK   O father Abram, what these Christians are,
       Whose own hard dealings teaches them suspect
       The thoughts of others! Pray you tell me this:
       If he should break his day, what should I gain
       By the exaction of the forfeiture?
165   A pound of man's flesh taken from a man
       Is not so estimable, profitable neither,
       As flesh of muttons, beefs or goats. I say
       To buy his favour, I extend this friendship:
       If he will take it, so, if not, adieu.
170   And for my love, I pray you wrong me not.

       ANTONIO   Yes Shylock, I will seal unto this bond.

---

141 kind kindness/natural behavior   142 were would be (indeed)   144 notary person
authorized to draw up contracts   145 single particular/**bond** that specifies that a sum of
money must be paid on an appointed day   148 condition contract   149 nominated for
named as   equal exact   155 dwell remain/exist   necessity need   161 suspect i.e. to
doubt   163 break his day miss the appointed date (for repayment)   164 exaction
enforcement   166 estimable valuable   169 so so be it

SHYLOCK   Then meet me forthwith at the notary's,
Give him direction for this merry bond,
And I will go and purse the ducats straight,
175   See to my house, left in the fearful guard
Of an unthrifty knave, and presently
I'll be with you.

ANTONIO   Hie thee, gentle Jew.   *Exit*
This Hebrew will turn Christian, he grows kind.

180   BASSANIO   I like not fair terms and a villain's mind.

ANTONIO   Come on, in this there can be no dismay.
My ships come home a month before the day.   *Exeunt*

Act 2 [Scene 1]   *running scene 4*

*Enter Morocco, a tawny Moor, all in white, and three or four followers
accordingly, with Portia, Nerissa and their train. Flourish cornets*

MOROCCO   Mislike me not for my complexion,
The shadowed livery of the burnished sun,
To whom I am a neighbour and near bred.
Bring me the fairest creature northward born,
5   Where Phoebus' fire scarce thaws the icicles,
And let us make incision for your love,
To prove whose blood is reddest, his or mine.
I tell thee, lady, this aspect of mine
Hath feared the valiant. By my love I swear,
10   The best-regarded virgins of our clime
Have loved it too: I would not change this hue,
Except to steal your thoughts, my gentle queen.

---

172 forthwith at once   173 direction instruction   174 purse bag up   175 See attend
fearful fear-inducing   176 unthrifty profligate/careless   knave scoundrel/servant
presently soon   178 Hie hurry   gentle courteous (may pun on "gentile")   179 kind
agreeable/generous/natural   2.1   *Location: Belmont*   *tawny* dark-skinned/of yellowish-
brown skin   *Moor* person of either African or Middle Eastern origin   *Flourish* fanfare
2 livery uniform/badge   burnished shining like polished metal   3 near bred closely related
5 Phoebus Roman sun god   6 make incision i.e. to let blood   7 reddest suggestive of
courage and vigor   8 aspect face   9 feared frightened   10 clime land   11 hue
color/appearance

PORTIA   In terms of choice I am not solely led
By nice direction of a maiden's eyes.
15   Besides, the lott'ry of my destiny
Bars me the right of voluntary choosing.
But if my father had not scanted me,
And hedged me by his wit to yield myself
His wife who wins me by that means I told you,
20   Yourself, renownèd prince, then stood as fair
As any comer I have looked on yet
For my affection.

MOROCCO   Even for that I thank you:
Therefore, I pray you lead me to the caskets
25   To try my fortune. By this scimitar
That slew the Sophy and a Persian prince
That won three fields of Sultan Solyman,
I would o'erstare the sternest eyes that look,
Outbrave the heart most daring on the earth,
30   Pluck the young sucking cubs from the she-bear,
Yea, mock the lion when he roars for prey
To win thee, lady. But alas the while!
If Hercules and Lichas play at dice
Which is the better man, the greater throw
35   May turn by fortune from the weaker hand:
So is Alcides beaten by his page,
And so may I, blind fortune leading me,
Miss that which one unworthier may attain,
And die with grieving.

40   PORTIA   You must take your chance,
And either not attempt to choose at all
Or swear before you choose, if you choose wrong

---

14 nice scrupulous/whimsical   **direction** guidance   **17 scanted** limited   **18 hedged**
protected/confined   **wit** wisdom   **19 His** as his   **20 then** would then have   **fair** i.e. fair a
chance (puns on the sense of "fair-skinned/attractive")   **22 For** of gaining/hoping for
25 scimitar short, curved sword   **26 Sophy** ruler (shah) of Persia   **27 fields** battles   **of**
from/against   **Solyman** Suleiman, sultan who fought against Persia   **28 o'erstare** outstare
33 Hercules Greek hero   **Lichas** Hercules' companion   **36 Alcides** another name for
Hercules

Never to speak to lady afterward
In way of marriage: therefore be advised.

45   MOROCCO   Nor will not. Come, bring me unto my chance.

PORTIA   First, forward to the temple. After dinner
Your hazard shall be made.

MOROCCO   Good fortune then!
To make me blest or cursed'st among men.

Cornets [and] exeunt

[Act 2 Scene 2]   *running scene 5*

Enter the Clown [Lancelet] alone

LANCELET   Certainly my conscience will serve me to run from
this Jew my master. The fiend is at mine elbow and tempts me,
saying to me, 'Gobbo, Lancelet Gobbo, good Lancelet', or
'Good Gobbo', or 'Good Lancelet Gobbo, use your legs, take the
5   start, run away.' My conscience says, 'No; take heed, honest
Lancelet, take heed, honest Gobbo', or, as aforesaid, 'Honest
Lancelet Gobbo, do not run, scorn running with thy heels.'
Well, the most courageous fiend bids me pack: 'Fia!' says the
fiend, 'Away!' says the fiend, 'For the heavens, rouse up a brave
10   mind', says the fiend, 'and run.' Well, my conscience, hanging
about the neck of my heart, says very wisely to me, 'My honest
friend Lancelet, being an honest man's son', or rather an
honest woman's son—for indeed my father did something
smack, something grow to, he had a kind of taste—well, my
15   conscience says 'Lancelet, budge not.' 'Budge', says the fiend.
'Budge not', says my conscience. 'Conscience,' say I, 'you

---

44 **advised** warned   45 **Nor will not** break my word, i.e. speak to a woman   47 **hazard**
risk/choice/fortune   **2.2**   *Location: Venice*   *Clown* a rustic, and/or comic character
Lancelet i.e. "little lance" (type of spear/penis); Sir Lancelot was famous for adultery with King
Arthur's wife; a "lance" was also a surgeon's instrument for piercing an abscess   1 **serve**
allow   3 **Gobbo** hunchback (Italian)   5 **start** advantage   7 **with thy heels** firmly (plays on
literal sense)   8 **courageous** purposeful/forceful/lusty   **pack** depart   **Fia!** *Via!* i.e. away
(Italian)   9 **For the heavens** i.e. in heaven's name   12 **honest** honorable (sense then shifts
to "chaste")   13 **something** somewhat/some thing (i.e. vagina)   14 **smack** have a taste
for/taste literally/have sex with   **grow to** become one with/tend toward/become erect
taste preference/literal taste

counsel well.' 'Fiend,' say I, 'you counsel well.' To be ruled by
my conscience, I should stay with the Jew my master, who,
God bless the mark, is a kind of devil; and to run away from the
20   Jew, I should be ruled by the fiend, who, saving your reverence,
is the devil himself. Certainly the Jew is the very devil
incarnation, and in my conscience, my conscience is a kind of
hard conscience to offer to counsel me to stay with the Jew; the
fiend gives the more friendly counsel. I will run, fiend. My
25   heels are at your commandment. I will run.

Enter Old Gobbo, with a basket

GOBBO   Master young man, you, I pray you which is the
way to Master Jew's?

LANCELET   O heavens, this is my true-begotten father,   *Aside*
who, being more than sand-blind, high-gravel-blind, knows
30   me not. I will try confusions with him.

GOBBO   Master young gentleman, I pray you which is the
way to Master Jew's?

LANCELET   Turn upon your right hand at the next turning, but
at the next turning of all, on your left; marry, at the very
35   next turning, turn of no hand, but turn down indirectly to
the Jew's house.

GOBBO   By God's sonties, 'twill be a hard way to hit. Can you
tell me whether one Lancelet, that dwells with him, dwell
with him or no?

40   LANCELET   Talk you of young Master Lancelet?—   *Aside*
Mark me now, now will I raise the waters.—Talk you of
young Master Lancelet?

GOBBO   No master, sir, but a poor man's son. His father,
though I say't, is an honest exceeding poor man and, God be
45   thanked, well to live.

19 God . . . mark i.e. excuse my language   20 saving your reverence i.e. begging your pardon
22 incarnation slip for "incarnate" (ironic, given that the Incarnation refers to the making of
Christ into flesh)   28 true-begotten honestly conceived (Lancelet means "real, true")
29 sand-blind half-blind (from "sam-blind," but Lancelet thinks "as if with **sand** in the eyes")
high-gravel-blind completely blind   30 confusions (appropriate) malapropism for
"conclusions"—i.e. "experiment"   35 of no hand i.e. neither left or right   indirectly along
a winding route (perhaps plays on the sense of "moral crookedness")   37 sonties saints
hit get right, find   41 raise the waters provoke tears   43 master gentleman or professional
tradesperson   45 well to live well-to-do/managing satisfactorily/healthy

LANCELET   Well, let his father be what a will, we talk of young
Master Lancelet.

GOBBO   Your worship's friend and Lancelet.

LANCELET   But I pray you *ergo*, old man, *ergo*, I beseech you talk
50   you of young Master Lancelet?

GOBBO   Of Lancelet, an't please your mastership.

LANCELET   *Ergo*, Master Lancelet. Talk not of Master Lancelet,
father, for the young gentleman—according to fates and
destinies and such odd sayings, the Sisters Three and such
55   branches of learning—is indeed deceased, or as you would
say in plain terms, gone to heaven.

GOBBO   Marry, God forbid! The boy was the very staff of my
age, my very prop.

LANCELET   Do I look like a cudgel or a hovel-post, a staff or a
60   prop? Do you know me, father?

GOBBO   Alack the day, I know you not, young gentleman,
but I pray you tell me, is my boy, God rest his soul, alive or
dead?

LANCELET   Do you not know me, father?

65   **GOBBO**   Alack, sir, I am sand-blind. I know you not.

LANCELET   Nay, indeed if you had your eyes you might fail of
the knowing me: it is a wise father that knows his own child.
Well, old man, I will tell you news of your son. Give   *He kneels*
me your blessing. Truth will come to light, murder cannot be
70   hid long, a man's son may, but in the end truth will out.

GOBBO   Pray you, sir, stand up. I am sure you are not
Lancelet, my boy.

LANCELET   Pray you let's have no more fooling about it, but
give me your blessing. I am Lancelet, your boy that was, your
75   son that is, your child that shall be.

GOBBO   I cannot think you are my son.

---

46 a he   48 friend and Lancelet Old Gobbo's polite way of rejecting the title "master" for
Lancelet   49 *ergo* "therefore" (Latin)   51 an't if it   53 father respectful form of address for
an old man   54 Sisters Three three Fates, goddesses who spin, measure, and cut the thread of
a person's life   59 hovel-post doorpost of a hovel   66 of the knowing to recognize   67 it . . .
child reversal of the proverb "it is a wise child that knows its own father"   74 your boy . . . be
comic paraphrase of the Gloria from the Book of Common Prayer: "As it was in the beginning,
is now, and ever shall be"

LANCELET   I know not what I shall think of that. But I am
Lancelet, the Jew's man, and I am sure Margery your wife is
my mother.

80 GOBBO   Her name is Margery, indeed. I'll be sworn, if thou
be Lancelet, thou art mine own flesh and blood. Lord
worshipped might he be! What a beard hast thou got! Thou
hast got more hair on thy chin than Dobbin my fill-horse has
on his tail.

85 LANCELET   It should seem, then, that Dobbin's tail   *He rises*
grows backward. I am sure he had more hair of his tail than
I have of my face when I last saw him.

GOBBO   Lord, how art thou changed! How dost thou and thy
master agree? I have brought him a present. How 'gree you
90 now?

LANCELET   Well, well. But for mine own part, as I have set up
my rest to run away, so I will not rest till I have run some
ground; my master's a very Jew. Give him a present? Give
him a halter! I am famished in his service. You may tell every
95 finger I have with my ribs. Father, I am glad you are come.
Give me your present to one Master Bassanio, who, indeed,
gives rare new liveries. If I serve not him, I will run as far as
God has any ground. O rare fortune! Here comes the man. To
him, father, for I am a Jew if I serve the Jew any longer.

Enter Bassanio, with a follower or two [including Leonardo]

100 BASSANIO   You may do so, but let it be so hasted   *To a Servant*
that supper be ready at the farthest by five of the clock. See
these letters delivered, put the liveries to making, and desire
Gratiano to come anon to my lodging.   *[Exit a Servant]*

LANCELET   To him, father.

105 GOBBO   God bless your worship!   *Comes forward*

BASSANIO   Gramercy! Wouldst thou aught with me?

---

80 **Margery** sometimes used as slang term for a whore, or vagina   83 **fill-horse** carthorse
("fills" were the shafts of a cart)   86 **backward** inward (i.e. is shorter)   **of** on   89 **agree**
get on   91 **set . . . rest** staked all   92 **rest** pause, stop   93 **very** thorough   94 **halter**
hangman's noose   **tell** count   95 **finger . . . ribs** Lancelet reverses **ribs** and **finger**   96 **Give
me** give for me/give (**me** is emphatic)   97 **rare** splendid   **liveries** uniforms (for servants)
99 **Jew** i.e. villain   100 **hasted** hastened   101 **farthest** latest   103 **anon** shortly
106 **Gramercy** many thanks   **aught** anything

GOBBO   Here's my son, sir, a poor boy—

LANCELET   Not a poor boy, sir, but the rich Jew's man, that would, sir, as my father shall specify—

110 GOBBO   He hath a great infection, sir, as one would say, to serve—

LANCELET   Indeed, the short and the long is, I serve the Jew and have a desire, as my father shall specify—

GOBBO   His master and he, saving your worship's reverence,
115 are scarce cater-cousins—

LANCELET   To be brief, the very truth is that the Jew, having done me wrong, doth cause me, as my father, being, I hope, an old man, shall frutify unto you—

GOBBO   I have here a dish of doves that I would bestow upon
120   your worship, and my suit is—

LANCELET   In very brief, the suit is impertinent to myself, as your worship shall know by this honest old man, and though I say it, though old man, yet poor man, my father.

BASSANIO   One speak for both. What would you?

125 LANCELET   Serve you, sir.

GOBBO   That is the very defect of the matter, sir.

BASSANIO   I know thee well, thou hast obtained thy suit.
Shylock thy master spoke with me this day,
And hath preferred thee, if it be preferment
130 To leave a rich Jew's service, to become
The follower of so poor a gentleman.

LANCELET   The old proverb is very well parted between my master Shylock and you, sir: you have the grace of God, sir, and he hath enough.

135 BASSANIO   Thou speak'st it well. Go, father, with thy son.
Take leave of thy old master and inquire
My lodging out.— Give him a livery   *To a Servant*
More guarded than his fellows'. See it done.

---

108 **poor** shifts sense from "unfortunate/humble" to "penniless"   110 **infection** malapropism for "affection" (i.e. desire)   115 **scarce** scarcely   **cater-cousins** good friends, close   118 **frutify** malapropism for "certify"   121 **impertinent** malapropism for "pertinent"   126 **defect** malapropism for "effect" (i.e. meaning, purport)   129 **preferred** recommended/promoted
132 **old proverb** "the grace of God is gear enough" (i.e. sufficient)   **parted** divided
136 **inquire . . . out** find out where my house is   138 **guarded** ornamented by braid trimmings

LANCELET   Father, in. I cannot get a service, no. I have ne'er a
140   tongue in my head. Well, if any man in Italy have a   *Points to*
fairer table which doth offer to swear upon a book,   *his palm*
I shall have good fortune. Go to, here's a simple line of life,
here's a small trifle of wives. Alas, fifteen wives is nothing!
Eleven widows and nine maids is a simple coming-in for one
145   man, and then to scape drowning thrice, and to be in peril
of my life with the edge of a feather-bed. Here are simple
scapes. Well, if Fortune be a woman, she's a good wench for
this gear. Father, come; I'll take my leave of the Jew in the
twinkling.   *Exit Clown [Lancelet with Old Gobbo]*

150   BASSANIO   I pray thee good Leonardo, think on this.   *Gives a list*
These things being bought and orderly bestowed,
Return in haste, for I do feast tonight
My best-esteemed acquaintance. Hie thee, go.

LEONARDO   My best endeavours shall be done herein.

Enter Gratiano

155   GRATIANO   Where's your master?

LEONARDO   Yonder, sir, he walks.   *Exit*

GRATIANO   Signior Bassanio!

BASSANIO   Gratiano!

GRATIANO   I have a suit to you.

160   BASSANIO   You have obtained it.

GRATIANO   You must not deny me. I must go with you to
Belmont.

BASSANIO   Why then you must. But hear thee, Gratiano,
Thou art too wild, too rude and bold of voice,
165   Parts that become thee happily enough
And in such eyes as ours appear not faults;
But where they are not known, why, there they show

---

141 **table** part of the palm   **book** i.e. Bible (on which oaths are sworn)   142 **simple**
ordinary/unremarkable   **line of life** the life-line on the palm supposedly records the length
and nature of a person's life   143 **trifle** insignificant amount   144 **simple** humble
coming-in income (puns on the sense of "having sex")   145 **scape** escape   146 **edge . . .
feather-bed** perhaps refers to the dangers of marriage (i.e. a wife's infidelity)   147 **scapes**
escapes/adventures/wrongdoings   148 **gear** matter   **the** i.e. a   151 **bestowed** stowed away
(on the ship bound for Belmont)   152 **feast** lay on a feast for   154 **herein** in this matter
160 **obtained it** i.e. been granted your request   164 **rude** raucous/coarse   165 **Parts**
qualities   **become** suit   167 **show** appear

Something too liberal. Pray thee take pain
To allay with some cold drops of modesty
170   Thy skipping spirit, lest through thy wild behaviour
I be misconstered in the place I go to,
And lose my hopes.

GRATIANO   Signior Bassanio, hear me:
If I do not put on a sober habit,
175   Talk with respect and swear but now and then,
Wear prayer-books in my pocket, look demurely,
Nay more, while grace is saying, hood mine eyes
Thus with my hat, and sigh and say 'Amen',   *Covers his face*
Use all the observance of civility,
180   Like one well studied in a sad ostent
To please his grandam, never trust me more.

BASSANIO   Well, we shall see your bearing.

GRATIANO   Nay, but I bar tonight. You shall not gauge me
By what we do tonight.

185   BASSANIO   No, that were pity.
I would entreat you rather to put on
Your boldest suit of mirth, for we have friends
That purpose merriment. But fare you well.
I have some business.

190   GRATIANO   And I must to Lorenzo and the rest,
But we will visit you at suppertime.   *Exeunt*

[Act 2 Scene 3]   *running scene 6*

Enter Jessica and the Clown [Lancelet]

JESSICA   I am sorry thou wilt leave my father so.
Our house is hell, and thou, a merry devil,
Didst rob it of some taste of tediousness;
But fare thee well. There is a ducat for thee.   *Gives money*

168 liberal licentious   **take pain** make an effort   **169 allay** diminish   **modesty** restraint/
propriety   **170 skipping** frivolous   **171 misconstered** misconstrued, misunderstood
174 habit demeanor/behavior/clothing   **175 but** only   **177 saying** being said   **180 studied
... ostent** practiced in a solemn appearance   **181 grandam** grandmother   **183 bar** exclude
gauge assess   **188 purpose** intend   **2.3 *Jessica*** probably a form of "Iscah," daughter of
Abraham's brother, Haran (Genesis 11:29)

5 And, Lancelet, soon at supper shalt thou see
   Lorenzo, who is thy new master's guest:
   Give him this letter. Do it secretly.   *Gives a letter*
   And so farewell. I would not have my father
   See me talk with thee.

10 LANCELET   Adieu! Tears exhibit my tongue, most beautiful
   pagan, most sweet Jew! If a Christian did not play the knave
   and get thee, I am much deceived; but adieu. These foolish
   drops do somewhat drown my manly spirit. Adieu.   *Exit*

   JESSICA   Farewell, good Lancelet.

15 Alack, what heinous sin is it in me
   To be ashamed to be my father's child!
   But though I am a daughter to his blood,
   I am not to his manners. O Lorenzo,
   If thou keep promise, I shall end this strife,
20 Become a Christian and thy loving wife.   *Exit*

[Act 2 Scene 4]   *running scene 7*

Enter Gratiano, Lorenzo, Salerio and Solanio

   LORENZO   Nay, we will slink away in suppertime,
   Disguise us at my lodging and return
   All in an hour.

   GRATIANO   We have not made good preparation.

5 SALERIO   We have not spoke us yet of torchbearers.

   SOLANIO   'Tis vile, unless it may be quaintly ordered,
   And better in my mind not undertook.

   LORENZO   'Tis now but four of clock. We have two hours
   To furnish us.— Friend Lancelet, what's the news?

Enter Lancelet, with a letter

10 LANCELET   An it shall please you to break up this,   *Gives him*
   shall it seem to signify.   *the letter*

---

10 exhibit express (malapropism for "inhibit," i.e. restrain)   **12 get** beget, conceive
18 manners behavior/character   **19 strife** i.e. internal conflict, turmoil   **2.4   1 in** during
5 spoke . . . of discussed/hired   **6 vile** degrading/worthless   **quaintly** skillfully   **ordered**
arranged   **9 furnish us** prepare   **10 An** if   **this** i.e. the letter's seal   **11 seem to signify** i.e.
tell you something

LORENZO   I know the hand. In faith, 'tis a fair hand,
And whiter than the paper it writ on
Is the fair hand that writ.

15   GRATIANO   Love-news, in faith.

LANCELET   By your leave, sir.   *Starts to leave*

LORENZO   Whither goest thou?

LANCELET   Marry, sir, to bid my old master the Jew to sup
tonight with my new master the Christian.

20   LORENZO   Hold here, take this. Tell gentle Jessica   *Gives money*
I will not fail her. Speak it privately.
Go, gentlemen,
Will you prepare you for this masque tonight?
I am provided of a torchbearer.   *Exit Clown [Lancelet]*

25   SALERIO   Ay, marry, I'll be gone about it straight.

SOLANIO   And so will I.

LORENZO   Meet me and Gratiano
At Gratiano's lodging some hour hence.

SALERIO   'Tis good we do so.   *Exit [Salerio with Solanio]*

30   GRATIANO   Was not that letter from fair Jessica?

LORENZO   I must needs tell thee all. She hath directed
How I shall take her from her father's house,
What gold and jewels she is furnished with,
What page's suit she hath in readiness.

35   If e'er the Jew her father come to heaven,
It will be for his gentle daughter's sake;
And never dare misfortune cross her foot,
Unless she do it under this excuse,
That she is issue to a faithless Jew.

40   Come, go with me, peruse this as thou goest.   *Gives the letter*
Fair Jessica shall be my torchbearer.   *Exeunt*

---

12 hand handwriting   **fair hand** attractive handwriting (sense then shifts to "beautiful pale hand")   **16 By your leave** with your permission (to go)   **18 sup** have supper   **22 Go** i.e. come   **23 masque** theatrical entertainment, usually involving music and dancing   **24 of with   28 some** about an   **31 must needs** must   **directed** instructed/described   **36 gentle** puns on "gentile"   **37 foot** step/path   **38 she** i.e. misfortune   **39 she** i.e. Jessica   **issue** child   **faithless** pagan/dishonest

[Act 2 Scene 5]

Enter [Shylock the] Jew and [Lancelet,] his man that was, the Clown

SHYLOCK   Well, thou shall see, thy eyes shall be thy judge,
The difference of old Shylock and Bassanio.—
What, Jessica!—Thou shalt not gormandize
As thou hast done with me— What, Jessica!—
5   And sleep and snore, and rend apparel out—
Why, Jessica, I say!

LANCELET   Why, Jessica!

SHYLOCK   Who bids thee call? I do not bid thee call.

LANCELET   Your worship was wont to tell me
10   I could do nothing without bidding.

Enter Jessica

JESSICA   Call you? What is your will?

SHYLOCK   I am bid forth to supper, Jessica.
There are my keys. But wherefore should I go?
I am not bid for love, they flatter me.
15   But yet I'll go in hate, to feed upon
The prodigal Christian. Jessica, my girl,
Look to my house. I am right loath to go.
There is some ill a-brewing towards my rest,
For I did dream of money-bags tonight.

20   LANCELET   I beseech you, sir, go. My young master doth expect
your reproach.

SHYLOCK   So do I his.

LANCELET   An they have conspired together. I will not say you
shall see a masque, but if you do, then it was not for nothing
25   that my nose fell a-bleeding on Black Monday last at
six o'clock i'th'morning, falling out that year on Ash
Wednesday was four year, in th'afternoon.

2.5   **2 of** between   **3 gormandize** eat excessively   **5 rend apparel out** wear out your clothes
9 wont accustomed   **12 bid forth** invited out   **13 wherefore** why   **15 upon** i.e. at the expense
of   **16 prodigal** wastefully extravagant   **17 to** after   **right loath** very reluctant   **18 ill**
harm/trouble   **19 tonight** last night   **20 expect** await   **21 reproach** malapropism for
"approach"; Shylock responds to what Lancelet has actually said   **25 nose fell a-bleeding**
considered to be a bad omen   **Black ... th'afternoon** a deliberately nonsensical series of details;
Lancelet pokes fun at superstitious attitudes such as Shylock's   **Black Monday** Easter Monday

SHYLOCK   What, are there masques? Hear you me, Jessica:
Lock up my doors, and when you hear the drum
30   And the vile squealing of the wry-necked fife,
Clamber not you up to the casements then,
Nor thrust your head into the public street
To gaze on Christian fools with varnished faces,
But stop my house's ears, I mean my casements.
35   Let not the sound of shallow fopp'ry enter
My sober house. By Jacob's staff, I swear,
I have no mind of feasting forth tonight,
But I will go. Go you before me, sirrah,
Say I will come.

40   LANCELET   I will go before, sir.— Mistress, look out   *Aside to Jessica*
at window, for all this,
There will come a Christian by,
Will be worth a Jewès eye.   [*Exit Lancelet*]

SHYLOCK   What says that fool of Hagar's offspring, ha?
45   JESSICA   His words were 'Farewell mistress', nothing else.

SHYLOCK   The patch is kind enough, but a huge feeder,
Snail-slow in profit, but he sleeps by day
More than the wild-cat. Drones hive not with me:
Therefore I part with him, and part with him
50   To one that I would have him help to waste
His borrowed purse. Well, Jessica, go in.
Perhaps I will return immediately.
Do as I bid you, shut doors after you.
Fast bind, fast find—
55   A proverb never stale in thrifty mind.   *Exit*

---

30 wry-necked played with the musician's head twisted away from the instrument
31 casements windows   **33 varnished faces** i.e. wearing masks   **34 stop** shut   **35 fopp'ry**
foolishness   **36 Jacob's staff** in the Bible, the only possession Jacob started out with
37 mind of inclination for   **forth** away from home   **41 for** despite   **43 a Jewès eye**
proverbial phrase for something very valuable; also plays on Jessica (a "Jewess") eyeing
Lorenzo   **44 Hagar's offspring** Abraham's Egyptian concubine Hagar gave birth to Ishmael;
both mother and son were outcast at Abraham's wife Sarah's request   **46 patch** fool, clown
47 profit progress   **48 Drones** non-workers (literally, bees whose only role is to impregnate the
queen)   **hive** live (in a hive)   **54 Fast . . . find** keep possessions securely and they'll always be
found quickly (proverbial)

JESSICA   Farewell, and if my fortune be not crossed,
I have a father, you a daughter lost.   *Exit*

[Act 2 Scene 6]   *running scene 9*

Enter the masquers, Gratiano and Salerio

GRATIANO   This is the penthouse under which Lorenzo
Desired us to make a stand.

SALERIO   His hour is almost past.

GRATIANO   And it is marvel he out-dwells his hour,
5   For lovers ever run before the clock.

SALERIO   O, ten times faster Venus' pigeons fly
To seal love's bonds new-made, than they are wont
To keep obligèd faith unforfeited!

GRATIANO   That ever holds: who riseth from a feast
10   With that keen appetite that he sits down?
.Where is the horse that doth untread again
His tedious measures with the unbated fire
That he did pace them first? All things that are,
Are with more spirit chasèd than enjoyed.
15   How like a younger or a prodigal
The scarfèd bark puts from her native bay,
Hugged and embracèd by the strumpet wind!
How like a prodigal doth she return,
With over-withered ribs and ragged sails,
20   Lean, rent and beggared by the strumpet wind!

Enter Lorenzo

SALERIO   Here comes Lorenzo. More of this hereafter.

56 crossed thwarted   2.6   1 penthouse projecting roof of a building   2 make a stand
i.e. wait   3 His . . . past i.e. he is almost late   4 marvel surprising   out-dwells his hour i.e. is
late   5 ever always   run . . . clock i.e. are early   6 Venus' pigeons doves that draw Venus'
chariot   8 obligèd contracted, pledged   unforfeited unbroken   9 ever always   holds
holds true   10 that with which   11 untread retrace   12 measures paces   unbated fire
undiminished keenness   15 younger younger son, as the **prodigal** was (sometimes emended
to "younker," fashionable youth)   16 scarfèd bark ship decorated with flags   puts from
leaves   17 strumpet lascivious/wild/changeable   19 over-withered ribs over-weathered
ship's timbers (i.e. damaged by waves)   20 rent torn   beggared made destitute

LORENZO   Sweet friends, your patience for my long abode:
Not I but my affairs have made you wait.
When you shall please to play the thieves for wives,
25   I'll watch as long for you then. Approach.
Here dwells my father Jew. Ho! Who's within?

[*Enter*] *Jessica above* [*in boy's clothes*]

JESSICA   Who are you? Tell me, for more certainty,
Albeit I'll swear that I do know your tongue.

LORENZO   Lorenzo, and thy love.

30   JESSICA   Lorenzo, certain, and my love indeed,
For who love I so much? And now who knows
But you, Lorenzo, whether I am yours?

LORENZO   Heaven and thy thoughts are witness that
thou art.

JESSICA   Here, catch this casket, it is worth the pains.
35   I am glad 'tis night, you do not look on me,
For I am much ashamed of my exchange.
But love is blind and lovers cannot see
The pretty follies that themselves commit,
For if they could, Cupid himself would blush
40   To see me thus transformèd to a boy.

LORENZO   Descend, for you must be my torchbearer.

JESSICA   What, must I hold a candle to my shames?
They in themselves, good sooth, are too too light.
Why, 'tis an office of discovery, love,
45   And I should be obscured.

LORENZO   So you are, sweet,
Even in the lovely garnish of a boy.
But come at once,
For the close night doth play the runaway,
50   And we are stayed for at Bassanio's feast.

---

22 your I beg your   abode delay   25 watch wait/keep watch   26 father father-in-law
28 tongue i.e. voice   36 exchange change (into boy's clothes)   38 pretty clever, artful
39 Cupid Roman god of love   42 hold . . . to stand and observe/illuminate   43 sooth truth
light immoral/evident/luminous   44 office of discovery i.e. torchbearing, because it involves
revealing things   47 garnish outfit/trimming (some editors emend "lovely" to "lowly")
49 close secretive/concealing   play the runaway i.e. pass quickly   50 stayed for awaited

JESSICA   I will make fast the doors and gild myself
With some more ducats, and be with you straight.

[Exit above]

GRATIANO   Now, by my hood, a gentle and no Jew.

LORENZO   Beshrew me but I love her heartily.

55   For she is wise, if I can judge of her,
And fair she is, if that mine eyes be true,
And true she is, as she hath proved herself,
And therefore, like herself, wise, fair and true,
Shall she be placèd in my constant soul.

Enter Jessica [below]

60   What, art thou come? On, gentlemen, away!
Our masquing mates by this time for us stay.

Exit [with Jessica and Salerio]

Enter Antonio

ANTONIO   Who's there?

GRATIANO   Signior Antonio?

ANTONIO   Fie, fie, Gratiano! Where are all the rest?

65   'Tis nine o'clock: our friends all stay for you.
No masque tonight, the wind is come about.
Bassanio presently will go aboard.
I have sent twenty out to seek for you.

GRATIANO   I am glad on't. I desire no more delight

70   Than to be under sail and gone tonight.   *Exeunt*

[Act 2 Scene 7]   *running scene 10*

[Flourish of cornets.] Enter Portia with [the Prince of] Morocco and
both their trains

PORTIA   Go, draw aside the curtains and discover
The several caskets to this noble prince.
Now make your choice.   *The curtains are opened*

---

51 **make fast** i.e. shut securely, lock   **gild** equip, adorn (literally, cover with gold)   53 **gentle**
dear one/gentile   54 **Beshrew** curse   56 **true** reliable   57 **true** constant   65 **stay** wait
66 **is come about** i.e. has changed (favorably for sailing)   **2.7** *Location: Belmont*   **trains**
retinues   1 **discover** reveal   2 **several** various, individual

MOROCCO   The first, of gold, who this inscription bears:
5   'Who chooseth me shall gain what many men desire.'
        The second, silver, which this promise carries,
        'Who chooseth me shall get as much as he deserves.'
        This third, dull lead, with warning all as blunt,
        'Who chooseth me must give and hazard all he hath.'
10   How shall I know if I do choose the right?
PORTIA   The one of them contains my picture, prince.
        If you choose that, then I am yours withal.
MOROCCO   Some god direct my judgement! Let me see.
        I will survey the inscriptions back again.
15   What says this leaden casket?
        'Who chooseth me must give and hazard all he hath.'
        Must give: for what? For lead? Hazard for lead?
        This casket threatens. Men that hazard all
        Do it in hope of fair advantages:
20   A golden mind stoops not to shows of dross,
        I'll then nor give nor hazard aught for lead.
        What says the silver with her virgin hue?
        'Who chooseth me shall get as much as he deserves.'
        As much as he deserves; pause there, Morocco,
25   And weigh thy value with an even hand:
        If thou be'st rated by thy estimation,
        Thou dost deserve enough, and yet enough
        May not extend so far as to the lady.
        And yet to be afeard of my deserving
30   Were but a weak disabling of myself.
        As much as I deserve? Why, that's the lady.
        I do in birth deserve her, and in fortunes,
        In graces and in qualities of breeding,
        But more than these, in love I do deserve.
35   What if I strayed no further, but chose here?

4 who which   5 Who whoever   8 dull not bright/blunt   blunt forthright/unrefined
12 withal with it   14 back over   20 dross rubbish/residue from melted metal   21 nor
neither   22 virgin hue possibly because **silver** is the color of the moon, ruled over by Diana,
goddess of chastity   25 weigh weigh up, assess   even fair/impartial   26 rated
valued/estimated   estimation reputation/value   30 disabling belittling

Let's see once more this saying graved in gold:
'Who chooseth me shall gain what many men desire.'
Why, that's the lady, all the world desires her.
From the four corners of the earth they come,
40 To kiss this shrine, this mortal breathing saint.
The Hyrcanian deserts and the vasty wilds
Of wide Arabia are as throughfares now
For princes to come view fair Portia.
The watery kingdom, whose ambitious head
45 Spits in the face of heaven, is no bar
To stop the foreign spirits, but they come,
As o'er a brook, to see fair Portia.
One of these three contains her heavenly picture.
Is't like that lead contains her? 'Twere damnation
50 To think so base a thought, it were too gross
To rib her cerecloth in the obscure grave.
Or shall I think in silver she's immured,
Being ten times undervalued to trièd gold?
O sinful thought! Never so rich a gem
55 Was set in worse than gold! They have in England
A coin that bears the figure of an angel
Stamped in gold, but that's insculped upon,
But here an angel in a golden bed
Lies all within. Deliver me the key:
60 Here do I choose, and thrive I as I may!
PORTIA   There, take it, prince, and if my form lie there,
Then I am yours.   *He unlocks the gold casket*
MOROCCO   O hell! What have we here?
A carrion Death, within whose empty eye
65 There is a written scroll; I'll read the writing.

---

36 graved engraved   40 mortal breathing i.e. living   41 Hyrcanian deserts Persian region
south of the Caspian Sea known for its wildness   desert deserted/isolated place   vasty vast
44 watery kingdom i.e. the sea   ambitious head i.e. waves   46 spirits courageous men
49 like likely   50 base unworthy (puns on lead as a **base** metal)   gross inferior/coarse/
earthly   51 rib enclose (as ribs do the internal organs)   cerecloth winding-sheet, shroud
obscure concealed/dark   52 immured enclosed   53 undervalued to less in value compared
with   trièd tested   55 set fixed, like a jewel   56 angel Archangel Michael who appeared on
a coin known as an "angel"   57 insculped engraved   61 form image   64 carrion
loathsome/skeletal/putrefying   Death death's head, skull

'All that glisters is not gold,   *Reads*
Often have you heard that told;
Many a man his life hath sold
But my outside to behold.
70 Gilded tombs do worms enfold.
Had you been as wise as bold,
Young in limbs, in judgement old,
Your answer had not been inscrolled:
Fare you well, your suit is cold.'
75 Cold, indeed, and labour lost.
Then farewell, heat, and welcome, frost!
Portia, adieu. I have too grieved a heart
To take a tedious leave. Thus losers part.

Exit [with his train. Flourish of cornets]

PORTIA   A gentle riddance. Draw the curtains, go.
80 Let all of his complexion choose me so.

[They close the curtains and] exeunt

[Act 2 Scene 8]   *running scene 11*

Enter Salerio and Solanio

SALERIO   Why, man, I saw Bassanio under sail.
With him is Gratiano gone along;
And in their ship I am sure Lorenzo is not.
SOLANIO   The villain Jew with outcries raised the duke,
5 Who went with him to search Bassanio's ship.
SALERIO   He comes too late, the ship was under sail;
But there the duke was given to understand
That in a gondola were seen together
Lorenzo and his amorous Jessica. Besides,
10 Antonio certified the duke
They were not with Bassanio in his ship.
SOLANIO   I never heard a passion so confused,

69 But only   72 in judgement old i.e. wise   73 inscrolled inscribed on a scroll   78 tedious lengthy   part depart   80 complexion temperament/skin color   2.8 *Location: Venice*   4 raised roused, woke up   12 passion passionate outcry

So strange, outrageous, and so variable,
As the dog Jew did utter in the streets:

15 'My daughter! O my ducats! O my daughter!
Fled with a Christian! O my Christian ducats!
Justice, the law, my ducats, and my daughter!
A sealèd bag, two sealèd bags of ducats,
Of double ducats, stol'n from me by my daughter!

20 And jewels, two stones, two rich and precious stones,
Stol'n by my daughter! Justice! Find the girl,
She hath the stones upon her, and the ducats.'

SALERIO   Why, all the boys in Venice follow him,
Crying, his stones, his daughter, and his ducats.

25 SOLANIO   Let good Antonio look he keep his day,
Or he shall pay for this.

SALERIO   Marry, well remembered.
I reasoned with a Frenchman yesterday,
Who told me, in the narrow seas that part

30 The French and English there miscarried
A vessel of our country richly fraught.
I thought upon Antonio when he told me,
And wished in silence that it were not his.

SOLANIO   You were best to tell Antonio what you hear;

35 Yet do not suddenly, for it may grieve him.

SALERIO   A kinder gentleman treads not the earth.
I saw Bassanio and Antonio part:
Bassanio told him he would make some speed
Of his return. He answered, 'Do not so,

40 Slubber not business for my sake, Bassanio,
But stay the very riping of the time.
And for the Jew's bond which he hath of me,
Let it not enter in your mind of love.

---

13 outrageous excessively fierce   **19 double ducats** twice the value of single ducats
20 stones jewels   **24 stones** plays on the sense of "testicles"   **25 look** be sure   **day** i.e. date
on which the loan is to be repaid   **28 reasoned** talked   **29 narrow . . . English** i.e. the English
Channel   **30 miscarried** came to harm/was destroyed   **31 fraught** laden   **32 upon** of
40 Slubber spoil/rush   **41 stay** wait (for)   **riping** ripening   **42 for** as for   **43 of** i.e.
concerned with

Be merry, and employ your chiefest thoughts
45 To courtship and such fair ostents of love
As shall conveniently become you there.'
And even there, his eye being big with tears,
Turning his face, he put his hand behind him,
And with affection wondrous sensible
50 He wrung Bassanio's hand, and so they parted.

SOLANIO   I think he only loves the world for him.
I pray thee let us go and find him out,
And quicken his embracèd heaviness
With some delight or other.

55 SALERIO   Do we so.   *Exeunt*

[Act 2 Scene 9]   *running scene 12*

Enter Nerissa and a Servitor

NERISSA   Quick, quick, I pray thee draw the curtain *The Servitor*
straight.   *opens the curtains*
The Prince of Aragon hath ta'en his oath,
And comes to his election presently.

Enter [the Prince of] Aragon, his train and Portia. Flourish of cornets

PORTIA   Behold, there stand the caskets, noble prince.
5 If you choose that wherein I am contained,
Straight shall our nuptial rites be solemnized.
But if thou fail, without more speech, my lord,
You must be gone from hence immediately.

ARAGON   I am enjoined by oath to observe three things:
10 First, never to unfold to anyone
Which casket 'twas I chose; next, if I fail
Of the right casket, never in my life
To woo a maid in way of marriage. Lastly,

---

45 **ostents** displays   46 **become you** be appropriate to you/dignify you   47 **there** i.e. then
49 **affection wondrous sensible** emotion extraordinarily evident   51 **he . . . him** i.e. Bassanio
is all he lives for   53 **quicken** revive/lighten   **embracèd heaviness** adopted sadness
2.9   *Location: Belmont**   **Servitor** servant   1 **straight** straight away   2 **Aragon** region of
northeastern Spain   3 **election** choice   **presently** at once   9 **enjoined** bound   10 **unfold**
reveal   12 **Of** i.e. to choose

If I do fail in fortune of my choice,
15   Immediately to leave you and be gone.
PORTIA   To these injunctions everyone doth swear
That comes to hazard for my worthless self.
ARAGON   And so have I addressed me. Fortune now
To my heart's hope! Gold, silver, and base lead.
20   'Who chooseth me must give and hazard all he hath.'
You shall look fairer, ere I give or hazard.
What says the golden chest? Ha? Let me see:
'Who chooseth me shall gain what many men desire.'
What many men desire—that 'many' may be meant
25   By the fool multitude that choose by show,
Not learning more than the fond eye doth teach,
Which pries not to th'interior, but like the martlet
Builds in the weather on the outward wall,
Even in the force and road of casualty.
30   I will not choose what many men desire,
Because I will not jump with common spirits
And rank me with the barb'rous multitudes.
Why, then to thee, thou silver treasure-house.
Tell me once more what title thou dost bear:
35   'Who chooseth me shall get as much as he deserves.'
And well said too, for who shall go about
To cozen fortune and be honourable
Without the stamp of merit? Let none presume
To wear an undeservèd dignity.
40   O, that estates, degrees and offices
Were not derived corruptly, and that clear honour
Were purchased by the merit of the wearer!
How many then should cover that stand bare!
How many be commanded that command!

---

18 addressed me prepared myself   **Fortune** good luck   **25 By** to signify   **fool** foolish
show appearance   **26 fond** foolish   **27 pries** peers closely   **martlet** swift/house-martin
28 in i.e. in a place exposed to   **29 force** turbulence/violence   **road** pathway   **casualty**
mischance   **31 jump** agree   **37 cozen** cheat   **40 estates, degrees** status, rank   **offices**
official roles   **41 clear** innocent, pure   **42 purchased** obtained   **43 cover . . . bare** i.e. keep
their hats on (social inferiors removed their hats in the presence of their superiors)

45   How much low peasantry would then be gleaned
     From the true seed of honour! And how much honour
     Picked from the chaff and ruin of the times
     To be new-varnished! Well, but to my choice:
     'Who chooseth me shall get as much as he deserves.'
50   I will assume desert; give me a key for this,
     And instantly unlock my fortunes here.   *He opens the silver casket*

PORTIA   Too long a pause for that which you find   *Aside?*
     there.

ARAGON   What's here? The portrait of a blinking idiot
     Presenting me a schedule! I will read it.
55   How much unlike art thou to Portia.
     How much unlike my hopes and my deservings.
     'Who chooseth me shall have as much as he deserves.'
     Did I deserve no more than a fool's head?
     Is that my prize? Are my deserts no better?

60 **PORTIA**   To offend and judge are distinct offices
     And of opposèd natures.

ARAGON   What is here?
     'The fire seven times tried this: *Reads*
     Seven times tried that judgement is
65   That did never choose amiss.
     Some there be that shadows kiss,
     Such have but a shadow's bliss.
     There be fools alive, iwis,
     Silvered o'er, and so was this.
70   Take what wife you will to bed,
     I will ever be your head.
     So begone: you are sped.'

---

45 gleaned stripped, culled   **46 seed** plant germ/descendants   **48 new-varnished** newly adorned, polished   **50 assume desert** claim worth   **54 schedule** scroll   **60 To . . . natures** i.e. Aragon must not assess his own case now that it has been judged; or, Portia says that she cannot comment, because she is the indirect cause of the offense   **63 this** i.e. the silver casket **64 judgement** i.e. God's judgment   **65 amiss** incorrectly   **66 shadows** images/illusions/ reflections   **68 iwis** indeed   **69 Silvered o'er** white-haired/decorated with ornamentation indicating military or court status   **71 I** i.e. the fool's head   **72 sped** (have) achieved your purpose/sent away with speed

Still more fool I shall appear
By the time I linger here.
75   With one fool's head I came to woo,
But I go away with two.
Sweet, adieu. I'll keep my oath,
Patiently to bear my wroth.   [*Exeunt Aragon and train*]

PORTIA   Thus hath the candle singed the moth.
80   O, these deliberate fools! When they do choose,
They have the wisdom by their wit to lose.

NERISSA   The ancient saying is no heresy:
Hanging and wiving goes by destiny.

PORTIA   Come, draw the curtain, Nerissa. *Nerissa closes the curtains*
Enter Messenger

85   MESSENGER   Where is my lady?

PORTIA   Here, what would my lord?

MESSENGER   Madam, there is alighted at your gate
A young Venetian, one that comes before
To signify th'approaching of his lord,
90   From whom he bringeth sensible regreets:
To wit, besides commends and courteous breath,
Gifts of rich value; yet I have not seen
So likely an ambassador of love.
A day in April never came so sweet
95   To show how costly summer was at hand,
As this fore-spurrer comes before his lord.

PORTIA   No more, I pray thee. I am half afeard
Thou wilt say anon he is some kin to thee,
Thou spend'st such high-day wit in praising him.
100   Come, come, Nerissa, for I long to see
Quick Cupid's post that comes so mannerly.

NERISSA   Bassanio, Lord Love, if thy will it be!   *Exeunt*

---

74 **By the time** i.e. the longer   78 **wroth** grief/anger   80 **deliberate** calculating   83 **wiving** marrying   **goes** is determined   86 **my lord** playful response to **my lady**   90 **sensible regreets** tangible greetings (i.e. **gifts**)   91 **To wit** that is to say   **commends** commendations **breath** speech   92 **yet** until now   95 **costly** bountiful   96 **fore-spurrer** one who has ridden ahead (i.e. messenger)   99 **high-day** holiday (i.e. elaborate)   101 **post** messenger

Act 3 [Scene 1]   *running scene 13*

Enter Solanio and Salerio

SOLANIO   Now, what news on the Rialto?

SALERIO   Why, yet it lives there unchecked that Antonio hath
a ship of rich lading wrecked on the narrow seas; the
Goodwins, I think they call the place, a very dangerous flat
5   and fatal, where the carcasses of many a tall ship lie buried,
as they say, if my gossip's report be an honest woman of her
word.

SOLANIO   I would she were as lying a gossip in that as ever
knapped ginger or made her neighbours believe she wept for
10   the death of a third husband. But it is true, without any slips
of prolixity or crossing the plain highway of talk, that the
good Antonio, the honest Antonio—O that I had a title good
enough to keep his name company!—

SALERIO   Come, the full stop.

15   SOLANIO   Ha, what sayest thou? Why, the end is, he hath lost
a ship.

SALERIO   I would it might prove the end of his losses.

SOLANIO   Let me say 'amen' betimes, lest the devil cross my
prayer, for here he comes in the likeness of a Jew. How now,
20   Shylock! What news among the merchants?

Enter Shylock

SHYLOCK   You knew, none so well, none so well as you, of my
daughter's flight.

SALERIO   That's certain. I, for my part, knew the tailor that
made the wings she flew withal.

25   SOLANIO   And Shylock, for his own part, knew the bird was

---

3.1   *Location: Venice*   **2 it . . . unchecked** an undisputed rumor is circulating   **3 lading**
cargo   **narrow seas** presumably the English Channel   **4 Goodwins** Goodwin Sands, off the
Kent coast   **flat** sandbank   **5 tall** lofty/gallant   **6 gossip** old friend/chatty woman
9 knapped nibbled at   **ginger** old women were proverbially fond of ginger   **10 slips of
prolixity** evasions into tedious explanation   **11 crossing** forestalling   **plain . . . talk** i.e. good,
honest communication   **14 Come . . . stop** i.e. get to the point and finish what you're saying
17 prove prove to be   **18 betimes** at once   **cross** thwart   **24 wings** (page's) costume/flying
apparatus

fledged, and then it is the complexion of them all to leave the
dam.

SHYLOCK   She is damned for it.

SOLANIO   That's certain, if the devil may be her judge.

30   SHYLOCK   My own flesh and blood to rebel!

SOLANIO   Out upon it, old carrion! Rebels it at these years?

SHYLOCK   I say, my daughter is my flesh and blood.

SALERIO   There is more difference between thy flesh and hers
than between jet and ivory, more between your bloods than
35   there is between red wine and Rhenish. But tell us, do you
hear whether Antonio have had any loss at sea or no?

SHYLOCK   There I have another bad match: a bankrupt, a
prodigal, who dare scarce show his head on the Rialto, a
beggar that was used to come so smug upon the mart. Let
40   him look to his bond. He was wont to call me usurer. Let him
look to his bond. He was wont to lend money for a Christian
courtesy. Let him look to his bond.

SALERIO   Why, I am sure if he forfeit, thou wilt not take his
flesh. What's that good for?

45   SHYLOCK   To bait fish withal. If it will feed nothing else, it will
feed my revenge. He hath disgraced me, and hindered me
half a million, laughed at my losses, mocked at my gains,
scorned my nation, thwarted my bargains, cooled my
friends, heated mine enemies, and what's the reason? I am a
50   Jew. Hath not a Jew eyes? Hath not a Jew hands, organs,
dimensions, senses, affections, passions? Fed with the same
food, hurt with the same weapons, subject to the same
diseases, healed by the same means, warmed and cooled by
the same winter and summer, as a Christian is? If you prick
55   us, do we not bleed? If you tickle us, do we not laugh? If you

26 fledged ready to fly/sexually ripe   complexion temperament   27 dam mother   29 devil
probably alludes to Shylock   30 flesh and blood i.e. daughter (Solanio plays on the sense of
"sexual desires")   31 Out upon it expression of irritation   carrion putrefying flesh   these
years i.e. your advanced age   34 jet and ivory i.e. black and white   37 match contract
39 mart market, i.e. the Rialto   40 look to heed, remember   41 for . . . courtesy out of
Christian charity/for a good deed in return   46 hindered me prevented me from earning
48 cooled alienated   49 heated angered   51 dimensions parts of the body   affections
inclinations/emotions/love   passions powerful emotions

poison us, do we not die? And if you wrong us, shall we not
revenge? If we are like you in the rest, we will resemble you
in that. If a Jew wrong a Christian, what is his humility?
Revenge. If a Christian wrong a Jew, what should his
60　sufferance be by Christian example? Why, revenge. The
villainy you teach me I will execute, and it shall go hard but
I will better the instruction.

Enter a man from Antonio

SERVANT　Gentlemen, my master Antonio is at his house and
desires to speak with you both.

65　SALERIO　We have been up and down to seek him.

Enter Tubal

SOLANIO　Here comes another of the tribe. A third cannot be
matched, unless the devil himself turn Jew.

Exeunt Gentlemen [Solanio, Salerio and Servant]

SHYLOCK　How now, Tubal, what news from Genoa? Hast thou
found my daughter?

70　TUBAL　I often came where I did hear of her, but cannot
find her.

SHYLOCK　Why, there, there, there, there! A diamond gone,
cost me two thousand ducats in Frankfurt! The curse never
fell upon our nation till now, I never felt it till now. Two
75　thousand ducats in that, and other precious, precious jewels.
I would my daughter were dead at my foot, and the jewels in
her ear! Would she were hearsed at my foot, and the ducats
in her coffin! No news of them? Why, so—and I know not
how much is spent in the search. Why, thou loss upon loss!
80　The thief gone with so much, and so much to find the thief,
and no satisfaction, no revenge, nor no ill luck stirring but
what lights o'my shoulders, no sighs but o'my breathing, no
tears but o'my shedding.

---

58 what . . . humility i.e. in what benevolent manner does he respond　　**59 his sufferance** the
Jew's endurance　　**61 go hard but** be highly unfortunate if I do not　　**62 better the instruction**
improve on the (Christian) example　　**65 up and down** everywhere　　**66 of the tribe** i.e. Jew
67 matched i.e. found to match them　　**68 Genoa** northwestern coastal Italian city
73 Frankfurt site of a famous jewelry fair　　**curse** God's curse on the Jews　　**77 hearsed** in a
coffin　　**81 satisfaction** compensation　　**82 lights** settles

TUBAL   Yes, other men have ill luck too. Antonio, as I heard
85   in Genoa—

SHYLOCK   What, what, what? Ill luck, ill luck?

TUBAL   —hath an argosy cast away, coming from Tripolis.

SHYLOCK   I thank God, I thank God. Is it true, is it true?

TUBAL   I spoke with some of the sailors that escaped the
90   wreck.

SHYLOCK   I thank thee, good Tubal, good news, good news!
Ha, ha, heard in Genoa?

TUBAL   Your daughter spent in Genoa, as I heard, one night
fourscore ducats.

95   **SHYLOCK**   Thou stick'st a dagger in me. I shall never see my
gold again. Fourscore ducats at a sitting, fourscore ducats!

TUBAL   There came divers of Antonio's creditors in my
company to Venice, that swear he cannot choose but break.

SHYLOCK   I am very glad of it. I'll plague him, I'll torture him.
100   I am glad of it.

TUBAL   One of them showed me a ring that he had of your
daughter for a monkey.

SHYLOCK   Out upon her! Thou torturest me, Tubal. It was my
turquoise, I had it of Leah when I was a bachelor. I would not
105   have given it for a wilderness of monkeys.

TUBAL   But Antonio is certainly undone.

SHYLOCK   Nay, that's true, that's very true. Go, Tubal, fee me
an officer, bespeak him a fortnight before. I will have the
heart of him, if he forfeit, for were he out of Venice I can
110   make what merchandise I will. Go, Tubal, and meet me at
our synagogue. Go, good Tubal, at our synagogue, Tubal.

Exeunt [separately]

---

87 **cast away** lost, shipwrecked   94 **fourscore** eighty   96 **at a sitting** in one go   97 **divers**
several   98 **break** fail to keep the bond/go bankrupt   101 **of** from   103 **Out upon her!**
expression of frustration and condemnation   104 **Leah** Shylock's wife   105 **wilderness** i.e.
large number   106 **undone** ruined   107 **fee** purchase, hire, secure   108 **officer** constable/
bailiff   **bespeak** engage   **before** i.e. before the date of Antonio's bond   110 **what** whatever
merchandise business dealings   **will** want

[Act 3 Scene 2]

Enter Bassanio, Portia, Gratiano, [Nerissa] and all their trains

PORTIA   I pray you tarry. Pause a day or two
             Before you hazard, for in choosing wrong
             I lose your company: therefore forbear awhile.
             There's something tells me, but it is not love,
5   I would not lose you, and you know yourself,
             Hate counsels not in such a quality;
             But lest you should not understand me well—
             And yet a maiden hath no tongue but thought—
             I would detain you here some month or two
10   Before you venture for me. I could teach you
             How to choose right, but then I am forsworn.
             So will I never be. So may you miss me.
             But if you do, you'll make me wish a sin,
             That I had been forsworn. Beshrew your eyes,
15   They have o'erlooked me and divided me.
             One half of me is yours, the other half yours,
             Mine own, I would say. But if mine, then yours,
             And so all yours. O, these naughty times
             Puts bars between the owners and their rights!
20   And so, though yours, not yours. Prove it so,
             Let fortune go to hell for it, not I.
             I speak too long, but 'tis to peise the time,
             To eke it and to draw it out in length,
             To stay you from election.
25   BASSANIO   Let me choose,
             For as I am, I live upon the rack.

3.2   *Location: Belmont*   1 tarry wait, delay   **2 in choosing** if you choose   **3 forbear**
desist, have patience   **6 quality** way   **8 And . . . thought** i.e. a modest young woman can
think but not speak what she feels   **10 venture** take a chance (i.e. with the caskets)
11 forsworn will have broken my promise   **12 So** that (i.e. forsworn)   **So** as a result   **miss
me** i.e. choose incorrectly   **15 o'erlooked** bewitched   **17 would** i.e. should   **18 naughty**
wicked   **19 bars** obstacles   **20 though . . . yours** i.e. although I am truly yours (by desire),
I am not so legitimately   **Prove it** if it turn out to be   **22 peise** delay (literally by weighing
down)   **23 eke** eke out, extend   **24 stay** prevent/dissuade   **election** choice   **26 rack**
torture instrument that stretched the limbs, used to elicit confessions from those suspected of
treason

PORTIA   Upon the rack, Bassanio? Then confess
What treason there is mingled with your love.

BASSANIO   None but that ugly treason of mistrust,
30   Which makes me fear the enjoying of my love.
There may as well be amity and life
'Tween snow and fire, as treason and my love.

PORTIA   Ay, but I fear you speak upon the rack,
Where men enforcèd do speak anything.

35   BASSANIO   Promise me life, and I'll confess the truth.

PORTIA   Well then, confess and live.

BASSANIO   'Confess and love'
Had been the very sum of my confession.
O happy torment, when my torturer
40   Doth teach me answers for deliverance!
But let me to my fortune and the caskets.

PORTIA   Away, then! I am locked in one of them.
If you do love me, you will find me out.
Nerissa and the rest, stand all aloof.
45   Let music sound while he doth make his choice,
Then if he lose, he makes a swan-like end,
Fading in music. That the comparison
May stand more proper, my eye shall be the stream
And wat'ry death-bed for him. He may win,
50   And what is music then? Then music is
Even as the flourish when true subjects bow
To a new-crownèd monarch. Such it is,
As are those dulcet sounds in break of day,
That creep into the dreaming bridegroom's ear,
55   And summon him to marriage. Now he goes,
With no less presence, but with much more love,
Than young Alcides, when he did redeem

29 **mistrust** worry, doubt   30 **fear** fearful, doubtful about   **enjoying** with sexual connotations   32 **as** as between   34 **enforcèd** compelled   36 **confess and live** plays on "confess and be hanged" (proverbial)   40 **deliverance** i.e. from death   41 **let me to** allow me (to deal with)   44 **aloof** to one side   46 **swan-like end** swans were thought to sing as they died   51 **flourish** trumpet fanfare   53 **dulcet** sweet   56 **presence** dignity/noble demeanor   57 **Alcides** i.e. Hercules, who rescued Hesione from a **sea-monster** and was rewarded by her father, the king of Troy, with a pair of magnificent horses, rather than the maiden's love

The virgin tribute paid by howling Troy
To the sea-monster. I stand for sacrifice,
60   The rest aloof are the Dardanian wives,
With blearèd visages, come forth to view
The issue of th'exploit. Go, Hercules!
Live thou, I live. With much, much more dismay
I view the fight than thou that mak'st the fray.   *Here music*

A song the whilst Bassanio comments on the caskets to himself

65   [SINGER]   Tell me where is fancy bred,
                Or in the heart, or in the head?
                How begot, how nourishèd?
                Reply, reply.
                It is engendered in the eyes,
70   With gazing fed, and fancy dies
                In the cradle where it lies.
                Let us all ring fancy's knell.
                I'll begin it—Ding, dong, bell.

        ALL   Ding, dong, bell.

75   BASSANIO   So may the outward shows be least themselves,
        The world is still deceived with ornament.
        In law, what plea so tainted and corrupt,
        But, being seasoned with a gracious voice,
        Obscures the show of evil? In religion,
80   What damnèd error, but some sober brow
        Will bless it and approve it with a text,
        Hiding the grossness with fair ornament?
        There is no vice so simple but assumes
        Some mark of virtue on his outward parts;
85   How many cowards, whose hearts are all as false
        As stairs of sand, wear yet upon their chins

---

58 **howling** grieving   59 **stand for** represent   60 **Dardanian** Trojan   61 **blearèd visages**
tear-stained faces   62 **issue** outcome   63 **Live thou** if you live   64 **fray** assault/din
65 **fancy** love   66 **Or** either   67 **begot** conceived   71 **the cradle** its infancy/the **eyes**
72 **knell** funeral bell   75 **themselves** i.e. like what they seem   76 **still** always   78 **gracious**
charming   80 **sober brow** i.e. solemn clergyman   81 **approve** support   **text** passage from
the Bible   82 **grossness** flagrant/coarse nature   83 **simple** small/basic   **assumes** acquires
84 **his** its

The beards of Hercules and frowning Mars,
Who, inward searched, have livers white as milk.
And these assume but valour's excrement
90   To render them redoubted. Look on beauty,
And you shall see 'tis purchased by the weight,
Which therein works a miracle in nature,
Making them lightest that wear most of it:
So are those crispèd snaky golden locks
95   Which makes such wanton gambols with the wind
Upon supposèd fairness, often known
To be the dowry of a second head,
The skull that bred them in the sepulchre.
Thus ornament is but the guilèd shore
100   To a most dangerous sea, the beauteous scarf
Veiling an Indian beauty; in a word,
The seeming truth which cunning times put on
To entrap the wisest. Therefore, then, thou gaudy gold,
Hard food for Midas, I will none of thee;
105   Nor none of thee, thou pale and common drudge
'Tween man and man. But thou, thou meagre lead,
Which rather threaten'st than dost promise aught,
Thy paleness moves me more than eloquence,
And here choose I. Joy be the consequence!
110   PORTIA   How all the other passions fleet to air,   *Aside*
As doubtful thoughts and rash-embraced despair
And shudd'ring fear and green-eyed jealousy!
O love, be moderate, allay thy ecstasy,
In measure rain thy joy, scant this excess.

---

87 **Mars** god of war   88 **searched** probed surgically   **livers . . . milk** the liver was thought to be the seat of courage; a coward's would be pale from lack of blood   89 **excrement** facial hair   90 **redoubted** dreaded/revered   **beauty . . . weight** cosmetics and hair were bought by the ounce   93 **lightest** most frivolous/least heavy   94 **crispèd** tightly curled   95 **wanton** playful/wild/lascivious   96 **fairness** beauty/brightness   97 **dowry . . . sepulchre** i.e. a wig made of a dead woman's hair   99 **guilèd** deceptive   101 **Indian** i.e. dark-skinned (the Elizabethans preferred fair complexions)   103 **gaudy** excessively showy/bright   104 **Midas** Phrygian king whose wish for everything he touched to turn to gold was granted only too literally   105 **thee** i.e. the silver casket   **drudge** lackey, because used in business transactions   110 **fleet** change/pass swiftly   111 **As** such as   **rash-embraced** recklessly adopted   114 **measure** moderation   **rain** pour (but could be "rein")   **scant** limit

115   I feel too much thy blessing. Make it less,
       For fear I surfeit.

       BASSANIO   What find I here?   *He opens the lead casket*
       Fair Portia's counterfeit! What demigod
       Hath come so near creation? Move these eyes?
120   Or whether, riding on the balls of mine,
       Seem they in motion? Here are severed lips,
       Parted with sugar breath, so sweet a bar
       Should sunder such sweet friends. Here in her hairs
       The painter plays the spider, and hath woven
125   A golden mesh t'entrap the hearts of men
       Faster than gnats in cobwebs. But her eyes—
       How could he see to do them? Having made one,
       Methinks it should have power to steal both his
       And leave itself unfurnished. Yet look how far
130   The substance of my praise doth wrong this shadow
       In underprizing it, so far this shadow
       Doth limp behind the substance. Here's the scroll,
       The continent and summary of my fortune.
       'You that choose not by the view   *Reads*
135   Chance as fair and choose as true.
       Since this fortune falls to you,
       Be content and seek no new.
       If you be well pleased with this
       And hold your fortune for your bliss,
140   Turn you where your lady is
       And claim her with a loving kiss.'
       A gentle scroll. Fair lady, by your leave,
       I come by note to give and to receive.
       Like one of two contending in a prize
145   That thinks he hath done well in people's eyes,

---

116 surfeit overindulge and become ill   **118 counterfeit** image   **demigod** i.e. the painter, or
creator of this perfect image   **119 eyes** i.e. the eyes of the portrait   **120 Or whether** or   **balls
of mine** i.e. my eyeballs   **121 severed** parted   **122 bar** barrier (i.e. **breath**)   **123 sunder**
separate   **126 Faster** more tightly   **128 it** i.e. the first painted eye   **129 unfurnished**
unfinished, unpartnered   **130 substance** subject (i.e. Portia)   **shadow** image, reflection
133 continent summation/container   **135 Chance as fair** guess as fortunately   **143 by note**
i.e. as directed by the scroll   **note** invoice/account   **144 prize** contest

Hearing applause and universal shout,
Giddy in spirit, still gazing in a doubt
Whether those peals of praise be his or no,
So, thrice-fair lady, stand I, even so,
150   As doubtful whether what I see be true,
Until confirmed, signed, ratified by you.

PORTIA   You see me, Lord Bassanio, where I stand,
Such as I am; though for myself alone
I would not be ambitious in my wish,
155   To wish myself much better, yet for you
I would be trebled twenty times myself,
A thousand times more fair, ten thousand times more rich,
That only to stand high in your account,
I might in virtues, beauties, livings, friends,
160   Exceed account. But the full sum of me
Is sum of nothing, which to term in gross
Is an unlessoned girl, unschooled, unpractisèd,
Happy in this, she is not yet so old
But she may learn. Happier than this,
165   She is not bred so dull but she can learn;
Happiest of all is that her gentle spirit
Commits itself to yours to be directed,
As from her lord, her governor, her king.
Myself, and what is mine, to you and yours
170   Is now converted. But now I was the lord
Of this fair mansion, master of my servants,
Queen o'er myself, and even now, but now,
This house, these servants and this same myself
Are yours, my lord. I give them with this ring,
175   Which when you part from, lose or give away,
Let it presage the ruin of your love
And be my vantage to exclaim on you.   *Puts a ring on his finger*

---

148 his for him   **151 confirmed, signed, ratified** language of commerce   **158 account** estimate/financial reckoning   **159 livings** possessions, livelihood   **160 account** calculation **sum** essence/financial amount   **161 term in gross** express overall, wholesale **162 unpractisèd** inexperienced/innocent   **170 converted** changed (also a legal term for wrongfully appropriating someone else's property for one's own use)   **But** just   **176 presage** indicate   **177 vantage** opportunity/superior position   **exclaim on** accuse/denounce

BASSANIO   Madam, you have bereft me of all words,
Only my blood speaks to you in my veins,
180 And there is such confusion in my powers,
As after some oration fairly spoke
By a belovèd prince, there doth appear
Among the buzzing pleasèd multitude,
Where every something being blent together,
185 Turns to a wild of nothing, save of joy
Expressed and not expressed. But when this ring
Parts from this finger, then parts life from hence.
O, then be bold to say Bassanio's dead!

NERISSA   My lord and lady, it is now our time,
190 That have stood by and seen our wishes prosper,
To cry, good joy: good joy, my lord and lady!

GRATIANO   My lord Bassanio and my gentle lady,
I wish you all the joy that you can wish,
For I am sure you can wish none from me.
195 And when your honours mean to solemnize
The bargain of your faith, I do beseech you,
Even at that time I may be married too.

BASSANIO   With all my heart, so thou canst get a wife.

GRATIANO   I thank your lordship, you have got me one.
200 My eyes, my lord, can look as swift as yours:
You saw the mistress, I beheld the maid.
You loved, I loved, for intermission
No more pertains to me, my lord, than you;
Your fortune stood upon the caskets there,
205 And so did mine too, as the matter falls,
For wooing here until I sweat again,
And swearing till my very roof was dry
With oaths of love, at last, if promise last,

---

179 blood blood/passion   **180 confusion** agitation   **powers** faculties   **184 something** i.e.
small utterance   **blent** blended   **185 wild** wilderness (i.e. confused sound, hubbub)   **save**
except   **186 expressed** articulated, comprehensible   **188 be bold** presume, feel certainty
190 That who   **194 wish none** require no more/want to detract from any of my joy
196 faith (love) promise   **197 Even** exactly   **198 so** provided   **201 maid** waiting-woman
202 intermission delay/respite (in loving)   **204 stood** depended   **205 falls** turns out
207 roof i.e. of the mouth   **208 last** endure (puns on **at last**)

I got a promise of this fair one here

210 To have her love, provided that your fortune

Achieved her mistress.

PORTIA Is this true, Nerissa?

NERISSA Madam, it is so, so you stand pleased withal.

BASSANIO And do you, Gratiano, mean good faith?

215 GRATIANO Yes, faith, my lord.

BASSANIO Our feast shall be much honoured in your
marriage.

GRATIANO We'll play with them the first boy for a thousand
ducats.

NERISSA What, and stake down?

GRATIANO No, we shall ne'er win at that sport, and stake down.

220 But who comes here? Lorenzo and his infidel?

What, and my old Venetian friend Salerio?

Enter Lorenzo, Jessica and Salerio

BASSANIO Lorenzo and Salerio, welcome hither,

If that the youth of my new interest here

Have power to bid you welcome. By your leave,

225 I bid my very friends and countrymen,

Sweet Portia, welcome.

PORTIA So do I, my lord. They are entirely welcome.

LORENZO I thank your honour. For my part, my lord,

My purpose was not to have seen you here,

230 But meeting with Salerio by the way,

He did entreat me, past all saying nay,

To come with him along.

SALERIO I did, my lord,

And I have reason for it. Signior Antonio

235 Commends him to you.   *Gives Bassanio a letter*

BASSANIO Ere I ope his letter,

I pray you tell me how my good friend doth.

SALERIO Not sick, my lord, unless it be in mind,

---

213 **so** provided   215 **faith** in truth/fidelity   217 **play . . . boy** bet who has the first son
218 **stake down** put the money down in advance   219 **sport** game/sex   **stake down** i.e. with
a non-erect penis   220 **infidel** i.e. Jessica   223 **youth** newness   **new interest** recently
acquired authority   225 **very** true   235 **Commends him** sends his regards   236 **ope** open

Nor well, unless in mind: his letter there

240   Will show you his estate.   *[Bassanio] opens the letter*

GRATIANO   Nerissa, cheer yond stranger, bid her welcome.
Your hand, Salerio. What's the news from Venice?
How doth that royal merchant, good Antonio?
I know he will be glad of our success,

245   We are the Jasons, we have won the fleece.

SALERIO   I would you had won the fleece that he hath lost.

PORTIA   There are some shrewd contents in yond same
paper,
That steals the colour from Bassanio's cheek.
Some dear friend dead, else nothing in the world

250   Could turn so much the constitution
Of any constant man. What, worse and worse?
With leave, Bassanio: I am half yourself,
And I must freely have the half of anything
That this same paper brings you.

255   BASSANIO   O sweet Portia,
Here are a few of the unpleasant'st words
That ever blotted paper! Gentle lady,
When I did first impart my love to you,
I freely told you all the wealth I had

260   Ran in my veins. I was a gentleman,
And then I told you true. And yet, dear lady,
Rating myself at nothing, you shall see
How much I was a braggart. When I told you
My state was nothing, I should then have told you

265   That I was worse than nothing, for indeed,
I have engaged myself to a dear friend,
Engaged my friend to his mere enemy,
To feed my means. Here is a letter, lady,
The paper as the body of my friend,

---

240 **estate** circumstances   241 **cheer** welcome   **yond** yonder, that   243 **royal** kingly,
magnificent   247 **shrewd** ominous/grievous   250 **constitution** mood   251 **constant**
consistent, stable   252 **leave** your permission   **half yourself** i.e. as his wife; the witnessed
betrothal was nearly as binding as marriage   262 **Rating** reckoning, estimating   264 **state**
estate, wealth   266 **engaged** pledged   267 **mere** total   269 **as** like

270   And every word in it a gaping wound,
      Issuing life-blood. But is it true, Salerio?
      Hath all his ventures failed? What, not one hit?
      From Tripolis, from Mexico and England,
      From Lisbon, Barbary and India?
275   And not one vessel scape the dreadful touch
      Of merchant-marring rocks?

SALERIO   Not one, my lord.
      Besides, it should appear, that if he had
      The present money to discharge the Jew,
280   He would not take it. Never did I know
      A creature that did bear the shape of man
      So keen and greedy to confound a man.
      He plies the duke at morning and at night,
      And doth impeach the freedom of the state,
285   If they deny him justice. Twenty merchants,
      The duke himself and the magnificoes
      Of greatest port have all persuaded with him,
      But none can drive him from the envious plea
      Of forfeiture, of justice and his bond.

290   JESSICA   When I was with him I have heard him swear
      To Tubal and to Chus, his countrymen,
      That he would rather have Antonio's flesh
      Than twenty times the value of the sum
      That he did owe him: and I know, my lord,
295   If law, authority and power deny not,
      It will go hard with poor Antonio.

PORTIA   Is it your dear friend that is thus in trouble?

BASSANIO   The dearest friend to me, the kindest man,
      The best-conditioned and unwearied spirit

---

272 hit success   274 Barbary Barbary Coast, North Africa   275 dreadful fear-inspiring
276 merchant-marring capable of damaging a merchant ship   278 should appear i.e. appears
279 present ready   discharge pay   280 He i.e. Shylock   282 confound destroy
284 impeach call into question   freedom civil liberty   286 magnificoes foremost noblemen
in Venice   287 port dignity/social standing   persuaded entreated   288 envious malicious
plea legal claim   289 forfeiture penalty   291 Chus a name found in Genesis 10:6, spelled
"Cush"   296 hard with badly for   299 best-conditioned best-natured

300   In doing courtesies, and one in whom
    The ancient Roman honour more appears
    Than any that draws breath in Italy.

PORTIA   What sum owes he the Jew?

BASSANIO   For me three thousand ducats.

305 **PORTIA**   What, no more?

    Pay him six thousand and deface the bond.
    Double six thousand and then treble that,
    Before a friend of this description
    Shall lose a hair through Bassanio's fault.

310   First go with me to church and call me wife,
    And then away to Venice to your friend,
    For never shall you lie by Portia's side
    With an unquiet soul. You shall have gold
    To pay the petty debt twenty times over.

315   When it is paid, bring your true friend along.
    My maid Nerissa and myself meantime
    Will live as maids and widows. Come, away!
    For you shall hence upon your wedding day.
    Bid your friends welcome, show a merry cheer,

320   Since you are dear bought, I will love you dear.
    But let me hear the letter of your friend.

BASSANIO   'Sweet Bassanio, my ships have all miscarried,   *Reads*
my creditors grow cruel, my estate is very low, my bond to
the Jew is forfeit, and since in paying it, it is impossible I

325 should live, all debts are cleared between you and I, if I might
see you at my death. Notwithstanding, use your pleasure, if
your love do not persuade you to come, let not my letter.'

PORTIA   O love! Dispatch all business, and be gone!

BASSANIO   Since I have your good leave to go away,

330   I will make haste; but till I come again,
    No bed shall e'er be guilty of my stay,
    No rest be interposer 'twixt us twain.   *Exeunt*

---

300 courtesies good services   **306 deface** obliterate   **318 hence** (go) from here   **319 cheer**
appearance/welcome   **320 dear** expensively (sense then shifts to "deeply")   **323 estate**
condition/status   **326 Notwithstanding** nevertheless   **use your pleasure** enjoy yourself/do
what you wish   **328 Dispatch** settle   **332 'twixt us twain** between us two

[Act 3 Scene 3]   *running scene 15*

Enter [Shylock] the Jew and Solanio and Antonio and the Jailer

SHYLOCK   Jailer, look to him, tell not me of mercy.
This is the fool that lends out money gratis.
Jailer, look to him.

ANTONIO   Hear me yet, good Shylock.

5   SHYLOCK   I'll have my bond. Speak not against my bond,
I have sworn an oath that I will have my bond.
Thou calledst me dog before thou hadst a cause,
But since I am a dog, beware my fangs.
The duke shall grant me justice. I do wonder,
10   Thou naughty jailer, that thou art so fond
To come abroad with him at his request.

ANTONIO   I pray thee hear me speak.

SHYLOCK   I'll have my bond. I will not hear thee speak.
I'll have my bond and therefore speak no more.
15   I'll not be made a soft and dull-eyed fool,
To shake the head, relent, and sigh, and yield
To Christian intercessors. Follow not,
I'll have no speaking. I will have my bond.   *Exit Jew*

SOLANIO   It is the most impenetrable cur
20   That ever kept with men.

ANTONIO   Let him alone.
I'll follow him no more with bootless prayers.
He seeks my life, his reason well I know;
I oft delivered from his forfeitures
25   Many that have at times made moan to me:
Therefore he hates me.

SOLANIO   I am sure the duke
Will never grant this forfeiture to hold.

3.3   *Location: Venice*   **1 look** see   **2 gratis** for no interest   **10 naughty** wicked   **fond**
foolish   **11 abroad** out of the jail/outside   **15 dull-eyed** easily deceived/stupid   **20 kept**
dwelt   **22 bootless** pointless   **25 made moan** complained, lamented (about debts to
Shylock)   **28 grant** allow   **hold** stand firm

ANTONIO   The duke cannot deny the course of law,
30   For the commodity that strangers have
With us in Venice, if it be denied,
Will much impeach the justice of the state,
Since that the trade and profit of the city
Consisteth of all nations. Therefore go.
35   These griefs and losses have so bated me,
That I shall hardly spare a pound of flesh
Tomorrow to my bloody creditor.
Well, jailer, on. Pray God, Bassanio come
To see me pay his debt, and then I care not.   *Exeunt*

[Act 3 Scene 4]   *running scene 16*

Enter Portia, Nerissa, Lorenzo, Jessica and [Balthasar,] a man of Portia's

LORENZO   Madam, although I speak it in your presence,
You have a noble and a true conceit
Of godlike amity, which appears most strongly
In bearing thus the absence of your lord.
5   But if you knew to whom you show this honour,
How true a gentleman you send relief,
How dear a lover of my lord your husband,
I know you would be prouder of the work
Than customary bounty can enforce you.
10   PORTIA   I never did repent for doing good,
Nor shall not now, for in companions
That do converse and waste the time together,
Whose souls do bear an equal yoke of love,
There must be needs a like proportion
15   Of lineaments, of manners and of spirit;
Which makes me think that this Antonio,

30 **commodity** (commercial) privileges   **strangers** outsiders (including Jews)   33 **Since that**
since   35 **bated** me diminished me/made me lose weight   **3.4**   *Location: Belmont*
2 **conceit** understanding   3 **godlike amity** divine friendship   5 **to whom** i.e. Antonio
6 **relief** financial aid   7 **lover** friend   9 **customary . . . you** ordinary generosity would make
you   12 **waste** spend/while away   14 **needs** of necessity   **like** similar, comparable
15 **lineaments** characteristics/physical features

Being the bosom lover of my lord,
Must needs be like my lord. If it be so,
How little is the cost I have bestowed
20   In purchasing the semblance of my soul
From out the state of hellish cruelty!
This comes too near the praising of myself:
Therefore no more of it. Hear other things.
Lorenzo, I commit into your hands
25   The husbandry and manage of my house
Until my lord's return; for mine own part,
I have toward heaven breathed a secret vow
To live in prayer and contemplation,
Only attended by Nerissa here,
30   Until her husband and my lord's return.
There is a monastery two miles off,
And there we will abide. I do desire you
Not to deny this imposition,
The which my love and some necessity
35   Now lays upon you.

LORENZO   Madam, with all my heart,
I shall obey you in all fair commands.

PORTIA   My people do already know my mind,
And will acknowledge you and Jessica
40   In place of Lord Bassanio and myself.
So fare you well till we shall meet again.

LORENZO   Fair thoughts and happy hours attend on you.

JESSICA   I wish your ladyship all heart's content.

PORTIA   I thank you for your wish, and am well pleased
45   To wish it back on you: fare you well Jessica.

                                   Exeunt [Jessica and Lorenzo]
Now, Balthasar,
As I have ever found thee honest-true,
So let me find thee still. Take this same letter,   *Gives a letter*
And use thou all the endeavour of a man

17 bosom lover intimate friend   20 semblance image   my soul i.e. Bassanio   25 husbandry
domestic administration   manage management   33 deny refuse   imposition command
38 people i.e. household servants   47 honest-true truthful and reliable

50 In speed to Padua. See thou render this
Into my cousin's hand, Doctor Bellario,
And look what notes and garments he doth give thee,
Bring them, I pray thee with imagined speed
Unto the traject, to the common ferry
55 Which trades to Venice; waste no time in words,
But get thee gone. I shall be there before thee.

BALTHASAR Madam, I go with all convenient speed. [*Exit*]

PORTIA Come on, Nerissa, I have work in hand
That you yet know not of; we'll see our husbands
60 Before they think of us.

NERISSA Shall they see us?

PORTIA They shall, Nerissa, but in such a habit,
That they shall think we are accomplishèd
With that we lack. I'll hold thee any wager,
65 When we are both accoutred like young men,
I'll prove the prettier fellow of the two,
And wear my dagger with the braver grace,
And speak between the change of man and boy
With a reed voice, and turn two mincing steps
70 Into a manly stride, and speak of frays
Like a fine bragging youth, and tell quaint lies,
How honourable ladies sought my love,
Which I denying, they fell sick and died.
I could not do withal. Then I'll repent,
75 And wish for all that, that I had not killed them;
And twenty of these puny lies I'll tell,
That men shall swear I have discontinued school
Above a twelvemonth. I have within my mind
A thousand raw tricks of these bragging Jacks,
80 Which I will practise.

---

50 **render** give   52 **look what** whatever   53 **imagined** all imaginable   54 **traject** crossing place/ferry   **common** public   55 **trades** i.e. crosses   62 **habit** clothing   63 **accomplishèd** equipped   64 **that we lack** i.e. penises (they will be disguised as men)   **hold** offer and maintain   65 **accoutred** dressed   67 **braver** bolder/more splendid   **grace** elegance/attitude   68 **between . . . voice** i.e. with an adolescent boy's reedy breaking voice   69 **mincing** dainty   70 **frays** fights   71 **quaint** ingenious   74 **do withal** help it   76 **puny** petty/inexperienced   78 **Above** more than   79 **raw** unrefined   **Jacks** fellows

NERISSA	Why, shall we turn to men?
PORTIA	Fie, what a question's that,

If thou wert near a lewd interpreter!
But come, I'll tell thee all my whole device
85   When I am in my coach, which stays for us
At the park gate; and therefore haste away,
For we must measure twenty miles today.   *Exeunt*

[Act 3 Scene 5]   *running scene 17*

Enter [Lancelet the] Clown and Jessica

LANCELET   Yes, truly, for look you, the sins of the father are to
be laid upon the children: therefore, I promise you, I fear you.
I was always plain with you, and so now I speak my agitation
of the matter: therefore be of good cheer, for truly I think you
5   are damned. There is but one hope in it that can do you any
good, and that is but a kind of bastard hope neither.

JESSICA   And what hope is that, I pray thee?

LANCELET   Marry, you may partly hope that your father got
you not, that you are not the Jew's daughter.

10   JESSICA   That were a kind of bastard hope indeed. So the sins
of my mother should be visited upon me.

LANCELET   Truly then I fear you are damned both by father and
mother: thus when I shun Scylla, your father, I fall into
Charybdis, your mother; well, you are gone both ways.

15   JESSICA   I shall be saved by my husband. He hath made me a
Christian.

LANCELET   Truly, the more to blame he. We were Christians
enow before, e'en as many as could well live one by another.

---

81 **turn to** become (Portia puns on the sense of "become sexually available to")   84 **device**
plan   87 **measure** cover/count out   **3.5   2 promise** assure   **fear you** fear for you   **3 plain**
honest   **agitation** agitated thoughts (possible malapropism for "cogitation")   **6 bastard**
mixed/illegitimate   **neither** nevertheless   **8 got** begot, conceived   **13 Scylla . . . Charybdis**
Odysseus had to navigate between these two dangerous points (the monster **Scylla** and
whirlpool **Charybdis**)   **fall into** with sexual connotations   **14 gone** ruined   **15 I . . .
husband** "the unbelieving wife is made acceptable to God by being united to her Christian
husband" (1 Corinthians 7:14)   **17 We . . . enow** there were enough of us Christians   **18 by**
alongside/off

This making of Christians will raise the price of hogs. If we
20   grow all to be pork-eaters, we shall not shortly have a rasher
on the coals for money.

Enter Lorenzo

JESSICA   I'll tell my husband, Lancelet, what you say. Here he
comes.

LORENZO   I shall grow jealous of you shortly, Lancelet, if you
25   thus get my wife into corners.

JESSICA   Nay, you need not fear us, Lorenzo. Lancelet and I
are out. He tells me flatly there is no mercy for me in heaven
because I am a Jew's daughter. And he says, you are no good
member of the commonwealth, for in converting Jews to
30   Christians, you raise the price of pork.

LORENZO   I shall answer that better to the commonwealth
than you can the getting up of the negro's belly. The Moor is
with child by you, Lancelet.

LANCELET   It is much that the Moor should be more than
35   reason, but if she be less than an honest woman, she is
indeed more than I took her for.

LORENZO   How every fool can play upon the word! I think the
best grace of wit will shortly turn into silence, and discourse
grow commendable in none only but parrots. Go in, sirrah,
40   bid them prepare for dinner.

LANCELET   That is done, sir, they have all stomachs.

LORENZO   Goodly lord, what a wit-snapper are you? Then bid
them prepare dinner.

LANCELET   That is done too, sir, only 'cover' is the word.

45   LORENZO   Will you cover then, sir?

LANCELET   Not so, sir, neither. I know my duty.

---

19 **raise . . . hogs** because Christians eat pork (unlike Jews)   21 **money** any price   25 **get . . .
corners** i.e. for sex   27 **are** have fallen   32 **getting . . . belly** making the **negro** pregnant
Moor African (woman)   34 **much** of concern   **more than reason** greater than is reasonable
(i.e. pregnant); **more** puns on **Moor**   35 **less . . . for** i.e. Lancelet does not think much of the
woman's morals (possibly he gets confused in his attempt to play on **Moor/more/less**)
honest chaste   38 **grace** virtue, quality   40 **them** i.e. the servants (but Lancelet takes the
sense of "diners")   41 **stomachs** appetites   42 **wit-snapper** wisecracker   44 **'cover'** lay the
table (Lancelet goes on to play on the sense of "cover one's head with a hat")   46 **my duty** i.e.
as a servant, who would remove his hat in the presence of superiors

LORENZO   Yet more quarrelling with occasion! Wilt thou show
the whole wealth of thy wit in an instant? I pray thee,
understand a plain man in his plain meaning: go to thy
50   fellows; bid them cover the table, serve in the meat, and we
will come in to dinner.

LANCELET   For the table, sir, it shall be served in: for the meat,
sir, it shall be covered: for your coming in to dinner, sir, why,
let it be as humours and conceits shall govern.

Exit, Clown [Lancelet]

55   **LORENZO**   O dear discretion, how his words are suited!
The fool hath planted in his memory
An army of good words, and I do know
A many fools that stand in better place,
Garnished like him, that for a tricksy word
60   Defy the matter. How cheerest thou, Jessica?
And now, good sweet, say thy opinion,
How dost thou like the lord Bassanio's wife?

JESSICA   Past all expressing. It is very meet
The lord Bassanio live an upright life,
65   For, having such a blessing in his lady,
He finds the joys of heaven here on earth.
And if on earth he do not merit it,
In reason he should never come to heaven.
Why, if two gods should play some heav'nly match
70   And on the wager lay two earthly women,
And Portia one, there must be something else
Pawned with the other, for the poor rude world
Hath not her fellow.

LORENZO   Even such a husband
75   Hast thou of me as she is for a wife.

---

47 **quarrelling with occasion** i.e. taking the opportunity for quibbling   50 **fellows** fellow
servants   52 **For** as for   **table** i.e. food   53 **covered** i.e. on a covered serving dish
54 **humours and conceits** whims and fancies   55 **discretion** judgment   **suited** adapted as
appropriate   58 **A many** many   **stand . . . place** have higher positions of employment
59 **Garnished** provided with a good supply of words/dressed   60 **Defy the matter** confuse the
meaning   **cheerest thou** are you feeling   63 **Past all expressing** beyond words   **meet**
suitable   68 **In reason** it stands to reason   70 **lay** bet, stake   72 **Pawned** pledged   **rude**
unrefined   73 **fellow** equal   74 **Even** just   75 **of** in

JESSICA	Nay, but ask my opinion too of that.
LORENZO	I will anon. First, let us go to dinner.
JESSICA	Nay, let me praise you while I have a stomach.
LORENZO	No, pray thee let it serve for table-talk,

80   Then, howsome'er thou speak'st, 'mong other things
I shall digest it.

| JESSICA | Well, I'll set you forth. | *Exeunt* |

Act 4 [Scene 1]   *running scene 18*

*Enter the Duke, the Magnificoes, Antonio, Bassanio and Gratiano
[with Salerio and others]*

DUKE	What, is Antonio here?
ANTONIO	Ready, so please your grace.
DUKE	I am sorry for thee. Thou art come to answer

A stony adversary, an inhuman wretch

5   Uncapable of pity, void and empty
From any dram of mercy.

| ANTONIO | I have heard |

Your grace hath ta'en great pains to qualify
His rigorous course, but since he stands obdurate

10   And that no lawful means can carry me
Out of his envy's reach, I do oppose
My patience to his fury, and am armed
To suffer with a quietness of spirit
The very tyranny and rage of his.

15 | DUKE | Go one, and call the Jew into the court. |
| SALERIO | He is ready at the door. He comes, my lord. |

Enter Shylock

| DUKE | Make room, and let him stand before our face. |

Shylock, the world thinks, and I think so too,

---

78 **stomach** appetite/inclination   81 **digest** consider/endure/swallow   82 **set you forth**
praise you/serve you up   **4.1** *Location: Venice*   3 **answer** face/defend yourself against
6 **From** of   **dram** tiny amount   8 **qualify** diminish, moderate   9 **stands obdurate** remains
inflexible   11 **envy's** malice's   14 **tyranny** cruelty   17 **our** the royal plural

That thou but lead'st this fashion of thy malice
20 To the last hour of act, and then 'tis thought
Thou'lt show thy mercy and remorse more strange
Than is thy strange apparent cruelty;
And where thou now exact'st the penalty,
Which is a pound of this poor merchant's flesh,
25 Thou wilt not only loose the forfeiture,
But, touched with humane gentleness and love,
Forgive a moiety of the principal,
Glancing an eye of pity on his losses,
That have of late so huddled on his back,
30 Enow to press a royal merchant down
And pluck commiseration of his state
From brassy bosoms and rough hearts of flints,
From stubborn Turks and Tartars, never trained
To offices of tender courtesy.
35 We all expect a gentle answer, Jew.

SHYLOCK   I have possessed your grace of what I purpose,
And by our holy Sabbath have I sworn
To have the due and forfeit of my bond.
If you deny it, let the danger light
40 Upon your charter and your city's freedom.
You'll ask me why I rather choose to have
A weight of carrion flesh than to receive
Three thousand ducats: I'll not answer that,
But say it is my humour; is it answered?
45 What if my house be troubled with a rat
And I be pleased to give ten thousand ducats
To have it baned? What, are you answered yet?
Some men there are love not a gaping pig,
Some that are mad if they behold a cat,

19 but . . . fashion only persist in this form/contrivance   20 last . . . act i.e. eleventh hour, final moment   21 remorse pity   strange surprisingly   22 strange unnatural/foreign   25 loose revoke, abandon   27 moiety portion/half   30 royal merchant merchant prince   32 brassy bosoms hard hearts   33 Turks and Tartars both considered pitiless infidels   35 gentle puns on "gentile"   36 possessed notified   38 due debt   39 danger damage   40 charter deed of privilege   42 carrion loathsome/putrefying   44 humour mood, inclination   answered explained satisfactorily   47 baned poisoned   48 love who love

50   And others when the bagpipe sings i'th'nose
    Cannot contain their urine, for affection,
    Mistress of passion, sways it to the mood
    Of what it likes or loathes. Now, for your answer:
    As there is no firm reason to be rendered,
55   Why he cannot abide a gaping pig,
    Why he, a harmless necessary cat,
    Why he, a woollen bagpipe, but of force
    Must yield to such inevitable shame
    As to offend, himself being offended.
60   So can I give no reason, nor I will not,
    More than a lodged hate and a certain loathing
    I bear Antonio, that I follow thus
    A losing suit against him. Are you answered?

BASSANIO   This is no answer, thou unfeeling man,
65   To excuse the current of thy cruelty.

SHYLOCK   I am not bound to please thee with my answer.

BASSANIO   Do all men kill the things they do not love?

SHYLOCK   Hates any man the thing he would not kill?

BASSANIO   Every offence is not a hate at first.

70 **SHYLOCK**   What, wouldst thou have a serpent sting thee
    twice?

ANTONIO   I pray you think you question with the Jew:
    You may as well go stand upon the beach
    And bid the main flood bate his usual height,
    Or even as well use question with the wolf
75   Why he hath made the ewe bleat for the lamb.
    You may as well forbid the mountain pines
    To wag their high tops and to make no noise
    When they are fretted with the gusts of heaven.
    You may as well do anything most hard

---

50 **i'th'nose** with a nasal twang   51 **affection** inclination   55 **he** one person   **gaping** i.e. roasted with its mouth open   56 **Why he** another person   **necessary** useful (for catching rats and mice)   61 **lodged** deep-rooted   **certain** definite, fixed   62 **follow** pursue   63 **losing** i.e. involving loss (for Antonio)   65 **current** course, flow   71 **think** realize   73 **main flood** sea at high tide   **bate** lessen   74 **use question** dispute   77 **wag** sway   78 **fretted** chafed   79 **hard** difficult (puns on the sense of "tough, firm")

80   As seek to soften that—than which what harder?—
            His Jewish heart: therefore, I do beseech you
            Make no more offers, use no further means,
            But with all brief and plain conveniency
            Let me have judgement and the Jew his will.

85 BASSANIO   For thy three thousand ducats here is six.

    SHYLOCK   If every ducat in six thousand ducats
            Were in six parts and every part a ducat,
            I would not draw them. I would have my bond!

    DUKE   How shalt thou hope for mercy, rend'ring none?

90 SHYLOCK   What judgement shall I dread, doing no wrong?
            You have among you many a purchased slave,
            Which, like your asses and your dogs and mules,
            You use in abject and in slavish parts,
            Because you bought them. Shall I say to you,
95   Let them be free, marry them to your heirs?
            Why sweat they under burdens? Let their beds
            Be made as soft as yours and let their palates
            Be seasoned with such viands? You will answer
            'The slaves are ours.' So do I answer you:
100   The pound of flesh which I demand of him
            Is dearly bought, 'tis mine and I will have it.
            If you deny me, fie upon your law!
            There is no force in the decrees of Venice.
            I stand for judgement. Answer: shall I have it?

105 DUKE   Upon my power I may dismiss this court,
            Unless Bellario, a learnèd doctor,
            Whom I have sent for to determine this,
            Come here today.

    SALERIO   My lord, here stays without
110   A messenger with letters from the doctor,
            New come from Padua.

    DUKE   Bring us the letters. Call the messenger.

---

80 than more than   83 conveniency convenience   88 draw collect/receive   89 rend'ring
yielding/giving back   90 no wrong i.e. nothing illegal   93 parts actions/duties   98 viands
food (as you eat)   104 stand for represent/uphold   109 stays without waits outside

BASSANIO   Good cheer, Antonio! What, man, courage yet!
            The Jew shall have my flesh, blood, bones and all,
115   Ere thou shalt lose for me one drop of blood.

ANTONIO   I am a tainted wether of the flock,
            Meetest for death. The weakest kind of fruit
            Drops earliest to the ground, and so let me;
            You cannot better be employed, Bassanio,
120   Than to live still and write mine epitaph.

Enter Nerissa [dressed like a law clerk]

DUKE   Came you from Padua, from Bellario?

NERISSA   From both. My lord Bellario greets your   *She gives*
            grace.   *the Duke a*

BASSANIO   Why dost thou whet thy knife so earnestly?   *letter while*

SHYLOCK   To cut the forfeiture from that bankrupt   *Shylock whets*
            there.   *his knife on*

125 GRATIANO   Not on thy sole, but on thy soul, harsh Jew,   *his shoe*
            Thou mak'st thy knife keen. But no metal can,
            No, not the hangman's axe, bear half the keenness
            Of thy sharp envy. Can no prayers pierce thee?

SHYLOCK   No, none that thou hast wit enough to make.

130 GRATIANO   O, be thou damned, inexecrable dog!
            And for thy life let justice be accused.
            Thou almost mak'st me waver in my faith
            To hold opinion with Pythagoras,
            That souls of animals infuse themselves
135   Into the trunks of men. Thy currish spirit
            Governed a wolf who, hanged for human slaughter,
            Even from the gallows did his fell soul fleet,
            And, whilst thou lay'st in thy unhallowed dam,
            Infused itself in thee, for thy desires
140   Are wolvish, bloody, starved and ravenous.

SHYLOCK   Till thou canst rail the seal from off my bond,

---

116 tainted diseased   **wether** sheep (specifically, castrated ram)   **117 Meetest** most fitting
126 keen sharp/eager   **127 hangman's** i.e. executioner's   **keenness** sharpness/eagerness/
severity   **130 inexecrable** unmovable/accursed   **131 thy life** the fact that you are alive
accused chastised   **133 Pythagoras** ancient Greek philosopher whose doctrine supported the
transmigration of souls   **135 currish** mean-spirited/snarling (like a dog)   **137 fell** savage
fleet leave, fly off   **138 unhallowed** unholy   **dam** mother   **141 rail** rant

Thou but offend'st thy lungs to speak so loud:
Repair thy wit, good youth, or it will fall
To endless ruin. I stand here for law.

145 DUKE   This letter from Bellario doth commend
A young and learnèd doctor in our court;
Where is he?

NERISSA   He attendeth here hard by,
To know your answer, whether you'll admit him.

150 DUKE   With all my heart. Some three or four of you
Go give him courteous conduct to this place.   [*Exeunt some*]
Meantime the court shall hear Bellario's letter.
'Your grace shall understand that at the receipt of   *Reads*
your letter I am very sick, but in the instant that your
155   messenger came, in loving visitation was with me a young
doctor of Rome. His name is Balthasar. I acquainted him
with the cause in controversy between the Jew and Antonio
the merchant. We turned o'er many books together. He
is furnished with my opinion, which—bettered with his
160   own learning, the greatness whereof I cannot enough
commend—comes with him, at my importunity, to fill up
your grace's request in my stead. I beseech you, let his lack of
years be no impediment to let him lack a reverend
estimation, for I never knew so young a body with so old a
165   head. I leave him to your gracious acceptance, whose trial
shall better publish his commendation.'

Enter Portia for Balthasar   *Dressed like a lawyer*

You hear the learnèd Bellario, what he writes,
And here, I take it, is the doctor come.
Give me your hand. Came you from old Bellario?

170 PORTIA   I did, my lord.

DUKE   You are welcome. Take your place.
Are you acquainted with the difference
That holds this present question in the court?

---

142 but offend'st merely harm   143 Repair restore   148 hard close   155 in loving visitation
on a friendly visit   159 furnished equipped   161 importunity urging   163 reverend respected,
worthy   165 whose trial the testing of whom   166 publish make known   commendation
recommendation/praise   172 difference dispute   173 present question current argument

PORTIA   I am informèd throughly of the cause.

175   Which is the merchant here, and which the Jew?

DUKE   Antonio and old Shylock, both stand forth.

PORTIA   Is your name Shylock?

SHYLOCK   Shylock is my name.

PORTIA   Of a strange nature is the suit you follow,

180   Yet in such rule that the Venetian law
Cannot impugn you as you do proceed.—
You stand within his danger, do you not?

ANTONIO   Ay, so he says.

PORTIA   Do you confess the bond?

185   ANTONIO   I do.

PORTIA   Then must the Jew be merciful.

SHYLOCK   On what compulsion must I? Tell me that.

PORTIA   The quality of mercy is not strained,
It droppeth as the gentle rain from heaven

190   Upon the place beneath. It is twice blest:
It blesseth him that gives and him that takes.
'Tis mightiest in the mightiest, it becomes
The thronèd monarch better than his crown.
His sceptre shows the force of temporal power,

195   The attribute to awe and majesty,
Wherein doth sit the dread and fear of kings.
But mercy is above this sceptred sway,
It is enthronèd in the hearts of kings,
It is an attribute to God himself;

200   And earthly power doth then show likest God's
When mercy seasons justice: therefore, Jew,
Though justice be thy plea, consider this,
That in the course of justice, none of us
Should see salvation. We do pray for mercy,

---

174 **throughly** thoroughly   180 **rule** proper discipline   181 **impugn** call into question
182 **danger** (power to) harm   184 **confess** acknowledge   188 **strained** forced, artificial;
also perhaps filtered/distilled (setting up rain imagery)   190 **is twice blest** bestows a double
blessing   194 **shows** represents   196 **dread** reverence/awe   197 **sceptred sway** royal
government   200 **likest** most like   201 **seasons** modifies   203 **justice** i.e. God's justice (if
He did not show mercy to humankind)

205   And that same prayer doth teach us all to render
       The deeds of mercy. I have spoke thus much
       To mitigate the justice of thy plea,
       Which if thou follow, this strict court of Venice
       Must needs give sentence 'gainst the merchant there.

210   SHYLOCK   My deeds upon my head! I crave the law,
       The penalty and forfeit of my bond.

       PORTIA   Is he not able to discharge the money?

       BASSANIO   Yes, here I tender it for him in the court,
       Yea, twice the sum. If that will not suffice,

215   I will be bound to pay it ten times o'er
       On forfeit of my hands, my head, my heart.
       If this will not suffice, it must appear
       That malice bears down truth. And I beseech you
       Wrest once the law to your authority.

220   To do a great right, do a little wrong,
       And curb this cruel devil of his will.

       PORTIA   It must not be; there is no power in Venice
       Can alter a decree establishèd.
       'Twill be recorded for a precedent,

225   And many an error by the same example
       Will rush into the state. It cannot be.

       SHYLOCK   A Daniel come to judgement! Yea, a Daniel!
       O wise young judge, how do I honour thee!

       PORTIA   I pray you let me look upon the bond.

230   SHYLOCK   Here 'tis, most reverend doctor, here it is. *Gives Portia the*

       PORTIA   Shylock, there's thrice thy money offered thee. *bond*

       SHYLOCK   An oath, an oath, I have an oath in heaven.
       Shall I lay perjury upon my soul?
       No, not for Venice.

235   PORTIA   Why, this bond is forfeit,
       And lawfully by this the Jew may claim

205 **render** perform in return   210 **My . . . head!** possible echo of the crowd's acceptance of responsibility for Jesus' death (Matthew 27:25)   212 **discharge** pay   213 **tender** offer   217 **must appear** will be evident   218 **bears down truth** overwhelms integrity   219 **Wrest once** for once, forcibly subject   224 **for** as   **precedent** i.e. on which future lawsuits can be based   227 **Daniel** in the Apocryphal story, Daniel judges Susannah correctly, despite his youth and the false witness of the Elders   **judgement** i.e. make judgment

A pound of flesh, to be by him cut off
Nearest the merchant's heart. Be merciful.
Take thrice thy money, bid me tear the bond.

240 SHYLOCK   When it is paid according to the tenure.
It doth appear you are a worthy judge;
You know the law, your exposition
Hath been most sound. I charge you by the law,
Whereof you are a well-deserving pillar,

245 Proceed to judgement. By my soul I swear,
There is no power in the tongue of man
To alter me. I stay here on my bond.

ANTONIO   Most heartily I do beseech the court
To give the judgement.

250 PORTIA   Why then, thus it is:
You must prepare your bosom for his knife.

SHYLOCK   O noble judge! O excellent young man!

PORTIA   For the intent and purpose of the law
Hath full relation to the penalty,

255 Which here appeareth due upon the bond.

SHYLOCK   'Tis very true. O wise and upright judge!
How much more elder art thou than thy looks!

PORTIA   Therefore lay bare your bosom.

SHYLOCK   Ay, his breast,

260 So says the bond, doth it not, noble judge?
'Nearest his heart', those are the very words.

PORTIA   It is so. Are there balance here to weigh
The flesh?

SHYLOCK   I have them ready.

265 PORTIA   Have by some surgeon, Shylock, on your charge,
To stop his wounds, lest he should bleed to death.

SHYLOCK   Is it so nominated in the bond?

PORTIA   It is not so expressed, but what of that?
'Twere good you do so much for charity.

270 SHYLOCK   I cannot find it, 'tis not in the bond.   *Looking at the bond*

---

240 **tenure** legal conditions, terms of the bond   254 **Hath . . . to** fully supports   262 **balance**
scales   265 **by** nearby   **on your charge** at your responsibility/expense   266 **stop** staunch

PORTIA   Come, merchant, have you anything to say?

ANTONIO   But little. I am armed and well prepared.
Give me your hand, Bassanio. Fare you well.
Grieve not that I am fall'n to this for you,
275   For herein Fortune shows herself more kind
Than is her custom. It is still her use
To let the wretched man outlive his wealth,
To view with hollow eye and wrinkled brow
An age of poverty, from which ling'ring penance
280   Of such misery doth she cut me off.
Commend me to your honourable wife.
Tell her the process of Antonio's end.
Say how I loved you; speak me fair in death.
And when the tale is told, bid her be judge
285   Whether Bassanio had not once a love.
Repent not you that you shall lose your friend,
And he repents not that he pays your debt.
For if the Jew do cut but deep enough,
I'll pay it instantly with all my heart.

290   BASSANIO   Antonio, I am married to a wife
Which is as dear to me as life itself,
But life itself, my wife, and all the world,
Are not with me esteemed above thy life.
I would lose all, ay, sacrifice them all
295   Here to this devil, to deliver you.

PORTIA   Your wife would give you little thanks for that,
If she were by to hear you make the offer.

GRATIANO   I have a wife, whom, I protest, I love.
I would she were in heaven, so she could
300   Entreat some power to change this currish Jew.

NERISSA   'Tis well you offer it behind her back,
The wish would make else an unquiet house.

---

272 **armed** i.e. prepared/fortified   276 **still** always (usually)   **use** practice   282 **process** course, manner   283 **me . . . death** favorably of me when I am dead   285 **love** i.e. loving friend   289 **with . . . heart** most willingly/literally, with my heart   291 **Which** who   295 **deliver** free   302 **else** otherwise

SHYLOCK   These be the Christian husbands. I have a daughter.
Would any of the stock of Barabbas   *Aside?*
305   Had been her husband rather than a Christian!
We trifle time. I pray thee pursue sentence.

PORTIA   A pound of that same merchant's flesh is thine.
The court awards it, and the law doth give it.

SHYLOCK   Most rightful judge!

310   PORTIA   And you must cut this flesh from off his breast.
The law allows it, and the court awards it.

SHYLOCK   Most learnèd judge! A sentence! Come, prepare!

PORTIA   Tarry a little, there is something else.
This bond doth give thee here no jot of blood,
315   The words expressly are 'a pound of flesh'.
Then take thy bond, take thou thy pound of flesh,
But in the cutting it, if thou dost shed
One drop of Christian blood, thy lands and goods
Are by the laws of Venice confiscate
320   Unto the state of Venice.

GRATIANO   O upright judge! Mark, Jew. O learnèd judge!

SHYLOCK   Is that the law?

PORTIA   Thyself shalt see the act,
For as thou urgest justice, be assured
325   Thou shalt have justice, more than thou desirest.

GRATIANO   O learnèd judge! Mark, Jew: a learnèd judge!

SHYLOCK   I take this offer, then. Pay the bond thrice
And let the Christian go.

BASSANIO   Here is the money.

330   PORTIA   Soft!
The Jew shall have all justice. Soft, no haste.
He shall have nothing but the penalty.

GRATIANO   O Jew! An upright judge, a learnèd judge!

PORTIA   Therefore prepare thee to cut off the flesh.
335   Shed thou no blood, nor cut thou less nor more

---

304 Would I wish   Barabbas a thief released by Pontius Pilate instead of Jesus at the people's
request   306 trifle waste   pursue proceed with   319 confiscate confiscated   321 Mark
take note   330 Soft! Wait a moment!   331 all only/complete

But just a pound of flesh. If thou tak'st more
Or less than a just pound, be it so much
As makes it light or heavy in the substance,
Or the division of the twentieth part

340 Of one poor scruple, nay, if the scale do turn
But in the estimation of a hair,
Thou diest and all thy goods are confiscate.

GRATIANO   A second Daniel, a Daniel, Jew!
Now, infidel, I have thee on the hip.

345 PORTIA   Why doth the Jew pause? Take thy forfeiture.

SHYLOCK   Give me my principal, and let me go.

BASSANIO   I have it ready for thee, here it is.

PORTIA   He hath refused it in the open court.
He shall have merely justice and his bond.

350 GRATIANO   A Daniel, still say I, a second Daniel!
I thank thee, Jew, for teaching me that word.

SHYLOCK   Shall I not have barely my principal?

PORTIA   Thou shalt have nothing but the forfeiture,
To be taken so at thy peril, Jew.

355 SHYLOCK   Why, then the devil give him good of it!
I'll stay no longer question.   *Starts to go*

PORTIA   Tarry, Jew.
The law hath yet another hold on you.
It is enacted in the laws of Venice,

360 If it be proved against an alien
That by direct or indirect attempts
He seek the life of any citizen,
The party gainst the which he doth contrive
Shall seize one half his goods, the other half

365 Comes to the privy coffer of the state,
And the offender's life lies in the mercy

---

337 **just** exact (plays on the sense of "fair, lawful")   338 **substance** amount/weight
340 **scruple** tiny amount   341 **estimation . . . hair** by a hair's breadth/weight   344 **on the
hip** at a disadvantage (wrestling term)   346 **principal** original capital sum, i.e. three thousand
ducats   349 **merely** only/absolute   352 **barely** i.e. at the very least   355 **good** good fortune
356 **stay** remain   **question** to argue the case   360 **alien** foreigner   363 **contrive** scheme
364 **seize** take legal possession of   365 **privy coffer** private treasury   366 **in** at

Of the duke only, gainst all other voice.
In which predicament, I say, thou stand'st,
For it appears, by manifest proceeding,
370   That indirectly, and directly too,
Thou hast contrived against the very life
Of the defendant, and thou hast incurred
The danger formerly by me rehearsed.
Down therefore, and beg mercy of the duke.

375   GRATIANO   Beg that thou mayst have leave to hang thyself,
And yet, thy wealth being forfeit to the state,
Thou hast not left the value of a cord:
Therefore thou must be hanged at the state's charge.

DUKE   That thou shalt see the difference of our spirit,
380   I pardon thee thy life before thou ask it.
For half thy wealth, it is Antonio's,
The other half comes to the general state,
Which humbleness may drive unto a fine.

PORTIA   Ay, for the state, not for Antonio.

385   SHYLOCK   Nay, take my life and all. Pardon not that.
You take my house when you do take the prop
That doth sustain my house. You take my life
When you do take the means whereby I live.

PORTIA   What mercy can you render him, Antonio?

390   GRATIANO   A halter gratis. Nothing else, for God's sake.

ANTONIO   So please my lord the duke and all the court
To quit the fine for one half of his goods,
I am content, so he will let me have
The other half in use, to render it,
395   Upon his death, unto the gentleman
That lately stole his daughter.
Two things provided more: that for this favour

---

367 **gainst . . . voice** despite any other appeals   369 **proceeding** course of action
373 **danger** damage/penalty   **rehearsed** related   374 **Down** i.e. on your knees   377 **cord**
rope   378 **charge** cost   381 **For** as for   383 **humbleness** remorse (on Shylock's part)
drive convert   384 **for . . . Antonio** i.e. the state's portion of the goods may be reduced to a
fine, but not Antonio's half   390 **halter** hangman's noose   391 **So** if it please   392 **quit**
cancel, release (Shylock) from   393 **so** provided that   394 **use** (legal) trust

He presently become a Christian.

The other, that he do record a gift

400 Here in the court of all he dies possessed

Unto his son Lorenzo and his daughter.

DUKE He shall do this, or else I do recant

The pardon that I late pronouncèd here.

PORTIA Art thou contented, Jew? What dost thou say?

405 SHYLOCK I am content.

PORTIA Clerk, draw a deed of gift.

SHYLOCK I pray you give me leave to go from hence,

I am not well. Send the deed after me,

And I will sign it.

410 DUKE Get thee gone, but do it.

GRATIANO In christening thou shalt have two godfathers.

Had I been judge, thou shouldst have had ten more,

To bring thee to the gallows, not to the font.   *Exit [Shylock]*

DUKE Sir, I entreat you home with me to dinner.   *To Portia*

415 PORTIA I humbly do desire your grace of pardon.

I must away this night toward Padua,

And it is meet I presently set forth.

DUKE I am sorry that your leisure serves you not.

Antonio, gratify this gentleman,

420 For in my mind you are much bound to him.

Exit Duke and his train

BASSANIO Most worthy gentleman, I and my friend

Have by your wisdom been this day acquitted

Of grievous penalties, in lieu whereof,

Three thousand ducats due unto the Jew

425 We freely cope your courteous pains withal.   *Offers money*

ANTONIO And stand indebted, over and above,

In love and service to you evermore.

PORTIA He is well paid that is well satisfied,

And I, delivering you, am satisfied

398 **presently** immediately   400 **possessed** possessed of   401 **son** i.e. son-in-law   403 **late** lately   412 **ten more** i.e. twelve, the number in a jury   413 **font** place of Christian baptism   415 **of** for   417 **meet** fitting, necessary   418 **your . . . not** you don't have time to stay   419 **gratify** show gratitude to/reward   423 **in lieu whereof** in exchange for which   425 **cope** give in recompense (for)

430   And therein do account myself well paid.

My mind was never yet more mercenary.

I pray you know me when we meet again.

I wish you well, and so I take my leave.   *Starts to leave*

BASSANIO   Dear sir, of force I must attempt you further.

435   Take some remembrance of us as a tribute,

Not as fee. Grant me two things, I pray you:

Not to deny me, and to pardon me.

PORTIA   You press me far, and therefore I will yield.

Give me your gloves, I'll wear them for your sake.   *To Antonio*

440   And, for your love, I'll take this ring from you.   *To Bassanio*

Do not draw back your hand, I'll take no more,

And you in love shall not deny me this.

BASSANIO   This ring, good sir, alas, it is a trifle!

I will not shame myself to give you this.

445 PORTIA   I will have nothing else but only this,

And now methinks I have a mind to it.

BASSANIO   There's more depends on this than on the value.

The dearest ring in Venice will I give you,

And find it out by proclamation.

450   Only for this, I pray you pardon me.

PORTIA   I see, sir, you are liberal in offers.

You taught me first to beg, and now methinks

You teach me how a beggar should be answered.

BASSANIO   Good sir, this ring was given me by my wife,

455   And when she put it on, she made me vow

That I should neither sell nor give nor lose it.

PORTIA   That 'scuse serves many men to save their gifts.

An if your wife be not a madwoman,

And know how well I have deserved this ring,

---

430 account consider (plays on the sense of "financial reckoning")   **432 know** remember (a private joke on the sense of "have sex with")   **434 attempt** tempt/persuade   **437 pardon me** i.e. excuse my insistence   **438 press** urge (plays on the sense of "enjoy sexually")   **yield** plays on the sense of "submit sexually"   **440 love** friendship (plays on the sense of "marital love")   **442 in** out of   **446 mind to** desire for   **448 dearest** most expensive   **451 liberal** free/over-generous

460   She would not hold out enemy forever
       For giving it to me. Well, peace be with you!

                                    Exeunt [Portia and Nerissa]

ANTONIO   My lord Bassanio, let him have the ring.
       Let his deservings and my love withal
       Be valued against your wife's commandment.

465 BASSANIO   Go, Gratiano, run and overtake him.
       Give him the ring, and bring him, if thou canst,
       Unto Antonio's house. Away, make haste!   *Exit Gratiano*
       Come, you and I will thither presently,
       And in the morning early will we both

470   Fly toward Belmont. Come, Antonio.   *Exeunt*

[Act 4 Scene 2]   *running scene 19*

       Enter Portia and Nerissa   *Still disguised*

PORTIA   Inquire the Jew's house out, give him this deed,
       And let him sign it. We'll away tonight   *Gives her a deed*
       And be a day before our husbands home.
       This deed will be well welcome to Lorenzo.

       Enter Gratiano

5 GRATIANO   Fair sir, you are well o'erta'en.
       My lord Bassanio upon more advice
       Hath sent you here this ring, and doth entreat
       Your company at dinner.   *Gives her the ring*

PORTIA   That cannot be;
10   His ring I do accept most thankfully,
       And so, I pray you tell him. Furthermore,
       I pray you show my youth old Shylock's house.

GRATIANO   That will I do.

NERISSA   Sir, I would speak with you.
15   I'll see if I can get my husband's ring,   *Aside to Portia*
       Which I did make him swear to keep for ever.

---

470 Fly hasten   4.2   1 Inquire . . . out find out where the Jew's house is   deed i.e. the
document stating Shylock will leave his possessions to Jessica and Lorenzo   3 be i.e. arrive
5 you . . . o'erta'en i.e. I'm glad I caught you   6 advice reflection

PORTIA   Thou mayst, I warrant. We shall have   *Aside to Nerissa*
      old swearing
      That they did give the rings away to men;
      But we'll outface them, and outswear them too.—
20   Away, make haste! Thou know'st where I will tarry.   *Aloud*

NERISSA   Come, good sir, will you show me to this house?

                                        Exeunt

Act 5 [Scene 1]   *running scene 20*

Enter Lorenzo and Jessica

LORENZO   The moon shines bright. In such a night as this,
      When the sweet wind did gently kiss the trees
      And they did make no noise, in such a night
      Troilus methinks mounted the Trojan walls
5   And sighed his soul toward the Grecian tents
      Where Cressid lay that night.

JESSICA   In such a night
      Did Thisbe fearfully o'ertrip the dew,
      And saw the lion's shadow ere himself,
10   And ran dismayed away.

LORENZO   In such a night
      Stood Dido with a willow in her hand
      Upon the wild sea banks and waft her love
      To come again to Carthage.

15 JESSICA   In such a night
      Medea gathered the enchanted herbs
      That did renew old Aeson.

---

17 old plenty of   **19 outface** defy/contradict/shame   **outswear** outdo in swearing
5.1   ***Location: Belmont***   **4 Troilus** separated from his lover, Cressida (**Cressid**), by the
Trojan War, he was subsequently abandoned by her   **8 Thisbe** at their meeting place Pyramus
discovered his lover Thisbe's cloak, dropped in fright at the sight of a lion; his mistaken belief
that she had been killed led to both their suicides   **o'ertrip** skip over   **9 ere himself** before the
lion itself   **12 Dido** Queen of **Carthage** who fell in love with, and was abandoned by, Aeneas
willow willow leaves; symbol of grief for lost love   **13 wild** unruly/cruel   **waft** wafted (i.e.
beckoned)   **16 Medea** lover of Jason; she helped him gain the golden fleece and restored the
health of his father, **Aeson**   **17 renew** rejuvenate/revive

LORENZO   In such a night
Did Jessica steal from the wealthy Jew
20   And with an unthrift love did run from Venice
As far as Belmont.

JESSICA   In such a night
Did young Lorenzo swear he loved her well,
Stealing her soul with many vows of faith,
25   And ne'er a true one.

LORENZO   In such a night
Did pretty Jessica, like a little shrew,
Slander her love, and he forgave it her.

JESSICA   I would out-night you, did nobody come.
30   But hark, I hear the footing of a man.

Enter [Stephano, a] Messenger

LORENZO   Who comes so fast in silence of the night?

STEPHANO   A friend.

LORENZO   A friend? What friend? Your name, I pray you, friend?

STEPHANO   Stephano is my name, and I bring word
35   My mistress will before the break of day
Be here at Belmont. She doth stray about
By holy crosses, where she kneels and prays
For happy wedlock hours.

LORENZO   Who comes with her?

40   STEPHANO   None but a holy hermit and her maid.
I pray you is my master yet returned?

LORENZO   He is not, nor we have not heard from him.
But go we in, I pray thee, Jessica,
And ceremoniously let us prepare
45   Some welcome for the mistress of the house.

Enter Clown [Lancelet]

LANCELET   Sola, sola! Wo ha, ho! Sola, sola!

LORENZO   Who calls?

---

19 **steal** run stealthily from/rob   20 **unthrift** extravagant   27 **shrew** troublemaker, ill-tempered woman   28 **love** lover   29 **out-night you** i.e. outdo you in our game of references to the night   **did** if   30 **footing** footfall   36 **doth stray about** is distracted by   37 **holy crosses** shrines by the road   46 **Sola** imitation of the sound of a messenger's horn/a hunting cry   **Wo ha, ho!** falconer's call to the hawk

LANCELET   Sola! Did you see Master Lorenzo?
And Master Lorenzo, sola, sola!

50   LORENZO   Leave hollowing, man! Here.

LANCELET   Sola! Where, where?

LORENZO   Here.

LANCELET   Tell him there's a post come from my master, with
his horn full of good news: my master will be here ere
55   morning.   [*Exit*]

LORENZO   Sweet soul, let's in, and there expect their coming.
And yet no matter. Why should we go in?
My friend Stephano, signify, pray you,
Within the house, your mistress is at hand,
60   And bring your music forth into the air.   [*Exit Stephano*]
How sweet the moonlight sleeps upon this bank!
Here will we sit and let the sounds of music
Creep in our ears. Soft stillness and the night
Become the touches of sweet harmony.
65   Sit, Jessica. Look how the floor of heaven   *They sit*
Is thick inlaid with patens of bright gold.
There's not the smallest orb which thou behold'st
But in his motion like an angel sings,
Still choiring to the young-eyed cherubins;
70   Such harmony is in immortal souls,
But whilst this muddy vesture of decay
Doth grossly close it in, we cannot hear it.
[*Enter Musicians*]
Come, ho, and wake Diana with a hymn!

---

50 hollowing shouting/urging on of dogs in the hunt   53 post messenger   54 horn
messenger's instrument/cornucopia, i.e. plentiful supply   56 in go in   expect await
58 signify make known   60 music i.e. musicians   air plays on sense of "melody"
64 Become suit   touches skillful playing (by plucking or fingering instruments)   65 floor of
heaven i.e. sky   66 patens shallow, circular dishes (on which communion bread is placed)
67 orb heavenly body (planet, star)   68 motion movement (heavenly bodies were thought to
be surrounded by hollow spheres; as they rotated they produced beautiful music)   69 Still
choiring continually singing in chorus   young-eyed with eternally clear sight   cherubins
cherubim, angels   71 muddy . . . decay i.e. clay-like mortal clothing (flesh)   72 grossly
physically, coarsely   close it in i.e. enclose the soul   73 Diana Roman goddess of the moon

With sweetest touches pierce your mistress' ear,

75   And draw her home with music.

JESSICA   I am never merry when I hear sweet music.

Play music

LORENZO   The reason is, your spirits are attentive.

For do but note a wild and wanton herd

Or race of youthful and unhandled colts,

80   Fetching mad bounds, bellowing and neighing loud,

Which is the hot condition of their blood.

If they but hear perchance a trumpet sound,

Or any air of music touch their ears,

You shall perceive them make a mutual stand,

85   Their savage eyes turned to a modest gaze

By the sweet power of music: therefore the poet

Did feign that Orpheus drew trees, stones and floods,

Since nought so stockish, hard and full of rage,

But music for time doth change his nature.

90   The man that hath no music in himself,

Nor is not moved with concord of sweet sounds,

Is fit for treasons, stratagems and spoils.

The motions of his spirit are dull as night

And his affections dark as Erebus.

95   Let no such man be trusted. Mark the music.

Enter Portia and Nerissa

PORTIA   That light we see is burning in my hall.

How far that little candle throws his beams!

So shines a good deed in a naughty world.

NERISSA   When the moon shone, we did not see the candle.

---

77 **spirits** mental faculties/feelings **attentive** i.e. preoccupied 78 **wanton** unrestrained, wild, boisterous 79 **race** company/herd **unhandled** untamed 80 **Fetching** performing **bounds** leaps 81 **hot condition** passionate nature **blood** spirit 82 **but** only **perchance** by chance/perhaps 83 **air** melody 84 **mutual stand** general pause 86 **the poet** i.e. Ovid 87 **feign** depict/invent **Orpheus** legendary Greek poet and musician who could charm all of nature with his music **drew** drew in, attracted **floods** rivers 88 **stockish** unfeeling/ stupid 92 **stratagems** schemes/bloody acts **spoils** destruction, pillaging 93 **motions** inner promptings **dull** dark/lifeless 94 **affections** feelings/disposition **Erebus** place of darkness between earth and the classical underworld 98 **naughty** wicked

100	PORTIA	So doth the greater glory dim the less.

A substitute shines brightly as a king
Until a king be by, and then his state
Empties itself, as doth an inland brook
Into the main of waters. Music! Hark!   *Music*

105   NERISSA   It is your music, madam, of the house.

PORTIA   Nothing is good, I see, without respect.

Methinks it sounds much sweeter than by day.

NERISSA   Silence bestows that virtue on it, madam.

PORTIA   The crow doth sing as sweetly as the lark

110   When neither is attended, and I think
The nightingale, if she should sing by day,
When every goose is cackling, would be thought
No better a musician than the wren.
How many things by season seasoned are

115   To their right praise and true perfection!
Peace, ho! The moon sleeps with Endymion
And would not be awaked.   *Music ceases*

LORENZO   That is the voice,
Or I am much deceived, of Portia.

120   PORTIA   He knows me as the blind man knows the cuckoo,
By the bad voice.

LORENZO   Dear lady, welcome home.

PORTIA   We have been praying for our husbands' welfare,
Which speed, we hope, the better for our words.

125   Are they returned?

LORENZO   Madam, they are not yet,
But there is come a messenger before,
To signify their coming.

PORTIA   Go in, Nerissa.

130   Give order to my servants that they take

---

102 by nearby   **his** i.e. the substitute's   **state** dignity/sovereignty   **104 main of waters**
sea   **106 respect** consideration of circumstance   **110 attended** paid attention to/heard
114 season occasion   **seasoned** improved/flavored   **116 Endymion** shepherd with whom
the moon goddess fell in love; she granted him eternal sleep so she could visit him   **124 speed**
succeed/hasten   **words** i.e. prayers   **127 before** ahead of them

No note at all of our being absent hence,

Nor you, Lorenzo, Jessica, nor you.   *A tucket sounds*

LORENZO   Your husband is at hand. I hear his trumpet.

We are no telltales, madam; fear you not.

135 PORTIA   This night methinks is but the daylight sick.

It looks a little paler. 'Tis a day,

Such as the day is when the sun is hid.

Enter Bassanio, Antonio, Gratiano and their followers

BASSANIO   We should hold day with the Antipodes,

If you would walk in absence of the sun.

140 PORTIA   Let me give light, but let me not be light,

For a light wife doth make a heavy husband,

And never be Bassanio so for me,

But God sort all! You are welcome home, my lord.

BASSANIO   I thank you, madam. Give welcome to my friend.

145 This is the man, this is Antonio,

To whom I am so infinitely bound.

PORTIA   You should in all sense be much bound to him,

For, as I hear, he was much bound for you.

ANTONIO   No more than I am well acquitted of.

150 PORTIA   Sir, you are very welcome to our house.

It must appear in other ways than words:

Therefore I scant this breathing courtesy.

GRATIANO   By yonder moon I swear you do me wrong.   *To Nerissa*

In faith, I gave it to the judge's clerk.

155 Would he were gelt that had it, for my part,

Since you do take it, love, so much at heart.

PORTIA   A quarrel, ho, already? What's the matter?

GRATIANO   About a hoop of gold, a paltry ring

That she did give me, whose posy was

160 For all the world like cutler's poetry

Upon a knife, 'Love me, and leave me not.'

---

132 tucket trumpet call   **138 should . . . Antipodes** would experience day at the same time as the other side of the world   **139 in . . . sun** i.e. at night (since Portia is like a second sun) **140 be light** be promiscuous   **141 heavy** sad (plays on the sense of "weighty")   **143 sort** arrange   **148 bound** imprisoned/indebted/legally bound   **149 acquitted of** repaid for/freed from   **152 scant** cut short   **breathing** i.e. verbal   **155 gelt** gelded, castrated   **for my part** as far as I'm concerned   **156 at** to   **159 posy** verse or motto inscribed on a ring

NERISSA   What talk you of the posy or the value?
You swore to me when I did give it you,
That you would wear it till the hour of death
165   And that it should lie with you in your grave.
Though not for me, yet for your vehement oaths,
You should have been respective and have kept it.
Gave it a judge's clerk! But well I know
The clerk will ne'er wear hair on's face that had it.
170   GRATIANO   He will, an if he live to be a man.
NERISSA   Ay, if a woman live to be a man.
GRATIANO   Now, by this hand, I gave it to a youth,
A kind of boy, a little scrubbèd boy,
No higher than thyself, the judge's clerk,
175   A prating boy, that begged it as a fee.
I could not for my heart deny it him.
PORTIA   You were to blame—I must be plain with you—
To part so slightly with your wife's first gift.
A thing stuck on with oaths upon your finger
180   And so riveted with faith unto your flesh.
I gave my love a ring and made him swear
Never to part with it, and here he stands.
I dare be sworn for him he would not leave it,
Nor pluck it from his finger, for the wealth
185   That the world masters. Now, in faith, Gratiano,
You give your wife too unkind a cause of grief.
An 'twere to me, I should be mad at it.
BASSANIO   Why, I were best to cut my left hand off   *Aside*
And swear I lost the ring defending it.
190   GRATIANO   My lord Bassanio gave his ring away
Unto the judge that begged it and indeed
Deserved it too. And then the boy, his clerk,
That took some pains in writing, he begged mine,
And neither man nor master would take aught
195   But the two rings.

166 Though i.e. if   **167 respective** careful, considerate   **173 scrubbèd** undersized
175 prating chattering   **178 slightly** easily   **180 riveted** bolted   **185 masters** possesses
187 mad enraged

PORTIA   What ring gave you my lord?
Not that, I hope, which you received of me.

BASSANIO   If I could add a lie unto a fault,
I would deny it. But you see my finger
200   Hath not the ring upon it. It is gone.

PORTIA   Even so void is your false heart of truth.
By heaven, I will ne'er come in your bed
Until I see the ring.

NERISSA   Nor I in yours till I again see mine.

205   BASSANIO   Sweet Portia,
If you did know to whom I gave the ring,
If you did know for whom I gave the ring,
And would conceive for what I gave the ring,
And how unwillingly I left the ring,
210   When nought would be accepted but the ring,
You would abate the strength of your displeasure.

PORTIA   If you had known the virtue of the ring,
Or half her worthiness that gave the ring,
Or your own honour to contain the ring,
215   You would not then have parted with the ring.
What man is there so much unreasonable,
If you had pleased to have defended it
With any terms of zeal, wanted the modesty
To urge the thing held as a ceremony?
220   Nerissa teaches me what to believe:
I'll die for't but some woman had the ring.

BASSANIO   No, by mine honour, madam, by my soul,
No woman had it, but a civil doctor,
Which did refuse three thousand ducats of me
225   And begged the ring; the which I did deny him
And suffered him to go displeased away—
Even he that had held up the very life

---

208 **conceive** understand   212 **virtue** power   214 **contain** retain   217 **If** that if   **pleased** wanted, attempted   218 **wanted** (so) lacking   **modesty** restraint   219 **urge** request persistently   **ceremony** sacred token   223 **civil doctor** doctor of civil law   226 **suffered** let 227 **held up** i.e. saved

Of my dear friend. What should I say, sweet lady?
I was enforced to send it after him.
230 I was beset with shame and courtesy.
My honour would not let ingratitude
So much besmear it. Pardon me, good lady!
And by these blessèd candles of the night,
Had you been there, I think you would have begged
235 The ring of me to give the worthy doctor.

PORTIA   Let not that doctor e'er come near my house.
Since he hath got the jewel that I loved,
And that which you did swear to keep for me,
I will become as liberal as you.
240 I'll not deny him anything I have,
No, not my body nor my husband's bed.
Know him I shall, I am well sure of it.
Lie not a night from home. Watch me like Argus.
If you do not, if I be left alone,
245 Now, by mine honour, which is yet mine own,
I'll have the doctor for my bedfellow.

NERISSA   And I his clerk: therefore be well advised
How you do leave me to mine own protection.

GRATIANO   Well, do you so. Let not me take him, then.
250 For if I do, I'll mar the young clerk's pen.

ANTONIO   I am th'unhappy subject of these quarrels.

PORTIA   Sir, grieve not you. You are welcome
notwithstanding.

BASSANIO   Portia, forgive me this enforcèd wrong,
And in the hearing of these many friends,
255 I swear to thee, even by thine own fair eyes,
Wherein I see myself—

PORTIA   Mark you but that!

232 it i.e. honor   233 candles . . . night i.e. stars   239 liberal generous   242 Know
recognize/have sex with   243 Argus monster with a hundred eyes   245 honour good
name/chaste reputation   yet still   247 be well advised take care   249 take catch
250 mar ruin   pen i.e. penis   251 th'unhappy the unlucky/miserable/trouble-causing

In both my eyes he doubly sees himself.
In each eye, one. Swear by your double self,
260   And there's an oath of credit.

BASSANIO   Nay, but hear me.
Pardon this fault, and by my soul I swear
I never more will break an oath with thee.

ANTONIO   I once did lend my body for thy wealth,—   To Bassanio
265   Which, but for him that had your husband's ring,   To Portia
Had quite miscarried. I dare be bound again,
My soul upon the forfeit, that your lord
Will never more break faith advisedly.

PORTIA   Then you shall be his surety. Give him this   She gives
270   And bid him keep it better than the other.   Antonio the ring

ANTONIO   Here, Lord Bassanio. Swear to keep this ring.

BASSANIO   By heaven, it is the same I gave the doctor!

PORTIA   I had it of him. Pardon, Bassanio,
For, by this ring, the doctor lay with me.

275   NERISSA   And pardon me, my gentle Gratiano,
For that same scrubbèd boy, the doctor's clerk,
In lieu of this last night did lie with me.   Shows her ring

GRATIANO   Why, this is like the mending of highways
In summer, where the ways are fair enough.
280   What, are we cuckolds ere we have deserved it?

PORTIA   Speak not so grossly. You are all amazed.
Here is a letter, read it at your leisure.   She gives a letter
It comes from Padua, from Bellario.
There you shall find that Portia was the doctor,
285   Nerissa there her clerk. Lorenzo here
Shall witness I set forth as soon as you,
And but e'en now returned. I have not yet
Entered my house. Antonio, you are welcome,

258 doubly sees himself sees himself reflected twice   259 double dual/deceitful   260 of
credit worth believing   266 quite miscarried entirely come to harm   268 advisedly
deliberately   269 surety guarantor   274 lay with slept with   277 lieu of exchange for
279 fair good, unmuddied (i.e. without needing repair)   280 cuckolds men with unfaithful
wives   281 grossly coarsely/foolishly   287 e'en just

And I have better news in store for you
290   Than you expect. Unseal this letter soon.   *Gives him a letter*
There you shall find three of your argosies
Are richly come to harbour suddenly:
You shall not know by what strange accident
I chancèd on this letter.

295   ANTONIO   I am dumb.

BASSANIO   Were you the doctor and I knew you not?

GRATIANO   Were you the clerk that is to make me cuckold?

NERISSA   Ay, but the clerk that never means to do it,
Unless he live until he be a man.

300   BASSANIO   Sweet doctor, you shall be my bedfellow.
When I am absent, then lie with my wife.

ANTONIO   Sweet lady, you have given me life and living;
For here I read for certain that my ships
Are safely come to road.

305   PORTIA   How now, Lorenzo?
My clerk hath some good comforts too for you.

NERISSA   Ay, and I'll give them him without a fee.
There do I give to you and Jessica,
From the rich Jew, a special deed of gift,
310   After his death, of all he dies possessed of.

LORENZO   Fair ladies, you drop manna in the way
Of starvèd people.

PORTIA   It is almost morning,
And yet I am sure you are not satisfied
315   Of these events at full. Let us go in,
And charge us there upon inter'gatories,
And we will answer all things faithfully.

GRATIANO   Let it be so. The first inter'gatory
That my Nerissa shall be sworn on is,

292 **richly** i.e. laden with expensive goods   295 **dumb** speechless   302 **living** livelihood
304 **road** harbor   311 **manna** during the Exodus, the food God provided for the Israelites in
the desert   314 **you . . . full** your curiosity will not be content until further details are revealed
316 **charge . . . inter'gatories** examine us under formal questioning   318 **inter'gatory**
question   319 **sworn on** under oath to answer truthfully

320 Whether till the next night she had rather stay,
    Or go to bed now, being two hours to day.
    But were the day come, I should wish it dark,
    Till I were couching with the doctor's clerk.
    Well, while I live I'll fear no other thing
325 So sore as keeping safe Nerissa's ring.   *Exeunt*

320 **stay** wait   323 **couching** in bed   325 **sore** greatly   **ring** gold band (plays on the sense of "vagina")

TEXTUAL NOTES

Q = First Quarto text of 1600
Q2 = Second Quarto text of 1619
F = First Folio text of 1623
F2 = a correction introduced in the Second Folio text of 1632
Ed = a correction introduced by a later editor
SD = stage direction
SH = speech heading (i.e. speaker's name)

List of parts = Ed

1.1.0 SD *Salerio and Solanio* = Ed. F = *Salarino, and Salanio* 8 SH SALE-RIO = Ed. F = *Sal.* Q = *Salarino.* *SHs for first three speeches of Antonio's friends reversed in F, due to confusing SHs in Q: Salarino, Salanio, Salar.* 15 SH SOLANIO = Q *(Salanio).* F = *Salar.* 28 docked = Ed. F = docks 62 SH SALERIO = Ed. F = *Sala. (his next two speeches: Sal.)* 70 SD *Salerio* = Ed. F = *Salarino* 116 Is = Ed. F = It is 118 are two = F. Q = are as two 158 do me now = Q. F = doe

1.2.6 small = F. Q = meane 15 be one = F. Q = to be one 19 reason is not in = F. Q = reasoning is not in the 22 Is it = Q. F = It is 39 Palatine = Q2. F = Palentine 44 rather to be = F. Q = rather be 47 Bon = Ed. F = *Boune* 52 throstle = Ed. F = Trassell 55 should = F. Q = shall 67 other = F. Q = Scottish. *Altered in F so as not to offend Scottish King James* 96 wish = F. Q = pray God grant 105 seek you = F. Q = seeke for you

1.3.33 Rialto = Ed. F = Ryalta 45 well-won = Q. F = well-worne 61 ye = Q. F = he 82 peeled *spelled* pil'd *in* F 111 spit *spelled* spet *in* F 121 should = F. Q = can 124 spat *spelled* spet *in* F 132 of barren = F. Q = for barren 135 penalties = F. Q = penaltie 151 it pleaseth = F. Q = pleaseth 180 terms = Q. F = teames

2.1.0 SD *Morocco spelled Morochus in* F 32 thee, lady = Q. F = the Ladie 36 page = Ed. F = rage

2.2.1 SH LANCELET = Ed. F = *Clo.* 3 Gobbo = Q2. F = *Iobbe (throughout scene)* 22 a kind = F. Q = but a kinde 48 Lancelet = F. Q = Lancelet sir 87 last = Q2. F = lost 156 SD *Exit placed two lines earlier in* F 167 where they = F. Q = where thou

2.3.9 talk = F. Q = in talk 11 did = Ed. F = doe 13 somewhat = F. Q = something

2.4.0 SD *Salerio* = Ed. F = *Slarino (Sal. for his SHs throughout this scene)*
  11 shall it = F. Q = it shall   **14 Is** = Q. F = I
2.5.1 SH SHYLOCK = Q2. F = *Iew*   **28 there** = Q. F = their   **43 Jewès** = Ed.
  F = Iewes   **47 but** = F. Q = and
2.6.0 SD *Salerio* = Ed. F = *Salino*   **2 a stand** = F. Q = stand   **7 seal** = Q. F =
  steale   **18 a prodigal** = F. Q = the prodigal   **46 you are** = F. Q = are you
  60 gentlemen = F. Q = gentleman
2.7.5 many men = Q. F = men   *Line accidentally printed twice in* F   **70 tombs**
  = Ed. F = *timber*
2.8.0 SD *Salerio* = Ed. F = *Salarino*   **6 comes** = F. Q = came   **8 gondola**
  spelled Gondilo *in* F   **34 You** = Q. F = Yo
2.9.7 thou = F. Q = you   **45 peasantry** = Q. F = pleasantry   **102 Bassanio,**
  Lord Love, = Ed. F = *Bassanio* Lord, loue
3.1.0 SD *Salerio* = Ed. F = *Salarino*   **6 gossip's** = F. Q = gossip   **33 blood** =
  F. Q = my blood   **50 what's the** = F. Q = what's his   **64 SH SERVANT** =
  Ed. *Not in* F   **71 of her** = Q. F = of ster   **80 how much** = F. Q = whats
  94 heard = Ed. F = here   **105 turquoise** = Ed. F = Turkies
3.2.0 SD *trains* = Q. F = *traine*   **17 if** = Q. F = of   **34 do** = Q. F = doth
  44 aloof = Q. F = aloose   **63 much, much** = Q. F = much   **69 eyes** =
  F. Q = eye   **83 vice** = Ed. F = voice   **152 me** = Q. F = my   **161 nothing** =
  F. Q = something   **174 lord** = F. Q = Lords   **199 have** = Q. F = gaue
  207 roof = Q2. F = rough   **213 is so** = F. Q = is   **323 SH BASSANIO** =
  Ed. *Not in* F   **326 might see** = F. Q = might but see   **333 No** = Q. F = Nor
3.3.2 lends = F. Q = lent
3.4.13 equal *spelled* egal *in* F   **50 Padua** = Ed. F = Mantua   **51 hand** = F. Q =
  hands   **54 traject** = Ed. F = Tranect
3.5.67–8 merit it, In = Ed. F = meane it, it Is. Q = meane it, it In   **75 a wife** =
  F. Q = wife
4.1.52 Mistress = Ed. F = Masters   **66 answer** = F. Q = answers
  75 Why . . . made = Q. *Not in* F   **78 fretted** = F. Q = fretten   **80 what** =
  F. Q = what's   **112 messenger** = Q. F = Messengers   **144 endless** = F. Q
  = cureless   **169 Came** = F. Q = Come   **208 court** = Q. F = course
  228 do I = F. Q = I do   **234 No, not** = F. Q = Not not   **266 should** = F. Q =
  doe   **267 Is it so** = Q. F = It is not   **271 Come** = F. Q = You   **286 not** = F. Q
  = but   **316 Then take** = F. Q = Take then   **337 it so** = F. Q = it but so
  344 thee = F. Q = you   **354 taken so** = F. Q = so taken   **411 thou shalt** =
  F. Q = shalt thou   **414 home with me** = Q. F = with me home
5.1.3 noise = Q. F = nnyse   **32 SH STEPHANO** = Ed. F = *Mes.*   **41 is** = Q. F =
  it   **returned** = Q. F = rnturn'd   **44 us** = Q. F = vs vs   **56 Sweet soul** = Ed.
  F *prints as last words of Lancelet's speech*   **58 Stephano** = Q2. F = *Stephen*
  pray = F. Q = I pray   **72 it in** = Q. F = in it   **89 time** = F. Q = the time
  164 the hour = F. Q = your hour   **168 But . . . know** = F. Q = no God's my
  Iudge   **233 And by** = F. Q = For by   **264 thy** = F. Q = his   **273 Pardon** =
  F. Q = Pardon me   **287 but e'en now** = F. Q = even but now

SCENE-BY-SCENE ANALYSIS

ACT 1 SCENE 1

Lines 1–115: Antonio confesses he is sad but cannot explain the reason. Salerio suggests he is worried about his ships, currently at sea, but Antonio says that he is not concerned about his merchandise. Salerio therefore suggests that it is because Antonio is "in love," establishing a link between two main themes: commerce and love. They are interrupted by Bassanio, Lorenzo, and Gratiano. Solanio and Salerio take their leave, joking that some "worthier company" has arrived, introducing the motif of "worth" (both of goods and people). Gratiano observes that Antonio looks unwell and Antonio's meta-theatrical response is that the world is a "stage where every man must play a part" and that his is "a sad one." Gratiano urges him not to put on sadness merely to seem wise, establishing the themes of disguise/appearance versus reality.

Lines 116–188: Bassanio observes that Gratiano "speaks an infinite deal of nothing" and that "His reasons are two grains of wheat hid in two bushels of chaff," images that reinforce the play's concerns with quantity and value. Antonio questions Bassanio about the lady he is in love with. Bassanio's response is elliptical, focusing instead on his lack of fortune and need to borrow money from Antonio, despite already being in debt to him "in money and in love," further reinforcing the link between these two themes. Bassanio describes Portia of Belmont, "a lady richly left," who has inherited a large fortune on her father's death, and who is "fair and, fairer than that word, / Of wondrous virtues." This raises the motif of "fairness," in terms of both beauty and justice. Bassanio needs money to court Portia. Antonio explains that his "fortunes are at sea" but will stand security if Bassanio borrows money.

ACT 1 SCENE 2

In Belmont, Portia is complaining of being "aweary of this great world," echoing Antonio in the previous scene. Under the terms of her dead father's will, she cannot choose her own husband, nor refuse one she dislikes if he passes the test set by her father. Each of Portia's suitors must choose between three caskets: one gold, one silver, and one lead. Only the man who chooses correctly shall marry Portia. She and Nerissa list her recent admirers: a "Neapolitan prince," a "French lord," a "young baron of England," and "the Duke of Saxony's nephew," emphasizing the competition that Bassanio faces, but also the play's concerns with cultural identities and differences. Portia dismisses each one, showing her quick wit and ability to reason. Nerissa reminds her of "a Venetian, a scholar and a soldier" (Bassanio) who visited their household while Portia's father was alive. The ladies agree he is "worthy" of praise. A servant announces that the four suitors have left, but that a fifth, "the Prince of Morocco," will arrive that night. Portia is unimpressed, commenting that her new suitor will have "the complexion of a devil," highlighting the racial/cultural boundaries that exist in the play.

ACT 1 SCENE 3

Bassanio and Shylock discuss a loan of "Three thousand ducats" for "three months." Bassanio assures Shylock that "Antonio shall become bound" in guarantee, but Shylock is unsure: Antonio's wealth is uncertain while his ships are still at sea. Antonio approaches and Shylock reveals his hatred in an aside: he hates Antonio "for he is a Christian," but more importantly because Antonio makes loans without charging interest, damaging Shylock's moneylending business. Finally, he points out that Antonio hates him because he is Jewish, and because he is a moneylender. This speech makes clear the opposing characters of Shylock and Antonio, contrasted throughout the play in terms of their faiths and characteristics.

When Antonio arrives, Shylock makes a show of civility. Antonio tells him that usually he does not "lend nor borrow," but that he is making an exception for Bassanio. Shylock remembers all the times that Antonio has "rated" him over his moneylending, and insulted him on the grounds of his faith, calling him a "misbeliever." He asks why he should lend money to someone who has "spat on" him and called him a "dog." Antonio replies that he is likely to do these things again and tells Shylock that he will be making a loan to his "enemy," who it will be easier to "Exact the penalties" from if he fails to pay. Shylock claims that he wants to "be friends," making the loan with no interest charges. He suggests, "in a merry sport," that if Antonio fails to pay back the money on the day stipulated, he will take a "pound" of Antonio's "fair flesh." Antonio agrees, despite Bassanio's protests. He points out that within two months he is expecting a return of "three times the value of this bond." Shylock tells them to meet him "at the notary's," where they will put the bond in writing, and leaves. Antonio observes that Shylock "grows kind," but Bassanio is less trusting, saying that Shylock has "a villain's mind." Antonio reiterates that his ships will come home "a month before the day," one of many references to time that create pace and tension.

ACT 2 SCENE 1

The Prince of Morocco begs Portia not to "Mislike" him on account of his complexion. She politely reminds him that, under the terms of her father's will, her marriage will be due to a "lott'ry" rather than her own choice. The prince's speeches are lover-like, but he is self-absorbed and boastful. Portia reminds him that the penalty for choosing wrongly is that he must remain unmarried. He agrees, and they go to dinner.

ACT 2 SCENE 2

Lines 1–99: Lancelet, the Clown, is contemplating running away from his master, whom he characterizes as a "fiend" and a "devil," recurring imagery used in conjunction with Shylock. As he finally decides to "run," he meets Old Gobbo, his father. Gobbo is blind and does not recognize his son, who decides to pretend to be someone else, a situation that creates comedy, but which also reinforces the other instances of concealed/exchanged identity in the play. Gobbo reveals that he is looking for Shylock's house and for his son, who Lancelet claims is dead, before revealing his true identity. Gobbo, however, will not believe that he is Lancelet. The confusion is resolved and Gobbo explains that he has brought Shylock a present, but Lancelet announces that he has run away from his master. He informs Gobbo that he intends to serve Bassanio, who gives "rare new liveries," and tells him to give Bassanio the present.

Lines 100–191: Bassanio enters, instructing a servant to have supper ready "by five of the clock," and to ask Gratiano to come to his lodging. Lancelet urges his father to give him the present, and comic confusion is created as both men try to ask Bassanio if he will take Lancelet into service. Bassanio clarifies matters and agrees. Lancelet and Gobbo leave. Gratiano arrives and asks Bassanio if he may accompany him to Belmont. Bassanio agrees, but insists that Gratiano must be more modest in his behavior.

ACT 2 SCENE 3

Jessica regrets that Lancelet is leaving, as he has made life in Shylock's house less tedious. She gives him money, and a letter to deliver to Lorenzo, a guest at Bassanio's house. Alone, Jessica reveals her "heinous sin": she is ashamed to be her "father's child." She declares that, although she is of Shylock's blood, she is not of "his manners," creating an important distinction between faith and character, explored throughout the play. She reveals her intention to "Become a Christian" and marry Lorenzo.

ACT 2 SCENE 4

Lorenzo and his friends prepare to disguise themselves as masquers and help Jessica escape from Shylock's house that evening. Lancelet delivers her letter to Lorenzo and tells them that he is going to Shylock's with an invitation to supper at Bassanio's. Lorenzo gives him money and a message to Jessica that he will not fail her, and sends

Salerio and Solanio to prepare. He tells Gratiano that Jessica will be waiting to elope with "gold and jewels" and will disguise herself as Lorenzo's torchbearer and escape as part of the masque.

ACT 2 SCENE 5

Shylock warns Lancelet that his "eyes shall be thy judge" of the differences between himself and Bassanio, raising a motif of sight/perception. He calls for Jessica and tells her that he is going out, although he is suspicious of Bassanio's motives in inviting him, and fears some "ill a-brewing." Lancelet tells him that there are to be masques that night, and Shylock warns Jessica to "Lock up" the house, and not to let the "sound of shallow fopp'ry enter / [His] sober house," emphasizing his separation from the prevailing Venetian culture. As Lancelet goes, he whispers to Jessica to look out for "a Christian" (Lorenzo) during the masque. Shylock leaves, reminding Jessica to lock the doors, and she secretly bids him goodbye.

ACT 2 SCENE 6

Gratiano and Salerio wait for Lorenzo. They are worried that he is late, particularly as "lovers ever run before the clock," but he joins them and calls for Jessica. She appears, above, disguised in boy's clothes, and throws Lorenzo a casket of money and jewels. She is embarrassed by her disguise, but Lorenzo urges her to "come at once." As they wait for her, Lorenzo tells Gratiano that Jessica is "wise, fair and true." She arrives and they go to join the masque, leaving Gratiano behind. Antonio arrives to tell Gratiano that "the wind is come about" and he must join Bassanio to sail for Belmont.

ACT 2 SCENE 7

Portia shows the Prince of Morocco the three caskets. He reads the inscription on each: he has a choice between gaining "what many men desire" (the gold casket), getting "as much as he deserves" (silver), or to "give and hazard all he hath" (lead). Portia tells him that the correct casket contains her portrait. The prince makes a long speech explaining his reasoning, but also, unwittingly, revealing his self-importance. He chooses the gold casket, which contains a skull "within whose empty eye / There is a written scroll" telling him that "All that glisters is not gold": he has judged by appearances, ironically given his request to Portia in Act 2 Scene 1. In contrast to his earlier verbosity, he tells Portia that he is "too grieved" to "take a tedious leave," and departs. Portia is pleased and expresses the wish that all of his "complexion" make a similar choice.

ACT 2 SCENE 8

Shylock has discovered the disappearance of Jessica and his money. We learn about his response through the biased, unsympathetic report of Salerio and Solanio. Shylock and the Duke of Venice went to search Bassanio's ship, which had already sailed. Antonio assured them that Lorenzo and Jessica were not on it. Solanio jeeringly reports Shylock's confused rage and shouts of "My daughter! O my ducats! O my daughter!," suggesting that he values them equally. Solanio observes that unless Antonio can "keep his day" for repaying Shylock financially, he will pay for these events. Salerio has heard that one of Antonio's ships may have been lost. They speak of Antonio's kind and generous nature, in direct contrast with the characterization of Shylock.

ACT 2 SCENE 9

The Prince of Aragon has come to take the test for Portia's hand. The process is repeated: the prince selects the silver casket and finds "The portrait of a blinking idiot," holding another scroll. He protests. Portia's observation that "To offend and judge are distinct offices / And of opposèd natures" emphasizes the theme of justice. The prince leaves, and Portia instructs Nerissa to "draw the curtain" on the caskets. A messenger brings news of the imminent arrival of a Venetian lord, who has sent greetings and gifts "of rich value." Portia is eager to see the visitor, and Nerissa hopes it is Bassanio.

ACT 3 SCENE 1

In Venice, Solanio and Salerio discuss the reported loss of another of Antonio's ships. Shylock approaches and Solanio observes that "the devil" "comes in the likeness of a Jew." Shylock accuses them of having a part in Jessica's elopement, and they torment him, before asking if he has heard about Antonio's losses at sea. Shylock recalls how "smug" Antonio has been in the past, and tells them that he must now "look to his bond." Salerio asks what good taking Antonio's flesh will do, to which Shylock replies "To bait fish," adding that it will "feed" his "revenge," showing his callousness. He argues that Antonio has "disgraced," "hindered" and "mocked" him, solely because he is Jewish. He makes an impassioned speech, pointing out that he is "hurt with the same weapons, subject to the same diseases, healed by the same means, warmed and cooled by the same winter and summer, as a Christian is."

This plea for tolerance highlights the complexities of the play in terms of the representation of the Jewish faith and of Shylock, intrinsically and separately, and the degree of the audience's sympathies for various characters, complicated here by Salerio and Solanio's evident prejudice and Shylock's evident desire for "revenge." They are interrupted by Antonio's servant, who asks Salerio and Solanio to go to his master. As they leave, Tubal arrives. Shylock asks for news of Jessica, but Tubal has not found her, although he reports that she is spending Shylock's money. He also reports that Antonio has lost another ship, and Shylock wavers between pleasure at Antonio's misfortune, and rage at his own losses.

ACT 3 SCENE 2

Lines 1–222: Portia asks Bassanio to wait "a day or two" before undertaking the task, as she does not want to lose him but he wants to choose immediately. He confesses his love and Portia agrees, calling for music to play while Bassanio is making his decision. As a song is sung, Bassanio considers the three caskets. Unlike the other suitors, he recognizes that "the outward shows be least themselves." Rejecting gold as "food for Midas" and silver as the money that passes

" 'Tween man and man," Bassanio selects the lead casket. Portia's aside reveals her happiness as he opens it to reveal her portrait. Portia makes Bassanio "her lord, her governor, her king" and master of her estate and fortune. To seal this, she gives him a ring, which he must never "part from, lose or give away" as this would signal the "ruin" of his love for her. He promises to wear it until he dies, another "bond" which must be upheld. Nerissa and Gratiano congratulate the couple and Gratiano reveals that he is in love with Nerissa, before asking permission to marry her. Bassanio and Portia agree. As they joke happily together, Lorenzo arrives, accompanied by Salerio and Jessica.

Lines 223–333: Bassanio and Portia welcome their visitors, and Salerio gives Bassanio a letter from Antonio. Gratiano says that Antonio will be pleased by the news of the betrothals, but Portia is watching Bassanio and comments that the letter "steals the color from Bassanio's cheek." Bassanio reveals the truth about the loan, and Antonio's bond, before questioning Salerio about the loss of Antonio's fortunes. Salerio tells him that even if Antonio could now find the money, Shylock is determined to have "forfeiture . . . justice and his bond." Jessica confirms that her father has often sworn that he would "rather have Antonio's flesh / Than twenty times the value of the sum." Bassanio describes Antonio to Portia as "the dearest friend" and "the kindest man." She says that Bassanio must pay as much as it takes to release Antonio, and offers him gold to "pay the petty debt twenty times over." She decides that they shall be married quickly, then Bassanio shall go back to Venice with Gratiano, while she and Nerissa "live as maids and widows" until their return. Bassanio reads Antonio's letter, which urges him to come and see him, as it is unlikely that he will live after paying the forfeit. Portia urges him to "be gone!" and Bassanio promises to return as soon as he can.

ACT 3 SCENE 3

Antonio is in jail. Shylock will not listen to requests for "mercy," and his bitterness seems to have driven him to the edges of sanity as he constantly repeats that he will "have [his] bond." He leaves, and Antonio resolves that he will stop begging, recognizing that Shylock wants him to die for the times he has helped people who owed him "forfeitures," although he does not acknowledge that the persecution of Shylock for his faith may have contributed to his desire for revenge. He knows that the duke cannot prevent Shylock from exacting the bond, because to do so would be to "impeach the justice of the state." Antonio sends Solanio away, hoping that Bassanio will come to see him "pay his debt."

ACT 3 SCENE 4

Lorenzo tells Portia that if she knew Antonio, she would be even "prouder" of her role in trying to save him. She replies that she sees saving Antonio as the same as saving Bassanio, and announces her intention to withdraw to a monastery with Nerissa, to live "in prayer and contemplation" while Bassanio is away. She asks Lorenzo and Jessica to take the place of Bassanio and herself until this time. Portia then hands Balthasar a letter to take to her cousin, Doctor Bellario in Padua, and instructs him to bring back "what notes and garments" the doctor gives him. Finally, alone with Nerissa, Portia reveals her plan for them to go to Venice, disguised as men.

ACT 3 SCENE 5

Lancelet tells Jessica that he fears for her soul because "the sins of the father are to be laid upon the children," but she argues that she has been "saved" by marriage to Lorenzo, who has made her a Christian. As they argue, Lorenzo arrives and Jessica repeats what Lancelet has said. Lorenzo, however, reports that Lancelet has got a Moorish servant pregnant. Lancelet merely responds with jokes until Lorenzo, annoyed, sends him to serve dinner. Lorenzo asks Jessica how she likes Portia, and she replies that the "world / Hath not her fellow." They go to dinner.

ACT 4 SCENE 1

Lines 1–166: In the courtroom, the duke sympathizes with Antonio, describing Shylock as "an inhuman wretch / Uncapable of pity."

Antonio is resigned, declaring that he will "oppose" Shylock's "fury" with "patience," and his "rage" with "a quietness of spirit," emphasizing the deliberate contrasting of the two characters. Shylock is shown in and the duke tells him that he is sure he will "show mercy" to Antonio. Shylock is unmoved, maintaining that he will have the "weight of carrion flesh" he is entitled to. He refuses to take the three thousand ducats instead, citing his "hate" and "certain loathing" of Antonio. Bassanio tries to reason with him and offers him more money, but Antonio tells him that it is pointless. The duke asks Shylock how he expects to receive mercy when he shows none. Shylock argues that he has no need of mercy when he is "doing no wrong": he is asking for justice, which must be given to him according to "the decrees of Venice." The duke has sent for "Bellario, a learnèd doctor" to determine the outcome, and Salerio reports that a messenger has arrived from Padua. Nerissa enters, disguised as a law clerk. As she hands the duke a letter, Shylock begins to sharpen his knife. The letter is from Bellario, who is unable to come but who has sent "A young and learnèd doctor," Balthasar, in his place. Portia enters, disguised as Balthasar.

Lines 167–270: Portia, as Balthasar, questions both Shylock and Antonio, concluding that "the Jew" must "be merciful." Shylock asks what "compulsion" there is to do so, and Portia responds that mercy cannot be forced: "It droppeth as the gentle rain from heaven / Upon the place beneath." Bassanio repeats that he now has the money to pay the bond "ten times o'er," and asks that the law be changed. Portia says that there is "no power in Venice" that can alter the law. Shylock is delighted. Portia asks to look at the bond and concludes that Shylock may "lawfully" "claim / A pound of flesh." Again, she urges Shylock to "be merciful" and again he refuses. He also declines to provide a surgeon to tend to Antonio afterward because " 'tis not in the bond," showing his determination to stick to the letter of the law.

Lines 271–356: Portia calls Antonio forward and he announces that he is "prepared." He takes Bassanio's hand and tells him to commend him to his "honourable wife" and tell her how much Antonio loved him. Bassanio declares that, although Portia is as "dear" to him "as life itself," he would "sacrifice" her to save Antonio. Gratiano makes a similar declaration, and Portia and Nerissa are both unimpressed by their husbands' claims. Portia announces that Shylock may cut the flesh from Antonio, but, as he goes to do so, she tells him to "Tarry." Using Shylock's own adherence to the wording of the bond against him, she reminds him that the "words" "expressly are 'a pound of flesh'"; he may take no "blood," and he must take exactly a pound. Anything else is against the law, and would result in Shylock having to surrender his "lands and goods" to the state. Shylock announces that he will take money instead, but Portia insists that he may only take his bond. Shylock accepts defeat and prepares to leave the court, but Portia calls him back.

Lines 357–413: Portia reminds Shylock of the penalty against "an alien" who "seek[s] the life of any citizen": he must forfeit all of his "goods," to be divided between the state and Antonio, and, unless the duke shows "mercy," he will be executed. In contrast to Shylock's own refusals to show mercy, the duke pardons his life and reduces his fine. Antonio is similarly merciful, returning his share of Shylock's fortune on the condition that he converts to Christianity and leaves his money to Jessica and Lorenzo. Shylock agrees, and leaves the court.

Lines 414–470: The duke invites "Balthasar" to dinner, but Portia says she must return to Padua. The duke tells Antonio that he should reward the "young man." Bassanio still does not recognize his own wife, ironically forgetting his own words on "outward shows" in Act 3 Scene 2, and offers the three thousand ducats. Portia declines the money, but Bassanio insists on giving some form of payment. Portia asks him for his gloves and the ring he wears. Bassanio gives the gloves, but refuses to hand over the ring, explaining the "vow" he made to his wife. Portia accepts this explanation, although she is sure his "wife" would know that Balthasar deserved the ring. After she and Nerissa have left, Antonio urges Bassanio to give the ring to Balthasar, and Bassanio agrees. He removes the ring, and sends Gratiano to deliver it.

ACT 4 SCENE 2

Still disguised, Portia and Nerissa arrange the deed bequeathing Shylock's wealth to Jessica and Lorenzo. Gratiano enters and gives Portia the ring. She asks Gratiano to show Nerissa where Shylock's house is, and Gratiano, not recognizing his own wife, agrees. Nerissa tells Portia in an aside that she, too, will try to get the ring that she gave to Gratiano. They look forward to hearing their husbands' explanations.

ACT 5 SCENE 1

Lines 1–137: In Belmont, Lorenzo and Jessica are declaring their love for each other, indicating the lighter, more comic tone of the final scene in comparison to the dark, complex emotions of the courtroom. They are interrupted by a messenger, who tells them that Portia and Nerissa will arrive soon. Lancelet brings the news that Bassanio and Gratiano will also be back before morning. Lorenzo calls for music to welcome Portia home, and as he and Jessica admire the stars, he muses that a man who cannot appreciate music is not to be trusted. Portia and Nerissa return, drawn by the light and the sounds of the music. Lorenzo greets them and tells them that Bassanio and Gratiano will soon be back. Portia asks that no one reveal that she and Nerissa have been away.

Lines 138–325: Bassanio and Gratiano return, accompanied by Antonio, and Portia welcomes them. As Portia speaks to Antonio, they are interrupted by Nerissa and Gratiano, quarreling. He is trying to explain that he gave her ring to "the judge's clerk," adding that it was only a "paltry" item. Nerissa argues that the value of the ring was not as important as his oath to always wear it, reminding us of the theme of "worth" and the various bonds entered into during the play. Portia claims that Bassanio would never have given away her ring, but Gratiano reveals that he did. Bassanio tries to explain, but both women accuse their husbands of giving the rings to other women, and claim their right to be unfaithful in their turn.

Antonio intervenes, blaming himself for the misunderstanding.

He offers to be "bound again," and will forfeit his "soul" if Bassanio ever breaks faith with Portia. Portia gives Bassanio a ring, telling him to "keep it better than the other." He recognizes it, and Portia pretends that Balthasar gave it to her for sleeping with him. Nerissa produces her ring, and claims that the clerk gave it to her for the same reason. Before the men can respond, however, Portia reveals the truth: she was Balthasar and Nerissa the clerk. She produces a letter from Bellario to prove this, and another letter for Antonio, revealing that three of his ships "are richly come to harbour." Lorenzo and Jessica are informed of Shylock's new will. The play ends happily for the three sets of lovers, but Antonio remains a solitary figure despite his restored fortune, and the treatment of Shylock throughout creates an ambiguous sense of resolution.

THE MERCHANT OF VENICE IN PERFORMANCE: THE RSC AND BEYOND

The best way to understand a Shakespeare play is to see it or ideally to participate in it. By examining a range of productions, we may gain a sense of the extraordinary variety of approaches and interpretations that are possible—a variety that gives Shakespeare his unique capacity to be reinvented and made "our contemporary" four centuries after his death.

We begin with a brief overview of the play's theatrical and cinematic life, offering historical perspectives on how it has been performed. We then analyze in more detail a series of productions staged over the last half century by the Royal Shakespeare Company. The sense of dialogue between productions that can only occur when a company is dedicated to the revival and investigation of the Shakespeare canon over a long period, together with the uniquely comprehensive archival resource of promptbooks, program notes, reviews, and interviews held on behalf of the RSC at the Shakespeare Birthplace Trust in Stratford-upon-Avon, allows an "RSC stage history" to become a crucible in which the chemistry of the play can be explored.

Finally, we go to the horse's mouth. Modern theater is dominated by the figure of the director, who must hold together the whole play, whereas the actor must concentrate on his or her part. The director's viewpoint is therefore especially valuable. Shakespeare's plasticity is wonderfully revealed when we hear directors of highly successful productions answering the same questions in very different ways. For this play, it is also especially interesting to hear the voice of those who have been inside the part of Shylock: we accordingly also include interviews with two actors who created the role to high acclaim.

FOUR CENTURIES OF *THE MERCHANT*: AN OVERVIEW

The performance history of *The Merchant of Venice* has been dominated by the figure of Shylock: no small feat for a character who
appears in fewer scenes than almost any other named character and
whose role is dwarfed in size by that of Portia. Nevertheless, tradition
has it that Richard Burbage, leading player of the Lord Chamberlain's Men, originated the role of Shylock. Quite how the character of
the Jewish moneylender was received on stage at the time has been
the subject of much debate and controversy. The actor-manager
William Poel, in his Elizabethan-practices production of 1898 at St.
George's Hall in London, played the character in the red wig and
beard, traditionally associated with Judas Iscariot, on the assumption that Shakespeare merely made use of an available stock type in
order that the vice of greed may "be laughed at and defeated, not primarily because he is a Jew, but because he is a curmudgeon."[1]

While more recent history makes the idea of the Jew as stock villain uncomfortable for modern audiences, it must be remembered
that, at the time of original performance, the Jewish people had been
officially excluded from England for three hundred years and would
not be readmitted until 1655. The play's original performances can
therefore be seen in a context of folk legend and caricature, as had
been recently perpetuated by Christopher Marlowe's *The Jew of Malta*,
with its explicitly Machiavellian villain Barabas epitomizing the fashionable type of the cunning Jew. Barabas was one of the great tragedian Edward Alleyn's leading roles, and may have provided the
incentive for Burbage, the other leading actor of the day, to take a
more complex spin on the stock Jewish figure. As recently as 2006,
New York's Theater for a New Audience played the two in repertory
together, drawing out the links and influences between the plays.

The play includes a part for William Kempe, the company clown,
as Lancelet Gobbo (the name interestingly referencing an earlier
Kempe role, Launce of *The Two Gentlemen of Verona*) and, in Portia,
his greatest challenge for a boy actor so far. Portia's role, comprising
almost a quarter of the play's entire text, required tremendous skill
and range from the young actor, and laid down the groundwork for

the great breeches-clad heroines of the mature comedies, Viola and Rosalind.

The play was played twice at court in February 1605, suggesting a popularity that had kept the play in the company repertory for the best part of a decade, but after this there is no record of the play being performed again in the seventeenth century. The play's history in the eighteenth century began, as with many of Shakespeare's works, as an adaptation, George Granville's *The Jew of Venice* (1701). While the title ostensibly shifts the focus from Antonio to Shylock, the company's leading actor, Thomas Betterton, took the role of Bassanio. Shylock, on the other hand, was played by Thomas Doggett, an actor best known for low comedy. The adapted play emphasized moral ideals: Shylock was a simple comic villain, Bassanio a heroic and romantic lover.

It was not until 1741 that Shakespeare's text was restored by Charles Macklin at Drury Lane. Macklin, like Doggett before him, was best known for his comic roles, but he deliberately set out to create a more serious interpretation of Shylock. John Doran, for example, notes that in the trial scene "Shylock was natural, calmly confident, and so terribly malignant, that when he whetted his knife . . . a shudder went round the house."[2] This Shylock posed a genuine threat that the earlier comic villains did not, and thus began the process of reimagining *The Merchant of Venice* as more than a straightforward comedy. Macklin performed Shylock until 1789 and redefined the role—and the play—for subsequent generations. To Alexander Pope is attributed the pithy tribute "This is the Jew that Shakespeare drew."[3]

With the notable exception of David Garrick, most of the major actor-managers of the eighteenth and nineteenth centuries attempted Shylock, with varying degrees of success. In 1814, at the age of twenty-seven, the then-unknown Edmund Kean made his mark at Drury Lane in which he responded to the tradition laid down by Macklin with a new reading of Shylock. Toby Lelyveld tells us "he was willing to see in Shylock what no one but Shakespeare had seen—the tragedy of a man."[4] Heavily influenced by Garrick's acting style, Kean's performance took the Romantic preoccupation with individual passion and applied it to Shylock, allowing audiences to experience sympathy and pity for the antagonist, as William Hazlitt noted in the *Morning Chronicle*: "Our sympathies are much oftener with him than with his enemies."[5]

Henry Irving's production ran for over a thousand performances from 1879 to 1905 in London and America, and its influence is still felt. Irving's Shylock was a direct descendant of Macklin and Kean's, consolidating and emphasizing the role as that of a tragic hero. The *Spectator* noted that "here is a man whom none can despise, who can raise emotions both of pity and of fear, and make us Christians thrill with a retrospective sense of shame."[6] The use of "us Christians" is revealing of audience responses to the play until this point: audiences expected to identify themselves with the Venetian Christians, and in opposition to the Jewish villain. Where Kean had begun to experiment with sympathy for the "other," Irving forced his audiences to take sides with Shylock and be outraged by his treatment.

Irving's production was additionally noted for the spectacle of its set, which followed the celebrated example of Charles Kean's 1858 staging by including a full-sized Venetian bridge and canal along which the masquers floated in a gondola. The historical locations of *The Merchant of Venice* have long held a deep fascination for directors and designers, and attempts to re-create elements of Venice have recurred throughout the play's performance history: even the production at Shakespeare's Globe in 2007 featured a miniature Bridge of Sighs extending into the yard. This fascination with the city reached its apogee in Michael Radford's 2005 film (see below).

Irving's Portia was Ellen Terry, the latest in a long line of prestigious Portias including Kitty Clive (1741), Sarah Siddons (1786), and Ellen Tree (1858, opposite her husband, Kean). However, the longstanding focus on Shylock had had the negative impact of restricting the opportunities available to even the better actresses. Act 5 was often cut during the nineteenth century in order to focus on Shylock's tragedy, along with the scenes featuring Morocco and Aragon, while much of the Bassanio and Portia plot was mercilessly pruned. Irving himself, in order to present the play as unambiguous tragedy, often replaced Act 5 with *Iolanthe*, a one-act vehicle for Terry which allowed her to finish the evening's entertainment without distracting from Shylock's tragedy.

1. Old Gobbo in Charles Kean's 1858 production, with stage set representing the real Venice.

Despite this, Terry's Portia set a precedent for imagining the heroine as independent and self-determining. Where Portia had usually been played as entirely subject to the fate dictated by her father, Terry gave reviewers the impression that she would take matters into her own hands if the man she loved failed to choose correctly. She also allowed Portia to spontaneously come up with the blood–flesh resolution to Shylock's demand in a last-minute moment of inspiration, demonstrating a greater presence of mind and inventiveness than usual for the character. With Portia's independence of spirit established, the character began to take control of her own story: Fabia Drake's Portia, at Stratford in 1932, began the tradition of giving clues to Bassanio by arranging the emphasis of the "bred-head-nourishèd-fed" sounds in the song that is played as he chooses, thereby suggesting the rhyme with "lead," and in doing so became manager of her own fate.

This 1932 production, directed by Theodore Komisarjevsky, subverted the established chain of actor-manager productions that had followed in Irving's vein. Herbert Beerbohm Tree's 1908 Stratford production was characterized primarily by its elaborate scenic effects, and Frank Benson continued the tradition of Victorian *Merchants* as late as May 1932. Two months later, Komisarjevsky's production turned the play into carnival. The acclaimed Russian director had been invited to mark the opening of the new Shakespeare Memorial Theatre, and did so with a production that satirized the lovers, utilized eclectic surrealist sets and, in the words of the *Daily Herald*, "had the courage to show Shylock what I always thought him to be—a terrible old scoundrel."[7] 1932 also saw John Gielgud direct the play at the Old Vic, with Malcolm Keen as Shylock and Peggy Ashcroft as Portia. *The Times* criticized both 1932 productions for not treating the play as "sacrosanct," particularly disliking the "air of burlesque" that Gielgud gave to the Belmont scenes, designed to give greater tragic weight to the Shylock scenes.[8]

The play's early twentieth-century history is unavoidably tainted by the horrors of the Second World War and the Holocaust. The oft-quoted belief that the play was appropriated as Nazi propaganda somewhat overstates the case: most pertinently, in Germany there were no major productions of the play for over thirty years after 1927, a production in which Fritz Kortner was not allowed to play the "inhuman" character he felt Shakespeare intended Shylock to be. However, productions of the play during the prewar and war years were inevitably political. In 1943, the Vienna Burgtheater presented Lotha Müthel's fiercely anti-Semitic production, which made

Jessica "acceptable" by turning her into the daughter of an affair between Shylock's wife and a non-Jew. By contrast, Leopold Jessner's Hebrew-language production of 1936 at the Habimah Theatre of Tel Aviv "occurred at an heroic moment, where national pathos was a standard theme."[9] Jessner was a Jewish exile from Berlin, yet even this production was vigorously protested, culminating in a public mock trial that vindicated Shakespeare from accusations of anti-Semitism. Tel Aviv hosted subsequent productions of the play in 1953 (Tyrone Guthrie), 1972 (Yossi Yzraeli), and 1980 (Barry Kyle), the last aiming to explore how "Shylock easily falls prey to revenge in succumbing to the logic and mentality of terrorism."[10] The play retains its potential for controversial and insightful political comment.

Productions of the play in North America have been similarly overshadowed by the Holocaust, and new productions continue to draw complaints from Jewish groups and campaigners, meaning that the treatment of Shylock is rarely unsympathetic. Fears about the play's potential to negatively influence spectators were sensationalized: during a performance at the 1984 Stratford Ontario Festival, a group of schoolchildren threw pennies at Jewish students, an incident which resulted in calls for the play to be banned from the Festival. The play was not mounted by an American company between 1930 and 1953, but thereafter grew in popularity and was mounted regularly across the country for the remainder of the century, acting to reaffirm American ideals of racial equality. In 1957, the Oregon Shakespeare Festival staged an Elizabethan-practices production that revived the red-wigged Shylock of William Poel: here, however, it was deliberately intended to be repugnant. Six years later, George Tabori's adaptation at the Stockbridge Playhouse in Massachusetts turned the play into an entertainment put on by concentration camp prisoners for their Nazi guards. Alvin Epstein switched continually between his roles as Jewish prisoner-actor and Shylock, utilizing Shakespeare's lines to articulate the prisoner's anger at his guards. During the trial scene, he cast aside his assumed role and attacked a guard with a real knife substituted for the prop one, and was killed in retaliation by the guards, bringing both the inner play and Tabori's production crashing to a close.

The most high-profile American casting of the latter half of the twentieth century was Dustin Hoffman, appearing first in London and then transferring to Washington and New York in Peter Hall's 1989 staging. While Hoffman's presence resulted in the play breaking West End box-office records for a straight play, Hall's interpretation was found dull and lacking in insight, and the *National Review* felt that Hoffman's Shylock "seems to have wandered in from a different production."[11] Peter Sellars' mounting for the Goodman Theater in Chicago in 1994 set the play in Venice Beach, California, with Latino actors as the Venetians, black actors in the Jewish roles, and Asian-Americans as the Belmont characters. This production lasted for over four hours and was unpopular with audiences, despite its laudable intentions.

The play maintained its popularity in Stratford-upon-Avon following Komisarjevsky's production, often opening the festival season; Iden Payne's stagings were revived frequently between 1935 and 1942. The star performances of Michael Redgrave and Peggy Ashcroft (still playing Portia twenty-one years after her Old Vic appearance) dominated coverage of Dennis Carey's 1953 production, with critics approving the contrast between Redgrave's "snarling and sneering and spitting old snake"[12] and Ashcroft's warm and dignified Portia.

Two more productions followed before the founding of the modern RSC: Margaret Webster (the first female director of the play in Stratford) with a poorly received Emlyn Williams as Shylock; and Michael Langham's 1960 production starring Peter O'Toole. O'Toole's Shylock was singled out for praise: passionate rather than intellectual, he "shows us a human being of stature, driven to breaking point by the inhumanity of others,"[13] while the *Evening News* saw him as "a dignified figure from the New rather than Old Testament—a Christ in torment."[14] The Old Vic staged the play less successfully in the same season. While Barbara Leigh-Hunt's Portia was singled out for praise, Robert Speaight criticized the director's pandering to "the vogue for an eighteenth century *Merchant*."[15] Speaight's remark is symptomatic of the increasing preference for productions that demonstrated the contemporary resonances of the play, as opposed to the historical recreations of the Victorian era.

2. Shakespeare Memorial Theatre, Stratford-upon-Avon, 1953: a snarling and spitting Michael Redgrave as Shylock with a warm and dignified Peggy Ashcroft as Portia.

London's National Theatre mounted two critically acclaimed productions in the later twentieth century, directed by Jonathan Miller (1970) and Trevor Nunn (1999), both subsequently televised. The two were closely related, both featuring a dignified Shylock integrated into a capitalist mercantile culture: other than his yarmulke, his costume in both identified him as a member of the Venetian community. This allowed the idea of his "outsider" status to be explored more subtly: Miller noted that by "allowing Shylock to appear as one among many businessmen, scarcely distinguishable from them, it made sense of his claim that, apart from his customs, a Jew is like everyone else."[16] Nunn followed this logic, as have many twenty-first-century directors of the play, such as Darko Tresnjak (Theater for a New Audience, 2007) and Tim Carroll (RSC, 2008).

Miller's production starred Laurence Olivier, whose key inspiration for his performance was Benjamin Disraeli. He dramatized the trials of an alien attempting to integrate himself into a new society, his abuses at Christian hands eventually unleashing a dignified and righteous rage. Henry Goodman's Shylock in Nunn's production was in a similar position, and emphasized the genial and fatherly aspects of the character: this was a good-natured and often humorous Shylock, whose trials were undeserved. For both Miller and Nunn, the key to demonstrating the insidiousness of racial prejudice was in setting the production in history recent enough to be uncomfortably familiar, but distant enough to provide a semblance of objectivity. Miller hearkened back to the late nineteenth century, while Nunn set his production in the 1930s. Both, too, used the character of Jessica to unsettle the harmony of Act 5. Miller made her "melancholy, not at all the giddy, venturesome girl one might expect,"[17] and at the end she could be heard singing the Kaddish offstage as a lament to her lost father. Gabrielle Jourdan's Jessica in the 1999 production was similarly discontented and closed the play by singing the same Yiddish prayer in a direct reference. Where the eighteenth-century star vehicles had relied on a tremendous Act 4 exit from Shylock to cast a pallor over the remaining scenes, Miller and Nunn's use of Jessica established a quieter and more universal epitaph for cultures violently subsumed.

A more recent trend in performance is to use the play as an exploration of male sexuality, often with the result of refocusing a production on the Merchant. Academics may argue that early modern platonic homosocial modes of behavior are easily confused with more modern understandings of homosexuality, but onstage it has become increasingly customary to explain Antonio's melancholy through feelings of unrequited (or once-requited) love for Bassanio, often with the suggestion that his sexuality makes him as much of an outsider as Shylock's religion does his. Bill Alexander's 1987 RSC production (discussed below) extended the homosexual theme to include most of the Venetian characters, and Michael Dobson notes that in Nunn's 1999 production David Bamber's Antonio's melancholy was occasioned by his "forlorn sexual yearnings for Bassanio [that] had long since been repressed."[18] Edward Hall's 2008 production with his all-male company Propeller relocated the play to the fictional Venice Prison, an exclusively male environment where the "female" characters were drag queens. Hall's production utilized Shakespeare's text to explore various incarnations of male–male relationships, from the negotiation of power and control to the simply romantic.

Despite Charles Edelman's assertion in 2002 that "given the sensitivity of the play's subject matter, it is very unlikely that [a major feature film] will ever be made,"[19] a full-scale film emerged only three years later, directed by Michael Radford and featuring an all-star cast including Al Pacino (Shylock), Jeremy Irons (Antonio), and Joseph Fiennes (Bassanio). Where the larger-scale Victorian stage productions had attempted to recreate the splendor of Venice onstage, Radford filmed on location in Venice itself, using dark alleys, open promenades, and claustrophobic courtrooms to impressive effect. Setting the production in the Venice of Shakespeare's time, Radford re-created the historical realities of Jewish life in the city, with Jews forced to wear red caps and live in ghettos. On television, as well as the screened versions of Miller and Nunn's National productions, the 1980 version for the BBC Shakespeare series directed by Jack Gold offered a very human, but not entirely sympathetic, Shylock in the Jewish actor Warren Mitchell, and drew attention for the uninhibited sexuality of Lorenzo and Jessica.

AT THE RSC

If ever there was a time when we should be asking the questions about humanity, greed, the outsider's place in society that are in this play it is now, in a time of decay.[20]

Race, Bigotry, and Alienation

The wrong question—"is it anti-Semitic?"—is always asked of *The Merchant of Venice*. The answer is: "only as far as is strictly necessary." Ask another question—"is it offensive?"—and the answer is an unequivocal "yes."[21]

Whatever their race or religion, Jewish or Christian, Muslim or Hindu, a member of the audience watching *The Merchant of Venice* in modern times is going to feel slightly uncomfortable in their seat. There is no doubt that Shakespeare's Jew is based on a stereotype, a vicious carica-

ture of a little understood and much maligned race. How does a post–
Second World War director tackle a play that links villainy with religion without being accused of racism? The answer, more often than
not, has been to make the Christian characters equally, if not more,
horrible than the Jew who decides their fate. Is this an imposition of
modern times? Does it distort the nature of Shakespeare's original
intention? The questions surrounding these issues have made *The Merchant of Venice* the real "problem play" of our times.

The playwright Arnold Wesker was compelled to give his opinion
after going to see the RSC's 1993 production directed by David
Thacker, which proved one too many *Merchants* for him:

> The strongest evidence offered in support of the view that
> Shakespeare did not create a stereotype are those widely trum-
> peted lines which he gives to Shylock as special pleading for his
> humanity: "Hath not a Jew eyes? . . ." For [John] Gross, as for
> many others, it is a noble piece of writing. Not for me! Far from
> vindicating the play, the sentiments betray it—self-pitying,
> patronising, and deeply offensive. Implied within them is
> medieval Christian arrogance, which assumed the right to
> confer or withdraw humanity as it saw fit.[22]

However, Shylock's statement of common "humanity" is delivered
with the express purpose of pleading his right to revenge, by very
inhumane means. Taken out of context both this speech and Portia's
speech on mercy are wonderful statements of humanity; taken in
the context of the play, however, they both echo with hypocrisy.

Shylock, unlike the Christian characters in the play, stands as an
embodiment of his race. Common Elizabethan myths about Jews,
which interestingly included the use of human sacrifice, of Christian
blood, in their rituals,* have directly influenced Shakespeare's characterization. The true offensiveness of this negative stereotype is evi-
denced when real Jewish beliefs are taken into consideration:

---

* Blood libel: an allegation, recurring during the thirteenth through sixteenth centuries, that
Jews were killing Christian children to use their blood for the ritual of making unleavened
bread (*matzah*). A red mold which occasionally appeared on the bread started this myth. From
The Jewish Virtual Library (www.jewishvirtuallibrary.org/index.html).

Jewish law includes within it a blueprint for a just and ethical society, where no one takes from another or harms another or takes advantage of another, but everyone gives to one another and helps one another and protects one another . . . We are commanded not to leave a condition that may cause harm, to construct our homes in ways that will prevent people from being harmed, and to help a person whose life is in danger. These commandments regarding the preservation of life are so important in Judaism that they override all of the ritual observances that people think are the most important part of Judaism.[23]

The difficulty for any actor playing Shylock today therefore resides in the portrayal of the character's Jewishness:

A photograph in *The Observer* shows that Eric Porter's Shylock [1965] was given bags under the eyes and a long hooked nose, while Emrys James [1971] depended for his repulsiveness less upon make-up than saliva. Described by one critic as ". . . barefoot, robed in old curtains, with a mouthful of spittle . . . ," James was "a medieval Jewish stereotype in a large, baggy kaftan, with grey ringlets spilling from beneath his skull cap." The same reviewer went on:

This is a Jew straight out of the Penny Dreadful magazines, literally salivating at the thought of his pound of Christian flesh.[24]

His individuality, his isolation from other Jewish characters in the play has also been emphasized to indicate that he is not the embodiment of a race but an individual aberration. In 1978 Patrick Stewart portrayed him as "a sour, loveless man, corroded by avarice, mutilated by money. Even his friend Tubal finds him faintly appalling."[25]

David Calder, in David Thacker's 1993 modern dress production, had played Shylock as a fully assimilated Jew, indistinguishable from the Christians by his mode of dress. He wore a business suit right up to the crucial scene where he discovered Jessica's elopement:

Wishing Jessica, "hearsed at my foot and the ducats in her coffin" [3.1.86], Shylock tore open his shirt to reveal the Star of David underneath (as Antonio's open shirt in the trial scene revealed a crucifix). By the trial scene, Shylock had turned himself into the image of a religious Jew, with skullcap and gabardine and with the Star of David now worn outside his collarless shirt. His use of the symbols of religion was now demonstrably an abuse of religion and race, becoming a Jew only because it focused his traumatised existence. It was Shylock himself who now appeared the anti-Semite . . . When Shylock announced "I will have the heart of him if he forfeit" [3.1.122–3], he put his hand firmly on an open book, a prayer book I presume, on his desk and Tubal registered horror at this abuse of religion.[26]

Some critics worried that overt Jewishness was being once again linked with villainy, but the majority of them believed that Shylock's change of costume signaled not only the character's anger at, but acceptance of, his alienation, his exclusion from a culture which had only been tolerating and patronizing him. Calder stated: "He believes that any attempt to alleviate racial intolerance is actually a mockery and what he must do is to become more Jewish and assert himself in that clear way."[27]

Part of the attraction of Shylock as a character is the fact that he is an "outsider." Like Othello, the question of whether he is a Jew or has black skin is important to a modern audience only in as much as it exposes the society from which he is estranged:

Racism is as much part of our world as it was [Shakespeare's]. The goal is not to sanitise or rehabilitate Shylock, but to see him as part of a society whose workings lead to cruel and outrageous acts.[28]

In 1978 Patrick Stewart made a conscious decision to tone down Shylock's Jewishness:

Apart from the yarmulke, the only other distinctive garment was a yellow sash, twisted round the waist and only just visible beneath the waistcoat. The ritual-like garment and its wearing was an invention of the designer's, though based on photographs of Russian Jews in the nineteenth century, who wore a yellow sash over a long frock coat. We wanted to avoid any excessive sense of Jewishness or foreignness in appearance but this detail, almost unnoticed in the earlier scenes could, in the court, be boldly worn over the frock coat as a proud demonstration of Shylock's racial difference. In the early scenes, however, I was anxious to minimize the impression of Shylock's Jewishness. Whenever I had seen either a very ethnic or detailedly Jewish Shylock I felt that something was lost. Jewishness could become a smoke-screen which might conceal both the particular and the universal in the role. See him as a Jew first and foremost and he is in danger of becoming only a symbol, although a symbol that has changed over the centuries as society's attitudes have changed.[29]

Stewart's Shylock was in effect a "bad Jew," totally motivated by money with little regard to the ethics of his religion. In this production the words "Jew" and "Christian" were merely labels, with neither set of characters demonstrating any of the traits of their creeds. Set in the late nineteenth century,

The Christians are, on the whole, a spoiled, boorish bunch, much given to throwing bread-rolls, shooting off cap-pistols, and other types of horseplay; and the shock provoked by their deep, instinctive prejudice is the shock of recognition, because they wear the suits some of our generation's grandfathers wore at public school or Oxbridge. The upper crust yob Gratiano, whose pet idiocy is dog-imitations, represents this faction at its most gruesome. And yet behind the witty, teasing front displayed by Patrick Stewart's Shylock, there festers a no less nasty temperament . . .[30]

One of the RSC's most controversial productions, directed by Bill Alexander in 1987,

3. Patrick Stewart as Shylock: not so obviously Jewish in appearance, but unashamedly motivated by money.

grappled with the play's offensive subject matter more daringly than any production in recent memory. Refusing to either rehabilitate Shylock as the play's moral standard-bearer . . . or to treat him from a safe historical distance as a comic "Eliza-bethan" Jew . . . Alexander courted controversy, seeming almost to invite accusations of racism. The controversy sprang in part from his refusal to honour the distinctions between romance and realism, comedy and tragedy, sympathy for and aversion to Shylock, from which stage interpreters have tradi-tionally felt they had to choose. By intensifying the problem-atic nature of the text, Alexander modulated the dynamics of audience response: he goaded audiences with stereotypes only to probe the nature of their own prejudices; he confronted them with alienation in different guises in order to reveal the motives of scapegoatism. His Shylock was grotesque—at once comic, repulsive, and vengeful. Yet he was made so in part by those Venetians who need someone on whom to project their own alienation; Venetians who, in their anxiety over sexual, religious, and mercantile values, were crucial to the transaction Alexander worked out between Shakespeare's text and contemporary racial tensions.[31]

Antony Sher, who played Shylock as a very exotic and very foreign-looking Jew, stated:

There have been a lot of productions set in the turn of the century—or in the last century—where he's dressed in a frock coat like everybody else and is an assimilated Jew. To me, that is nonsense, because clearly he sticks out like a sore thumb in society . . . We chose to make him a Turkish Jew using a Turkish accent. What we were doing with that was trying to extend the racism and by just making him a very unassimilated foreigner, very foreign, rather than very Jewish, we hoped to slightly broaden the theme of racism. We also wanted to make the racism as explicit and as brutal as described in the text, but never normally done. You don't normally see Christians spitting at him or kicking him or doing all the things that he says they do.[32]

The first appearance of Sher's Shylock was of him

turbaned, baggy-panted and first seen squatting cross legged on an ottoman in his black tent . . . Mr Sher's Shylock also is tremendously volatile: when he describes "the work of generation" among Laban's sheep, he pummels his left palm with his right fist in mimic procreation. When Antonio makes the fateful bargain, Mr Sher runs his hand over the outline of his body like a butcher sizing-up a carcass. There is nothing sentimental about this Shylock: he is out for blood. But you understand why, when Antonio picks up his abacus, hurls it to the floor and spits at his departing figure on "Hie thee, gentle Jew." Too much? Not if you look at the text, which tells us that Antonio publicly calls Shylock a misbeliever and cut-throat dog at every opportunity. The trial scene is more exciting than I ever remember it. The appearance of this Shylock almost provokes a race-riot, with the Christians indulging in anti-Semitic chants. Tubal has even providentially brought a cloth with which his colleague can wipe the spit from his face. As Mr Sher prepares to extract the pound of flesh, he intones a Hebrew sacrificial prayer specially invented for this production.[33]

In this volatile setting Shylock's defiance almost represented "a perverted act of courage."[34] Nevertheless, Shylock was "not a tragic hero: he is proof that racism breeds revenge."[35] According to the critics, there was more spit in this production than in any other before, or since. The spit directed at the Jew was an important symbol of hatred and returned in the trial scene in which

> Shylock is seen whetting his knife *with his own spit*. This image might well be the visual equivalent of his line: "The villainy you teach me I will execute."[36]

Kit Surrey's design ensured that the audience did not at any stage forget the racial tensions affecting the behavior of the play's characters:

> The back wall was crumbling plaster broken away to reveal the brickwork beneath, and on that wall were two images of religious conflict: an ornate shrine for the Madonna and a Star of David daubed in yellow paint. The Venice scenes were dimly lit through smoke to suggest danger and decay. By contrast Belmont was lit brilliantly . . . [however], the image of Belmont was marred by the presence of the back wall: by not having the two warring images removed, there could never be a true sense of peace.[37]

Portia offered no redemption from this brutality, racism, and underlying sense of conflict:

Deborah Findlay's intriguing Portia is a tart, astringent figure constantly boxing people's ears and guilty, to put it mildly, of social tactlessness, in dismissing Morocco with "Let all of his complexion choose me so" in front of her own black servant.[38]

[She] has nothing of the healer, or seer, or Desdemona in her. She wants her husband white, bright, and speaking the right Latin tongue . . . Even if the blood beneath everyone's skin is red, her father could surely not have wanted all her elegant curls, flounced dresses and milky looks to be married to a black face. She cuffs her Negro servant with a relish which looks customary, and she keeps a polite but distinguishing distance from Lorenzo's new bride.[39]

Findlay found this too harsh a reading of the character and after the play transferred to London, changed her performance to what she believed was more in line with Shakespeare's original conception:

As an experienced actress she felt that she had a right to the part, that it had an essence which she had intuited: "Portia is never mean. Any choice you make about motivation for this character has to be made with all the generosity of spirit that you can muster. She is as loving, as intelligent, as witty, as brave, as compassionate, as everything as you can make her." Who is right here? The actress who with all her talent, training, and experience undertakes the part and inhabits it as it makes sense to her, or the director whose vision of the whole play necessitates a re-vision of the heroine? There is of course no simple answer, though the problem is peculiar to the twentieth century and the age of the director.[40]

Mercy and Love

Bill Alexander's brutal reading of the play left the audience without a redeeming character. Most other modern productions have been less clear-cut in their depictions, but have opted for psychological depth and elements of sympathy to be found in key love relationships. Both Portia and Jessica's lives are governed by overprotective and domineering fathers—the decree of one and the finances of the other act as the catalyst for the action of the play. Are Portia and Jessica viewed as commodities by their fathers, or are they genuinely concerned about their welfare? What effect does this have on the characters of their daughters?

When playing Shylock, David Suchet described the importance of the one domestic scene Shakespeare gives us of his home life:

> Shakespeare gives us the shortest scene in the play, which is the domestic relationship between Shylock and Jessica and none of it suggests her life is hell. It is equally wrong to impose such an interpretation of Jessica, and it is also wrong to show a great deal of love because that is not there either. But because of there being a third person present all the time, Gobbo, it is not anyway just a straight scene between father and daughter, it is elevated by the presence of the third person. You see Shylock hesitating as to whether or not to go to dinner, disciplining Jessica over not looking on the Masques, shutting the windows and doors and so on and leaving Jessica to look after the house. She is, for him, both wife and daughter . . . There are thousands of boys and girls today who want to run away from home and live with someone with whom they've fallen in love. Your sympathies can lie either way. He has met these men in the street who, he realizes, asked him to dinner so his daughter could be taken away. I don't think this is the moment for a great speech of sympathy about the race. He lets out a great stream of bitterness, anger and disillusion about mankind . . . This is not the same Shylock we have seen before.[41]

Does Shakespeare give us enough evidence to judge Shylock's emotional capabilities? Patrick Stewart believed that with regards to Jessica,

> The real, natural warm, human, affectionate, loving responses have been cauterised in the man and she is a victim of it. So it is impossible for him to show the undoubted love that lies there

underneath. It's so far down it can never be tapped. In our production . . . we had a controversial moment when I struck her
very hard. After the blow I made some attempt at reconcilia-
tion . . . But by then the damage had been done and she was
bound to reject him.[42]

In Gregory Doran's 1997 production, actor Philip Voss

had come to excuse Shylock's behaviour towards Jessica as
deriving from the absence of a mother's moderating influence . . . [We've] decided—that Shylock's wife died about five
years before—making Jessica, I think, about thirteen. To
explain how Jessica has come to loathe her father so much, you
need a certain amount of time for his oppressive behaviour to
have affected her to that degree. Because, I mean, I see Shylock
as a perfectly nice man . . . The reason that Jessica hates him,
I think, is because he is oppressive, because he is a widower,
because he has lost his wife, and that she is the woman in the
house and he has just demanded too much of her, both in her
religion and domestically. And then in every way he has
absolutely fed off her, I think. And, if she's that age, she just
wants to get away—the house is hell, because it's no fun . . .[43]

Voss's Shylock was destroyed by the loss of his daughter (rather
than his ducats). Doran intensified the audience's awareness of Shylock's pain by having him witness her elopement:

Shylock ran into the raucous and nightmarish carnival which
had modulated grotesquely from the same masque that he had
watched as an entertainment laid on for his meal with Bassanio and Antonio. Apparently coming home after leaving the
Christians, Voss's Shylock stumbled unwittingly into the
obscene and drunken cavorting of the Christians' street party.
Attempting without success to avoid the lunging pigs' heads,
the old man was jostled and pushed around on the stage, until,
at a point when the goading was at its height, the music
stopped and he suddenly saw his daughter, dressed improperly

4. Emma Handy as Jessica, "who has come to loathe her father," an "oppressive" Philip Voss as Shylock, in Gregory Doran's 1997 production.

in boy's clothes and carried high on her lover's shoulders. Screaming her name, he was dragged into his house and spun around as it revolved in a nightmare sequence which saw him thrown from one wall to another as his daughter made her escape.[44]

In David Thacker's 1993 modern dress production, he included an extra scene in which Shylock was seen looking lovingly at his wife's picture while listening to classical music. Shylock's grief and loneliness at the loss of his wife signaled his capacity for love and heightened the audience's sympathy for him. It also threw "an enormous light on the bond between Jessica and her father":[45]

His private world contains touchstones—Jessica his daughter being the most important. His love of his daughter is tainted by over protectiveness, which is endemic to many societies . . . When his daughter is stolen from him by a Christian the profound pain, insult and shame push him onto a road from which there is no return.[46]

As a reminder to the audience in the trial scene, "a sob escapes this Shylock as he recalls his daughter":[47] "and when he is finally tricked of justice, Calder's hollow laughter and sudden physical frailty leave no doubt that here is a man with a broken heart with nothing left to live for."[48]

Sinead Cusack (1981) played Portia as a woman in a state of grief over the death of her father. She even wore her father's shabby raincoat in order to relate herself to "the wise and 'ever virtuous' old man who understood the law and money and marriage."[49] The casket test was put in place in order to stop her from marrying someone who would treat her as a commodity, to weed out opportunist fortune hunters (ironically, like Bassanio). However, even here Portia's father's test succeeds, as Bassanio finds his own true worth in this match:

> Receiving her suitors almost in a melancholic trance, Sinead Cusack invests Portia with translucent intelligence. The caskets are simple boxes thrown vigorously aside as Bassanio picks the right one. At last this Portia comes alive, dropping her inhibitions with her grey cloak and, turning on Bassanio, blossoming as an ecstatic vision in primrose. The liberation of Portia continues through the court scene, where Miss Cusack's lawyer is less an impersonation than a revelation of her true crop-haired self. In the exchanging of the rings she asserts her independence, for Bassanio now sees he is married to a woman of wit, steadfastness and resource.[50]

Other Portias have been less fortunate, with their Bassanios' sexual ambiguity becoming one hurdle too far to happiness. Of Clifford Williams' 1965 production, one critic commented on the treatment of Antonio and Bassanio:

> in this production it's clear from the start that between him and Bassanio there is what is euphemistically described as a romantic friendship. Brewster Mason's heavy, ageing Antonio is the counterpart of today's wealthy bachelor stockbroker with a big house in Surrey and aberrations so tidily exercised that only his more intimate friends know about them . . . Even

in imminent danger from Shylock's knife, he keeps his eyes affectionately fixed on the boyfriend whose extravagance has brought him to this situation. Peter McEnery, a graceful, handsome, very young Bassanio, fond of his old protector, who has given him so much—fonder, in fact, than he is of Portia. I suspect he's not really very fond of Portia at all; but she's a rich and "with it" girl, and marrying her will be a smart thing to do. So when he is with her, when he is actually professing his love for her, his eyes wander round the company to see what kind of impression he's making. There is a lot of Lord Alfred Douglas* in this Bassanio . . .[51]

Despite his centrality to the plot, Antonio comes across as a despicable racist to a modern audience. Again to redress the balance and find elements of sympathy, directors have emphasized the character's loneliness, also making him an outsider by dint of his sexuality. In 1987 John Carlisle's Antonio "became agitated as Portia became a threat to his homoerotic love for Bassanio. Carlisle remained on stage as the scene changed from Belmont and fixed Portia with a confrontational glare."[52] His moroseness was attributed to his unrequited love for Bassanio; like Orlando at the start of *Twelfth Night*, he was lovesick to the point of suicide:

But the strength of the production . . . is that the action springs from a precise social and psychological context; and one of the undoubted beneficiaries is John Carlisle's excellent Antonio, presented as a tormented closet-gay.

That is not especially original. What is new is the idea that in such a rabidly conformist world Antonio would actually prefer death to restricted life; and Mr Carlisle greets his salvation with sullen, angry resentment.[53]

In these interpretations the genuineness of Bassanio's feelings is called into question, leaving the audience to ponder whether Portia will receive the expected happiness at their union. In 1971:

* Lord Alfred Douglas was the lover of the famous Irish writer Oscar Wilde, and went on to marry heiress and poet Olive Eleanor Custance.

[As] Tony Church plays him there is no question of his love for Bassanio, but it is a melancholy undemanding love with no physical expression; thus it becomes acceptable within the production's romantic terms . . . in scenes like that following the trial, where he tries to hold polite conversation while on the brink of nervous collapse, he makes old situations brand new . . . [Michael Williams' Bassanio] makes an opening display of smothering Antonio in grateful kisses, but after that he reverts to the perfect lover: while [Judi] Dench turns her radiant resources on Portia so as to burn up personal characteristics in the sheer experience of love.[54]

Due to the inherent doubts over Bassanio's motivations—he makes it clear that he is initially out for a wealthy match, and at the trial states that his love for Antonio is greater than his love for his new bride—the portrayal of the wooing of Portia has also become a means of differentiating Bassanio from her other suitors. In Barton's 1978 production:

The first two suitors approached her from behind, avoiding eye contact, whereas Bassanio knelt in front and addressed her directly over the caskets . . . creating a silent moment of human contact . . . The exchange of lovers' rings occurred underneath a central spotlight emphasising the importance of the exchange and creating a strong image that would later prove significant . . . an important learning process . . .

Antonio rejoined the lovers' hands, reconciling the worlds of Belmont and Venice, and the rings were once again held in the central light used during the betrothal scene. This was evidence of a greater understanding gained through experience, and as Portia pronounced, "It is almost morning" [5.1.313] it promised an understanding that would develop and mature in future.[55]

Deborah Findlay (1987) pointed out that in the wooing scenes:

Both Morocco and Aragon want to dominate Portia, Morocco by machismo and Aragon by a patronizing approach. We felt

that Morocco would treat a wife as his property, appropriate
her physically, so there was a bit of manhandling in the scene
which Portia reacted against. This may have been seen as
reacting against his colour but it is much more to do with
being treated as a sexual object—an interesting conundrum:
who is the oppressor?[56]

In this production both Jew and woman were the oppressed races, at
the mercy of the charity of the white Christian male. This was driven
home by a very startling final image of Antonio and Jessica, two
characters who themselves will always remain outsiders because of
sexuality and race. However, Antonio, being a man and a Christian,
powerfully demonstrated which sex and which religion remained on
top. Jessica was left

> . . . half kneeling before Antonio, trying to get back the long
> chain and cross she has dropped in her haste to keep up with
> Lorenzo. Antonio draws it from her, mastering for a moment a
> victim who is still nothing but a Jew and a woman. And then
> there is darkness.[57]

The link between Portia and Shylock has been emphasized in
many productions. Of John Barton's 1981 revival of his 1978 production, Sinead Cusack explained:

> A lot of people ask why then does Portia put everyone through
> all that misery and why does she play cat-and-mouse with Shy-
> lock. The reason is that she doesn't go into the courtroom to
> save Antonio (that's easy) but to save Shylock, to redeem
> him—she is passionate to do that. She gives him opportunity
> after opportunity to relent and to exercise his humanity . . . It
> is only when he shows himself totally ruthless and intractable
> (refusing even to allow a surgeon to stand by) that she offers
> him more justice than he desires.[58]

One critic commented:

> Besides her apt resemblance to a fairytale princess Miss Cusack
> is one of the rare Portias who can stay in character while

enlarging on the quality of mercy (which she plays as a strictly forensic argument) . . . There is no trace of the bitch or the boss lady. All the essential characteristics are there, but for once human accuracy does not disfigure the fable.[59]

Portia's reaction to Antonio's demand that Shylock renounce his faith can also be a key moment in which to demonstrate her innate decency. In David Thacker's 1993 production, Penny Downie played her "with glowing intelligence, as a decent woman visibly upset by Shylock's forced conversion to Christianity."[60]

This reaction again came from an empathy with Shylock's plight as a victimized section of society: "[She] subtly and generously portrays a Portia who is both imperious and victimised, a woman who knows she has been made into a bargaining counter and clings to her dignity as to a lifebelt."[61]

The actor playing Portia has the difficulty of creating a character that a modern audience can believe has an immense capacity for love and generosity of spirit, despite the many dubious lines Shakespeare has given her. As a result, it is often Portia herself who is on trial in the courtroom, as she will be judged by her actions and reactions to the bigoted Venetian mentality. Surely Shakespeare's intention was to have us believe that "Belmont becomes the soul which Venice has lost."[62] As director David Thacker explained: "Belmont offers us something that can renew and reform. It allows the quality of mercy to spread throughout the whole civilization and heal."[63]

THE DIRECTOR'S CUT: INTERVIEWS WITH DAVID THACKER AND DARKO TRESNJAK

David Thacker's directing career spans more than thirty years, during which time he has directed over a hundred productions. He is particularly known for his close working relationship with the American playwright Arthur Miller, directing the British premieres of four of his plays. He has been artistic director of the Young Vic and Lancaster's Dukes theater as well as director in residence at the RSC, for whom he has directed *The Two Gentlemen of Verona, Julius*

Caesar, *The Merchant of Venice* (discussed here), *Coriolanus*, and *Pericles*, which won the Olivier Awards for Best Director and Best Revival. At the Young Vic he directed *An Enemy of the People*, *Ghosts*, *Some Kind of Hero* by Les Smith, *A Touch of the Poet* by Eugene O'Neill, and *Comedians* by Trevor Griffiths. He also works prolifically in television, having directed more than thirty TV productions. In 2008 he was appointed artistic director of the Octagon Theatre in Bolton.

Darko Tresnjak is a prominent American theater director. He has received the Alan Schneider Award for Directing Excellence and several other awards. Born in the city of Zemun, Yugoslavia (now Serbia), he emigrated to the United States with his mother when he was ten years old. He graduated from Swarthmore College in 1988, then attended the Columbia University School of the Arts MFA theater directing program. From 2004 to 2007 he was artistic director of the Old Globe Shakespeare Festival in San Diego, California, where he is now resident artistic director. His productions there have included *Pericles*, *The Winter's Tale*, *Hamlet*, *A Midsummer Night's Dream*, *Titus Andronicus*, *The Comedy of Errors*, *The Two Noble Kinsmen*, and *Antony and Cleopatra*. He talks here about his modern dress (Wall Street–style) production of *The Merchant of Venice* with Theater for a New Audience in New York, which transferred to Stratford-upon-Avon in 2007 as part of the RSC Complete Works Festival. Shylock was F. Murray Abraham, winner of an Oscar for his role as Salieri in the movie *Amadeus*.

The Merchant of Venice is the play that has changed in our common estimation and viewpoint probably more than any other, because of twentieth-century history. What implications did that have for your production? Does the play demand that you take a particular line on it?

THACKER: It had very profound implications for the production. I'm not sure I'd ever describe it as a particular "line," but I think that you have particular responsibilities in directing that play. Your primary responsibility is to William Shakespeare. When you do any production of a Shakespeare play you have a profound responsibility to try to understand the play and to try to express it as richly and as powerfully as you can. Having said that, I think every play is responsive not only to the time in which it was written, but also the time in which you perform it. And certain things that are acceptable to one generation are not acceptable when time moves on. Because of the extent of anti-Semitism in our society, and because of what Jewish people have had to suffer historically, coming to a terrible climax in the Holocaust, I think it is vital that you approach this play with enormous care and sensitivity.

When I'm directing any play by Shakespeare I try to approach it as if William Shakespeare was in the rehearsal room with us. If I was working with a living playwright I would be in constant dialogue about the meaning of the play and what the playwright was trying to achieve, and how we might express that most effectively. With Shakespeare, self-evidently, you can't speak to him or conjure him up, so all you can do is proceed honestly and with integrity in relation to that play. I believe that if Shakespeare were alive now he would not give permission for the play to be performed uncut—I'm certain that he would rewrite it. It's the only Shakespeare play I've ever directed where I said at the beginning of the rehearsal period, "I'm going to make some cuts." The context has changed so drastically that I think that the play needs delicate *attention*. I think that does affect the meaning of the play, and so I was very clear in my own mind that this was a conscious decision I would take. These weren't massive changes and to a lot of people might have been totally imperceptible. It was partly, for example, a number of judicious prunings of the word "Jew," particularly when uttered by Portia. Although it's fashionable to turn Portia into a kind of rich bitch, she is clearly the life force at the heart of the play. She is the person who argues passionately for redemption, for the classic Shakespearean themes—particularly as his achievement grew to full maturity in the Late Plays—of mercy, redemption, forgiveness. But in that scene I don't know how many times we cut the word "Jew." It becomes like a hammer banging on a nail, "Jew," "Jew," "Jew," "Jew," all with a slight pejorative edge to it. It inevitably affects what one's sensitivities are in relation to the character, so there was a slight pruning there.

People might think we were oversensitive to the use of "Jew," but if you look at the rest of Shakespeare's canon, leaving *The Merchant of Venice* out, there are only six other uses of the word "Jew," and every one is pejorative. Launce's wonderful comic speech in *The Two Gentlemen of Verona*, telling the audience about his dog, says "A Jew would have wept!"—but not the dog. Even a Jew would have wept, therefore this dog is even worse than a Jew—that is the joke. This is the stuff of normal comedy within Shakespeare—you can't hide from the fact that the rest of his work regards the word "Jew" and therefore being Jewish in a negative light. Having said that, it indicates what a fantastic achievement *The Merchant of Venice* is, because Shakespeare makes Shylock, in so many senses, so sympathetic. "Hath not a Jew eyes?" It's almost like Shakespeare, because of his own humanity, is digging as deep as he could possibly dig to show us a Jewish person in a sympathetic light, but even within that context he couldn't quite rid himself of his own culture and the limitations of his own society, his personal history, all the rest of it. Therefore I would say the proper responsibility of an artist in relation to that is to make a personal decision that says "I really don't believe that Shakespeare would want this." You might think that is a terribly arrogant thing to say, but any choice you make about any Shakespeare production is an assumption about what you believe he would have wanted. Nothing is neutral, you make crucial interpretive decisions all the way along, so it's essentially only a decision of that kind to say, "I just don't think Shakespeare would want this."

I found it an utterly delightful experience doing the play and I was proud of it and proud of the work that everybody did. I was blessed with an exceptional cast, in particular to have David Calder playing Shylock, because what David brings to the table is not just his skill as an actor but his intelligence, something Penny Downie [who played Portia] shares as well. They helped me enormously in the developing conception of the show. It was the collective endeavor, I think, of that group of actors, that turned it into something that I think we all thoroughly believed in, and believed was very special.

5. "[I]t became even clearer why Shylock, a devout, sensitive, and serious man, would have such difficulty with drunken lager-louts and Christians" —David Thacker production, 1993.

TRESNJAK: It had enormous implications, especially in New York, where our production originated and where staging the play is still far more controversial than staging it in England. From the earliest planning phases to the opening night we worked extensively with James Shapiro, the author of *Shakespeare and the Jews.* His insights were invaluable—not just about the text but about the entire production history of the play. In many discussions, the word that we kept coming back to was *exclusion.* How are the characters in *The Merchant of Venice* marginalized or excluded—because of their religion, gender, age, race, sexuality, or economic status? In a workshop that took place six months before the actual production, I got to play around with the ways in which the text could support various forms of exclusion, and I found that this approach nourished both the tragic and the comic aspects of the play. (Granted, much of the humor was rather cruel.) Most of all, it helped me see Shylock as a part of the universe that Shakespeare creates in *The Merchant of Venice.* And, directing the play in 2007, that seemed to me like a worthwhile goal, to reincorporate Shylock into the general fabric of the play.

How did you and your designer represent the contrasting settings of Venice and Belmont?

THACKER: I had the inspiration to do *Merchant* on Black Wednesday, because, like the events of that day, things happen in the play so rapidly. That's when the idea of setting it in a modern London came. We modeled the world of Venice on the Lloyd's building, so it was the world of the stock exchange, big business, suits, money, computers, mobile phones, all that sort of stuff. The challenge with all of Shakespeare is to invent a world that you believe is the world of the play. With Belmont, which is always tricky, what we most wanted the audience to focus on was the caskets. So if there was a criticism of the production in retrospect, I'd say I think Venice was, in design terms, very powerful and persuasive, and Belmont might not have resonated so powerfully.

TRESNJAK: According to the critic Marjorie Garber, *The Merchant of Venice* presents us with "the opposites that are increasingly similar" during the course of the play. One of those seeming opposites is Venice versus Belmont. Both worlds are ultimately ruled by financial considerations. So for me, the most important practical concern was to move swiftly from one setting to the other, because I did not want the textual similarities and the thematic connections to get obliterated by long and elaborate scenic changes.

The constant in John Lee Beatty's set design for the play were three sleek desks with three Apple PowerBooks on top of them. Above each desk was a flatscreen monitor. In Venice, we projected stock market quotes on the monitors. I was inspired by the Internet cafés of New York City and by the trading floor down on Wall Street. The characters would tune out of conversations to check their e-mail or to answer their cell phones. (Today, technology is another way that we exclude and marginalize each other on a moment-to-moment basis.) The bulk of our fourteen-member cast was featured in these scenes. The characters smashed into each other throughout. I wanted to create a rude and congested urban setting. In Belmont, the three PowerBooks represented the three caskets and we projected Shakespeare's riddles on the monitors above them. Working on an off-Broadway budget, I had to turn our own financial con-

6. F. Murray Abraham as Shylock and Tom Nelis as Antonio in Darko Tresnjak's 2007 production, set in a modern financial center, with flatscreen monitors and Apple PowerBooks.

siderations into a dramatic statement. So Portia's entire household staff consisted of Nerissa and Balthasar, who we thought of as Portia's IT guy. I imagined Belmont as a hi-tech haven that Portia's father had left her, isolated, under-populated, and eerie.

Bassanio sometimes seems like a gold-digger rather than a romantic lead. Are there _any_ social relations in this play that aren't dependent on money?

THACKER: I think he is a gold-digger, but I also think he falls in love! I don't think that if he wasn't massively attracted to Portia to begin with he'd ask Antonio to lend him the money. I think he can't believe his luck really. There's nothing that I remember from directing the play that implies he doesn't love her. I think Bassanio is a really tough part because he has some very difficult speeches to handle, like the speech when he chooses the lead casket. Technically that's a very difficult speech to get the hang of. But I felt that he became more and more attractive and charismatic as the play develops. I think we grow to like Bassanio very much by the end, and I think because Portia loves him we forgive him a lot. I don't think he's one of Shakespeare's greatest creations: if you asked me to list all the male hero leads in order of preference, he'd be way down the list somewhere. He can't compare with Romeo, Hamlet, and God knows how many other young men that Shakespeare created, but I think he works in this play.

TRESNJAK: Our production ended with the three couples swaying to the Rosemary Clooney recording of "How Am I to Know?" The lyrics of the Dorothy Parker/Jack King song struck me as rather appropriate:

> Oh
> How am I to know
> If it's really love
> That found its way here?
> Oh
> How am I to know
> Will it linger on
> And leave me then?
> I'll dare not guess
> At this strange happiness
> But oh
> How am I to know
> Can it be that love
> Has come to stay here?

So I think that not being able to answer your question is, for me, the whole point of the play. The characters themselves are not in the position to answer it. Along the way, they all make compromising choices, choices that haunt even the most innocent relationships. I am thinking especially of Lorenzo and Jessica. They always struck me as the youngest, the most innocent characters in the play. We certainly cast the roles in our production that way. The decision to steal Shylock's possessions haunts them, and I think that the unease that it creates between them is right under the surface of the famous "In such a night as this" exchange at the top of the last scene.

As for Bassanio, he reminds me of Chance Wayne, the male lead in Tennessee Williams' *Sweet Bird of Youth*—a tarnished angel, still appealing yet also somewhat pathetic. Frayed. I think that the last train is about to leave the station and he needs to catch it however he can. The moment in the first scene when Bassanio is about to ask Antonio for money—when he talks about his school days and uses the analogy of the lost arrow—it always made me squirm in the best possible way. It's wonderfully icky—an innocent, youthful appeal by someone who's neither innocent nor all that youthful.

The play is called *The Merchant of Venice*, and yet Antonio has a smaller part than Portia, Shylock, Bassanio, and even by some counts Gratiano and Lorenzo! Why is that, and does it present peculiar problems for casting (and for the actor playing the merchant)?

THACKER: We had a much older actor playing Antonio and it was very clear that this was in that tradition of gay men who love young men, but would never dream of being sexual with them, or indeed of imposing upon the young man anything that would be discomforting. There's a pattern that as a heterosexual man I've been quite familiar with in my life, of older gay men having wonderfully respectful relationships with young heterosexual men, whom they perhaps do desire but would never risk allowing anything sexual to spoil that relationship. That's how I imagined Antonio's relationship with the younger men. I think he's very sad that he doesn't have his own partner; probably he can't confess his own homosexuality anyway in the society in which he lives. But he also has his own serious failings, like the nature of his aggression toward Shylock at the beginning and his overt anti-Semitism, which I think was clear enough just by playing it straight down the line. There didn't strike me as being any problem about the casting of him or carrying through the logic of the relationships.

TRESNJAK: I don't think that the size of the role is problematic since any actor playing Antonio has to deal with the mystery of his sadness, the nature of his relationship with Bassanio, and the source of his hatred for Shylock. At this stage in my career, I am increasingly intrigued by Shakespeare's shorthand, by those moments where something seems to be withheld from the audience. Antonio's reticence—what it implies about his position in the Venetian society, his relationship with Bassanio, and his hatred for Shylock—is rather intriguing.

In casting the roles of Antonio and Bassanio, I decided that I had to be completely honest about the fact that we were going to explore the sexual ambiguity of their relationship. Acknowledging that dimension of *The Merchant of Venice* is an essential part of how I see the play, just as much a part of it as Shylock's Jewishness.

The "choice of casket" motif is like something out of a fairy tale, but Portia is a flesh-and-blood woman, no fairy-tale princess: is that tough to reconcile stylistically?

THACKER: In the context of a modern dress production set in the city of London, Portia has got to be an intelligent modern woman. She is clearly the most intelligent person in the play anyway: she thinks on her feet, she's quick-witted, she's intelligent, but most important, she is the moral center of the play. It is through Portia that we understand how to consider everybody else's behavior and actions. She's yet another of those wonderful Shakespearean women who are warm, kind, passionate, sexy, intelligent, and have such integrity that it is through them that we understand how human beings should behave. I'm very positive about Portia. I think she's meant to be a young woman, imprisoned by an obsessive father who has tried to trap her in a way that, certainly in lots of cultures, is very easy for us to understand now. So, no, I didn't find it difficult to reconcile, I found it a pretty straightforward choice.

TRESNJAK: I believe that, regardless of how one chooses to stage *The Merchant of Venice*, Portia herself has a choice from the very beginning of the play. To stay in Belmont, accept her father's will, keep her fortune, and potentially end up with a jackass of a husband. Or to leave Belmont, get disinherited, and discover her own path in the world at large. (That, too, is a common fairy-tale motif.) So, in my opinion, for all her moping in the first scene, Portia is a compromised, complicated character from the outset, and not exactly a fairy-tale princess. In our production, I tried to highlight this by making it clear that Nerissa was a working girl, mostly supportive but at times bewildered and infuriated by Portia—especially after her racist remark about the Prince of Morocco.

It's sometimes said that whereas Barabas in Christopher Marlowe's _The Jew of Malta_ is the stereotypical villainous Jew, Shylock is humanized, for example by "Hath not a Jew eyes?" and the reference to Leah's ring which he would not have given away for "a wilderness of monkeys." But you can't get much more stereotypically villainous than threatening to cut off a pound of someone's flesh. How did you and your Shylock reconcile this?

THACKER: I think it's very clear that for a large part of the play Shakespeare is reasonably hostile in his attitude to Shylock: "I hate him for he is a Christian" (Act 1 Scene 3). If someone said in a play, "I hate him because he is a Muslim," for example, you'd think that was a pretty unpleasant line for anyone to utter. Also, "If I can catch him once upon the hip." These things are unquestionably there in the play, so either you let them flourish or you slightly adjust them. I was enormously influenced when I directed the play by the fact that at the time I'd just directed the British premiere of Arthur Miller's play _Broken Glass_. _Broken Glass_ is essentially about a Jewish person who's subjected to a degree of what we would now call institutional racism, and responds by trying to assimilate himself totally into New York business society by completely _denying_ his Jewishness. Arthur Miller creates a counterpoint Jewish character, the doctor, who's so completely well adjusted about his own Jewishness that at the end of the play when they come together it's a bit of a debate on whether you assimilate or whether you don't. That was one of the inspirations for our production, which was to allow Shylock to assimilate, or to need or want to assimilate as fully as possible within the Christian world, so that he would be able to be successful. That seemed to be a truthful way of approaching the play given where we set it. Therefore Shylock inevitably became a modern businessman, and so it all sat very comfortably.

In the play there is a suggestion that Shylock doesn't like music, which would be very unlikely for a modern Jewish person, particularly an educated person. That's another element of Shylock being unsympathetic, because later in the play Lorenzo says, "The man that hath no music in himself, / Nor is not moved with concord of sweet sounds, / Is fit for treasons." In our production we saw Shylock, when safely in his home, listening to music, and clearly very devout in his culture privately. At home the trappings of his own culture were present, therefore it became even clearer why Shylock, a devout, sensitive, and serious man, would have such difficulty with drunken lager-louts and Christians, and, just like there were in the 1980s, serious money-type city slickers, and why he would not want his daughter to be involved in any of that.

When Shylock finds out about his daughter having eloped, it's very clear and it would be very difficult to avoid if you played the complete text, that he is more worried about losing his money than losing his daughter. Therefore we had some judicious pruning which actually addressed that balance and made clear he was more worried the other way around. David Calder played it that the realization that his daughter had left him was the most terrible thing that had happened to him; for example, he ripped his clothes, as Jewish people do when someone is dead. She was effectively dead to him, it was the worst possible kind of betrayal.

In a post-Holocaust world, one of the things that I think was very powerful and very successful about the production was that it worked almost as an analogy for the state of Israel, and the fact that after the Holocaust one could almost forgive any mistake of Israel. But in the course of doing that, what happens is the oppressed becomes the oppressor. So the bombing of Gaza, for example, isn't a valid response to the Holocaust. In a similar kind of way it became very clear in our production that Shylock was oppressed. The costume design was absolutely crucial here because he started off by trying to assimilate as much as possible into the Venetian world, but after his daughter was taken away he became more and more orthodox. He went from being a man in a suit and there being no trace of his Jewishness, to, by the end of the play, being dressed almost like an orthodox Jew, and being guilty of very, very cold-hearted savagery. David Calder had a wonderful idea, which was to actually mark out the place, with a felt-tip pen, on Antonio's heart, where he was going to cut the flesh. By this time this was an act of such cold-hearted revenge that I now think what the production successfully revealed—and I'm not sure I believe it to be true in its intention, but the production made it very clear—was that Shylock, having been oppressed so terribly, gets to breaking point and then becomes a man whose actions have to be stopped. There has to be another way, and that way is the quality of mercy, the quality of forgiveness. I think you get from Portia this wonderful, very passionate plea for mercy in a modern world. The production was very highly rated in Israel, because they felt it was a truthful demonstration of how the oppressed becomes the oppressor.

TRESNJAK: The only answer that I can give is a theatrical one and not a bit rational. But if it all came down to being rational we certainly would not need theater, and I think that Shakespeare understood the appeal of the irrational gesture on stage more than any playwright before or since. I think that Shylock unleashes a hurt, isolated, and vengeful part inside of all of us, and I can't say that either F. Murray Abraham or I tried to soften his jagged edges. It is one of those strange paradoxical roles where you gain the audience's sympathy by not asking for it. The worst thing to do is try to be ingratiating. In the universe of *The Merchant of Venice*, Shylock's quest for the pound of flesh cuts through the layers of hypocrisy. Theatrically, it is as potent and as irrational as the statue of Hermione coming to life at the end of *The Winter's Tale*. But it connects to a different, darker side of our fantasy life, the desire to maim as opposed to heal.

"The quality of mercy" is one of the great speeches in Shakespeare, but does Portia's (cross-dressed) courtroom performance come from the same place in her as her behavior and language in Belmont?

TRESNJAK: I don't think that Portia could have uttered "The quality of mercy" speech before meeting Bassanio. The first moment that we see them together on stage, she speaks her other famous monologue ("I pray you tarry. Pause a day or two . . ."). I think that Shakespeare is telling us something about the transformative power of love. It makes Portia more eloquent. It gives her courage to go on a big adventure, travel to Venice, put on a disguise, and save the day. But the irony is that she knows so little about Venice, Shylock, Antonio, and even her new husband. And by the end of the scene, her plea for mercy will seem rather perverse.

In *Shakespeare After All*, Marjorie Garber writes: "on the level of sheer beauty of language and power of dramaturgy, the play is disturbingly appealing, just at those moments when one might wish it to be unappealing. The most magnificent of its speeches are also, in some ways, the most wrongheaded." I thought about this notion throughout the rehearsal process, especially during the trial scene, where we see Portia at her most eloquent and her most ignorant.

Lancelet Gobbo is not Shakespeare's most memorable clown, but he at the very least has an important structural role, doesn't he?

THACKER: I was very lucky indeed to have a wonderfully gifted comic actor, Chris Luscombe, who's now a director, playing Lancelet Gobbo. I did think, "How am I going to make this work in a modern dress production?" It was one of the things I just couldn't see working. We did cut quite a lot to help it along, but he made it work brilliantly, he was so funny and so real, and I have to say all the credit has to go to him. He solved the problem for me, and he was utterly credible within the context of this play. I was a very lucky director to find someone who made a very tricky situation not only not difficult, but effortlessly real and funny.

TRESNJAK: I find him intriguing because he seems like a rather ambitious young clown. From Shylock to Bassanio to Belmont, he pops up all over the place. He is both literally and upwardly mobile. He'll do well.

Lorenzo and Jessica: why does Shakespeare take them to Belmont and give them that poetic and musical exchange at the beginning of the fifth act?

THACKER: Bear in mind this is quite an early play in Shakespeare's development as a playwright. As he got older he was able to bring things to a harmonious conclusion in a way that came completely organically out of the play. I think Act 5 has fundamentally a healing function. That's why it is so beautiful and so poetic and should be, I think, very real and very moving. It's hard to get right, but it should be a transition into healing. But of course there are two characters in it who are uncomfortable: one is Jessica, because of her betrayal of her roots and her father, and the other is Antonio, because of the trauma he's just been through and his being left on the stage by himself when everyone else is paired up. He is the only man left there, the gay man when all the couples have gone off and happily got married, so there's a bittersweet moment there, but I think these are subtle nuances that should be allowed to be there without banging them into people's faces.

TRESNJAK: I find that this is the hardest scene to write about and the most intriguing scene to stage. One can interpret it and stage it a hundred different ways, all of them equally valid. But regardless of the staging, there is something genuinely startling and heartbreaking about hearing such gorgeous poetry after the appalling ending of the trial scene. The radical shift in tone is its own reward. Near the end of their exchange, Lorenzo speaks three lines that, to me, were the thesis statement for our production:

Such harmony is in immortal souls,
But whilst this muddy vesture of decay
Doth grossly close it in, we cannot hear it.

Is there a risk of the final act, with the business of exchanging rings, sagging after the drama of the courtroom scene, particularly as audiences who aren't familiar with the play might expect the courtroom scene to represent its climax?

THACKER: I think that Shakespeare's imagination probably ran away with him: that he loved so much the writing of Shylock, and he turns out to be such a wonderful character, that you might think that in one sense the play is unbalanced in terms of what was probably the original impulse to write it. How the audience reacts to Shylock being made a Christian is pretty crucial. I think Shakespeare probably thought of it as a good thing, a gift. It's very difficult for our modern sensibilities to accept that and the natural consequence of that action was for the audience to be shocked at that point. I was very happy for them to be shocked, but we tried to make it clear that Portia was herself shocked at the outcome. Portia gives Shylock every possible chance. We tried to make that completely clear in the play—she gives him so many opportunities to be forgiving that he doesn't take.

TRESNJAK: I think that the effectiveness of the final act depends entirely on the choices that are made during the trial scene. At the very least, Portia and Nerissa are going to hear Bassanio and Gratiano profess that their esteem for Antonio is greater than their love for their new wives. In addition to that, Shakespeare gives Gratiano the most vicious attacks on Shylock. Add to that the possibility that Portia notices some homoerotic overtones in Bassanio's interactions with Antonio. Then there is also the possibility that Nerissa may not approve of Portia's actions during the trial. And the result is a fifth act that's brimming with tensions: between Portia and Nerissa; Portia and Bassanio; Nerissa and Gratiano; and Portia and Antonio. (The moment when Portia welcomes Antonio to Belmont strikes me as wonderfully curt and cryptic.) In our production, I thought of the last act as a brief reversal of *The Taming of the Shrew*, or *The Shaping of the Husbands*, as I like to call it. I think the audience truly enjoyed watching Bassanio and Gratiano squirm when Portia and Nerissa went after them.

At the end of our *Merchant*, the three couples went off to party and Antonio was left alone, contemplating Shylock's yarmulke that, earlier in the scene, fell out of Portia's pocket. I wanted to show that, by the end of the play, both Shylock and Antonio are outsiders.

PLAYING SHYLOCK: INTERVIEWS WITH ANTONY SHER AND HENRY GOODMAN

Sir Antony Sher was born in Cape Town in 1949, and trained as an actor at the Webber Douglas academy in London. He joined the

Liverpool Everyman theater in the 1970s, working with a group of gifted young actors and writers which included Willy Russell, Alan Bleasdale, Julie Walters, Trevor Eve, and Jonathan Pryce. He joined the RSC in 1982 and played the title role in *Tartuffe* and the Fool in *King Lear*. In 1984 he won both the Evening Standard and Laurence Olivier awards for his performance in the RSC's *Richard III*. Since then he has played numerous leading roles in the theater as well as on film and television, including *Stanley* and *Primo* at the National Theatre and on Broadway (*Stanley* winning him a second Olivier Award, and *Primo* two New York Awards), and, at the RSC, *Tamburlaine*, *Cyrano de Bergerac*, and *Macbeth*, as well as Prospero in *The Tempest*, Iago in *Othello*, and Shylock in *The Merchant of Venice*, directed by Bill Alexander, which he discusses here. He also writes books and plays, including the theatrical memoirs *Year of the King* (1985), *Woza Shakespeare: Titus Andronicus in South Africa* (1997, cowritten with his partner Gregory Doran), and his autobiography, *Beside Myself* (2001). As an artist, his recent exhibitions have included the London Jewish Cultural Centre (2007) and the National Theatre (2009).

Henry Goodman was born in 1950. After graduating from RADA he moved to South Africa, running Athol Fugard's Space Theatre in Cape Town. Returning to England in the 1980s he quickly made a name for himself in a remarkably versatile range of roles, winning the Olivier Award for Best Actor in 1993 for his role in Stephen Sondheim's *Assassins*. At the RSC his work includes *Richard III*, *Volpone*, *The Comedy of Errors*, and *They Shoot Horses, Don't They?* At the National Theatre he won his second Olivier Award for his portrayal of Shylock in Trevor Nunn's production of *The Merchant of Venice*, discussed here, as well as playing Nathan Detroit in *Guys and Dolls*, Roy Cohn in *Angels in America*, and Philip Gellburg in *Broken Glass*. In the West End his roles include *Duet for One*, Billy Flynn in *Chicago*, Freud in *Hysteria*, and Eddie in *Feelgood*, and on Broadway his work includes *Tartuffe* and *Art*.

His television and film work includes *The Damned United*, *Churchill*, *Colour Me Kubrick*, *Notting Hill*, *Mary Reilly*, and *The Mayor of Casterbridge*.

Shylock is a major role, but he is on stage for very few scenes, so there is little opportunity for gradual evolution of his character: is that a particular challenge?

AS: I think that Shylock is extremely well structured as a role, with one exception (I wish he had a final scene, an Act 5 Scene 2, after all the lightweight comedy about missing rings in 5.1), but there is still ample opportunity to develop his character. To summarize: in Act 1 Scene 3, we see him as he normally is in public, treading a tightrope with the Christians, now being humble, now resentful, now darkly humorous; in Act 2 Scene 5, we see him as he is in private—paranoid and strict (as a father); in Act 3 Scene 1, we see this troubled man explode, almost splitting into two—shaken senseless by his daughter's elopement, while rejoicing crazily at Antonio's misfortunes; in Act 3 Scene 3, we see how he has now hardened, the split personality fused into a single immovable force; in Act 4 Scene 1, the "Trial Scene," we see a horrible spectacle—the new monstrous Shylock ruling supreme at first, and then being cut down, piece by piece, till he is a shadow of his former self, and finally loses everything. What a journey.

HG: No, because what you get in *Merchant* are huge events in the offstage life that forcefully inform and cause the remarkable things you see. The sparing use of the actual presence of Shylock onstage means that the huge events that happen in his family life, in his home, in his social milieu, in a broader sense socially and politically, but in a very direct sense in his daily life, are immediate and active catalysts that we witness in his development when he is onstage. For example, with the taunting of the young lads-about-town, the irritation with his servant at home, Gobbo, and then the huge upheaval in his family life after Jessica elopes with a Christian, all of these events are like an emotional tidal wave that expose the bare foundations and leave him naked and visceral. I think he's sparingly used, but when he does come on he is just overwhelming in force to everybody else around him. In theater, as in life, situation always breeds character; how people deal with challenges, pressures, or opportunities reveals who they really are.

Villain or victim?

AS: He is both victim and villain, strictly in that order, and epitomizes a syndrome which fascinates me, and has featured often in my work, both as an actor and a writer: the persecuted turning into the persecutor. I witnessed it in my native South Africa. In colonial times, the Boers were persecuted by the British, who, during the Anglo-Boer War, invented the concentration camp, starving and killing thousands of Boer women and children. But then when the Boers gained power, becoming the Afrikaners, they created Apartheid, and persecuted the blacks. Meanwhile, my family fled anti-Semitic persecution in Eastern Europe, settled in South Africa, gradually prospered, and ended up supporting the racist Afrikaner government. Seldom do human beings seem to learn from experience, seldom do they draw the obvious comparisons between what they have previously suffered and now go on to inflict. As with Shylock. In his first scene, he describes how the Christians treat him as a second-class citizen, their form of "kaffir": "You call me misbeliever, cutthroat dog, / And spit upon my Jewish gaberdine." To be spat upon is a small, physically harmless, yet particularly foul form of humiliation (as I learned during the Jew-baiting scenes in our production). Surely someone who has endured this outrage wouldn't want it done to others? No, indeed—Shylock wants worse. He wants a pound of flesh cut from Antonio. It's a worthless thing, inedible to man, "a weight of carrion flesh" as he says himself, but, now that he has the upper hand, this bruised and battered victim simply wants revenge of the most violent kind.

HG: I cannot help but be deeply affected by Shakespeare, as with all his writing, showing many sides of the picture—many more than simply continuing the notion that all foreigners are evil and dangerous. He's far more balanced and sophisticated than that, and it's only by going more deeply into the details of the text that we can explore that. I did a great deal of reading around the history of the production and I found all that liberating, because you realize that everyone who ever played the role is trying to deal with the essential problem of whether you fall into the trap of deciding, am I villain or victim?

The key is the inner experience he is having. I feel he's a victim of *himself*. There are many people treated harshly by life who manage to stop themselves from becoming vicious and ugly because they have the inner resources or countervailing warmth and generosity of spirit within them to offset the poison. But Shylock hasn't—he has been poisoned by the pressure of the reality he lives in. I think we see that in the scene with Jessica and Gobbo in his home. The home, I think we should believe from Jessica's words, is a prison. She may belong to his nation, but not to his manner, and in that wonderful speech that she has, she hates him for his hatred. It's clearly more than natural teenage rebellion, it's religious repression: there's something in the orthodoxy of Shylock's behavior that really upsets her deeply. It's a type of fanaticism. For Shylock there's a sense that your home is a retreat from the world. Jessica wants it to be open, to be a passport to the world in every sense. But then you have to understand that their home is in a ghetto. In this the details are important: by sunset every night you have to be inside with the doors firmly closed; if you're not inside you have to pay a huge fine to the authorities. They are locked in on the site of an old iron foundry (the Italian is *barghetto*, where *ghetto* comes from). Every night this community of people that would have come from all over the Mediterranean, Persia, France, Jews from Europe, Russia, the Ottoman Empire and other exotic places, would have to get out of the city and into the ghetto. What binds them is an enforced identity as aliens. So they take solace from that very otherness—solace and, crucially, strength. In Shylock, a potentially villainous, fanatical, justified strength of thought, strength of righteousness. A strength that is self-harming and eventually condones, with right and God on its side, murder. There's a wonderful book by Cecil Roth on the history of the Jews which gives a great insight into the lives of their dynamic and exciting cultures throughout Europe (in the late sixteenth century). Shakespeare doesn't concentrate on that aspect, and this is the interesting thing: what Shakespeare does is show the effect of the political and the social on the private man. The individual tortured by society. He shows how that very society "breeds" its own monsters, monsters that will wound it deeply. Also, in a similar way, domestically: that's why Shakespeare goes out of his way to show that this man has no wife. Jessica *is* his wife: his daughter has to be mature beyond her years; she not only lives in a very orthodox, repressive regime, but emotionally her father is a disturbed man. He is obsessed, not just by money-making but by protecting himself from the savagery of the awfulness of the life out there on the streets. There is a psychological ghetto in the home scenes as much as the physical ghetto outside.

Though often regarded as an especially isolated character, we see Shylock with Tubal, and his family is obviously very important to him (his relationship with Jessica, his memory of his wife Leah): did you seek to convey both these aspects?

AS: It is vitally important for the actor playing Shylock to make him as detailed and complex a character as possible, and to show his humanity. No better chance comes than when Tubal reports that Shylock's eloped daughter, Jessica, has traded one of his rings for a monkey. Numb with shock, Shylock suddenly mentions his late wife (in the action there's no Mrs. Shylock to help him, like there's no Mrs. Lear or Mrs. Prospero), and he speaks with a strange, blurred eloquence: "I had it of Leah when I was a bachelor. I would not have given it for a wilderness of monkeys." The fact that he says this to Tubal indicates a trust, a friendship between the men, and the fact that they agree to meet later at their synagogue gives a glimpse of their social and spiritual life. These may just be tiny moments, but they're valuable.

More specifically, how did you and your Jessica play the relationship with each other?

AS: The opportunity to play the Shylock/Jessica relationship lies not so much in their one short scene together as in its aftermath. Deborah Goodman and I played the scene rather formally, an Orthodox Jewish father and daughter; he stern, she dutiful. Then, during the elopement, she revealed how oppressed she had felt under his rule, and how liberated she was now. He, in turn, learning about her betrayal, unleashed the kind of primal passion you only feel about those closest to you: "I would my daughter were dead at my foot, and the jewels in her ear!" Later, during the banter about rings in Act 5,

7. Henry Goodman as Shylock with Gabrielle Jourdan as Jessica: huge affection, though sometimes expressed, as affection often is, in violence.

Jessica became increasingly isolated, and then at the end of the play, we created an extra moment, like most modern productions do (to compensate for what I call "the missing Shylock scene")—she dropped her newly acquired crucifix, and it was retrieved by Antonio. He held it in front of her with ambiguous intent: was he returning it, or was he questioning her right to wear it? Two lonely outsiders. He deprived of his beloved Bassanio, she of her father and her racial identity.

HG: Well, the key to any hatred is love gone wrong. They love each other deeply and they need each other. But they don't need the way the other behaves and they don't need the other's needs! Shylock needs Jessica to be everything that he believes in: to be respectful, true to rules and to the traditions of Jewish orthodox behavior, to live in the denial of pleasure that he lives in, against the society from which he earns his living. There is an issue, beneath the play, of moral superiority, of who's right, the New Testament or the Old. You can say that he is learning to be a mother, and he can't. Gabrielle Jourdan, who played Jessica, brought a huge intelligence and yearning. There wasn't just a naughty young girl there, there was somebody who had a desire to be supportive, kind, and understanding, but also a love of life that was being stifled. We tried to show, I think instinctively, that there was huge affection between them which was expressed, as affection often is, in violence. Losing temper with the ones you love. Disturbing and treating horribly the ones you care about. Love is dysfunctionally expressed, and that is the link with the society outside. When events take the course they do, he has not got the control or that surface carapace that he normally has on the Rialto.

"Hath not a Jew eyes?" is one of those famous speeches, like "To be or not to be," that everyone is waiting for and on which an actor perhaps needs a new angle to keep it fresh: what did you discover in the speech?

AS: The "Hath not a Jew eyes?" speech was born out of the very center of the production: the violence of prejudice. In Act 2 Scene 8, the audience has learned that Shylock is running through the streets, shouting: "My daughter! O my ducats! . . . two rich and precious stones / Stol'n by my daughter!" Also they learn that "all the boys in Venice follow him / Crying, his stones, his daughter, and his ducats." So in Act 3 Scene 1, the director Bill Alexander and I decided to have Shylock enter in a disheveled state, his forehead bleeding (as though actually stoned by the boys), and to have Solanio and Salerio attack him, verbally and physically. Then the great speech just came out as a spontaneous and deeply felt response. Here, especially, we wanted to show the victim before he becomes the villain, the persecuted before he becomes the persecutor.

HG: Actually in performance it flows out from the action organically, but yes, it is a burden. To avoid self-consciousness I needed to find the context out of which he is driven. We've a man who has worked on the Rialto for many years and when he's outside he smiles, he's genial. Then he goes home to this sour, dark temple, where he can spit about the society outside. There's this dichotomy, this schism emotionally within him. At home, as I did in my performance, he smacks his daughter round the face, he is violent, he's aggressive and ugly. He is not a nice man. He cannot express love. Yes, we know why and we can understand why he's not a nice man, but he's not a well-balanced, pleasant man. It is not right to avoid that in trying to portray him honestly. The actor should avoid at all costs mollifying him or making him a villain for politically correct motives. What the play is really saying, I think, is that society buys its own outcomes. The notion of value and what we buy in life is central to the play.

Off the script, but intuited from it, consider this: the sense of grievance, and I believe grief, at the death of his wife Leah is the soil out of which this articulate human challenge comes. "Why me? Please, not more grief and pain and insult and disgrace and loss. Please explain to me . . . it's just not fair" is a paraphrase I would use to shape that inner sense of being wronged beyond endurance.

Shylock is in the habit of expecting Antonio to treat him in a certain way, to spit on him and insult him, but when the tables are turned and Antonio needs the loan it is fascinating. Antonio is a bold public figure who confidently entertains his friends by his derision

toward the Jews. He has a very strong sense of religious commitment, and I think this is very important. Antonio is a very committed
Christian, he's a good Christian, and to be a good Christian is to stop
Jews being Jews. The pope has at this time condoned, by law, burning
them, let's recall! That all religion is dangerous is something the play
reveals and explores. Shylock in a certain sense has an equally
indomitable commitment to religion. This is the New Testament versus the Old. So when Antonio needs to borrow the money it brings
out in Shylock a sense of opportunism, a savagery. For years he has
demonstrated a patient acceptance of how you deal with life, of *years*
of habitually being spat on, and he makes it quite clear he's dealt
with it patiently. It really is remarkable, and I think that is a secret
about Shylock: he has learned a carapace of survival in this society,
of smiling, laughing. On the surface a certain sense of bonhomie,
but inside a deep sense of self-denigration, shame, guilt about that
very carapace. Then the leading Merchant of Venice, Antonio, who
is the champion of all of these anti-alien, anti-Jewish behaviors, who
encourages the young bloods in this mercantile city, suddenly HE
needs money! It is like the Lockerbie bomber needing a loan from the
parents of those he killed. The irony unleashes something unique
emotionally, an opportunity to rebalance the books. On the surface
you can say that's just revenge and hatred, but I think it's also a certain sort of justice. I think all of that context is swimming underneath: the loss of his money, his diamonds, his daughter, his wife,
and then the ring, which he was given as a bachelor by his wife-to-
be, Leah, who means a great deal to him and whose death has devas-
tated Shylock. And the only memory of this human being is the ring.
I think before Shylock speaks those powerful words he's reached a
stage of primal, lucid, almost existential thinking. I don't think he's
ever been in this state before. He's asking *himself* the question; it's not
just rage at these two racists that spit on him and laugh at him and
taunt him. The emotional impact of his daughter becoming a Christian, running away with the enemy and taking the ring, puts him in
a state when he says those lines which is absolutely new for him. It's
not just an old habit coming out, it's something absolutely new. The
thoughts are newly discovered because of a traumatized state, and
that's why they're great. That's what shapes the rhetorical bite of his

thought. Newness of discovery is why any Shakespeare speech becomes great: people reach a point of understanding about themselves that shapes their thoughts and language. I think that's the way to understand that speech; he's been pushed to a point where he's almost for a moment gone beyond just anger. Yes, there's huge emotional heft in the scene, but there's also a sense of unavoidable truthfulness, lucidity.

Shylock's implacability in the trial scene is pretty unremitting: how do you as an actor empathize with the man who insists on his pound of flesh?

AS: I had no difficulty at all empathizing with him in the trial scene—he's been badly damaged by his treatment, and now he's insane with rage. We intensified his mental state by having him perform a (totally invented) Jewish ritual while he prepared to cut the pound of flesh from Antonio, chanting away in Hebrew, as though this was some ancient sacrificial rite. But I have to confess that my commitment to the frenzied attack was shaken one night when a lady in the front row said of John Carlisle, playing Antonio, and the slimmest of actors, "Oh, you'll never get a pound of flesh off him!"

HG: I think what's important is that before he goes into the trial scene we learn from the scene on the street that the jailer has been breaking the rules and allowing Antonio to come begging for mercy. Antonio is so powerful in this town that people are fighting on his behalf; even the duke has clearly spoken to Shylock on Antonio's behalf. So before he gets in the courtroom, people are on the streets calling out "You vicious Jew, how can you try and bring down one of our leading men of Venice?" The whole city has turned against him. He goes home to an empty house; everywhere he looks, hatred looks back at him. I'm very conscious before he gets into that public space of the private nightmare of his life. However bad it was before, it is now a million times worse. And, crucially, he now has legitimate opportunity and inner need for justice (some say revenge). Think of it: sitting at home, on his own, without his daughter or wife, even Tubal his sole Jewish friend has started to think "You're going too far." He's lonely, he's isolated, and in his isolation he becomes very

8. Antony Sher as Shylock in the trial scene, intoning his (invented) Hebrew sacrificial prayer.

dangerous. I also think it's important that Shylock is a very clever, canny man. He's read the Old Testament in all of its rich, proverbial allegories and stories. He's a market trader at the highest level—that sense of playing the long game, almost mental chess, working out numbers, planning when ships come in, how much a piece of cloth will be; he plays hedge funds in his head. He thrives when challenged with complex situations. Emotionally, he rubs his soul with joy when people take him on. He's held his sense of injustice back and spat about it inside the ghetto, but now he can actually look at it, deal with it. That's what I was interested in exploring. He enjoys taking them on in a way that he never did before. Then there is the very key issue of his innate temperament, his "humour" in the contemporary Elizabethan medical sense. Early in the play, well before bile is aroused, he can't stop himself from saying, "Signior Antonio, many a time and oft / In the Rialto you have rated me / About my moneys and my usances . . . What should I say to you?," etc. He can't stop himself from being ironical, and prodding, because he knows he's got these guys in a corner intellectually, and they're hypocrites. Now put that into a political, social, emotional, life-and-death situation, a man who thinks and says, "I fight for my tribe." He even says in the trial, which a lot of people forget, "I follow thus / A losing suit against him." I am fighting a losing situation—he uses those words. "A pound of flesh. What good is that to me? But now I will have him." And that's why all this insight comes under pressure: "You bought your slaves. If I said to you, why don't you let them sleep in your beds and marry your daughters, would you do it? No, you wouldn't, because you *bought* them. You *own* them. Well I *bought* the right to hate this man. My hatred is 'dearly bought.'" It's a remarkable statement. He knows what he's saying. He *loves* the legal precedents, that's why the notion of Daniel, the great thinker, the great judge in the great biblical tradition, is so important to him—and also Jacob, the father of the nation—because these were thinkers. Daniel was a wise, powerful, clever man. So all of that is in that room. It's the chance to bite back. And in the moment of playing, you're not aware at all of playing the big speeches, or big problems, you've just got the heft of all of these events and history behind you, just speaking out from an unavoidable inner insight and pressure. The phrase "affection / Mistress of passion, sways it to the mood / Of what it like or loathes": my paraphrase would be "I am—we are all—at the mercy of this effect (as Freud called it!), this drive. I can't stop myself as Shylock—like people who pee whenever they hear the bagpipes!"

Were physical characteristics an important part of your creation of the character?

AS: In researching the Jewish ghetto in Venice (Jan Morris' book on that city was particularly useful), I was interested to learn that a significant part of its population was Turkish. Bill Alexander and I became drawn to the idea that it wasn't just Shylock's religion that made him very foreign, very alien, to the Christians. Since they were being played in RP British accents, Shylock developed a very Turkish sound, and look—with long hair and beard, and a large purple djellaba—and a heavy, almost brutal walk. I thought of him as a simple, relatively uneducated man, a peasant turned businessman, used to receiving blows, and now ready to return them.

HG: I feel very strongly that in the writing there's a different rhythm in the way he speaks. There were not a lot of Jews in London when Shakespeare wrote the play, so they were a little bit alien, but there were a great many foreigners with foreign accents. London in that sense was like Venice: it benefited from them, even though there was a huge, fearful mentality and a terror of being at war. I think one of the things that hit me were the sounds of the writing and the rhythm of the writing; there's a rhythmic shape and pattern. In our production, the sensibility was to put it pre-Holocaust, otherwise it becomes unwatchable and in bad taste. Trevor found a way to put it in Europe, in Vienna or in Budapest; it wasn't explicit, probably in the late 1920s, early 1930s, before things had really got out of hand. And one of the lovely ideas that Trevor had which affected the social, political milieu was that Shylock, when he went off for dinner, went off to meet Antonio to seal the deal, met them at the cabaret, which is really louche and sexy and naughty, and which for Shylock is utterly abhorrent and uncomfortable. And there was Gobbo, whom he has just sacked, on the microphone saying "My master's an old

Jew . . ." Once again, there it is: all the hatred, from his own servant, who's now dressed a little better, working for Bassanio, whom Shylock has just lent a load of money to. It's a wonderful irony and a great idea of Trevor's.

Did historical research into the status of Jews in Shakespeare's time play a part in your preparation of the role?

AS: No, though I knew of course that Jews were officially banned from England at the time Shakespeare wrote the play. So his fully rounded and compassionate view of Shylock came either from encounters with Jews elsewhere, or, more likely, his fully rounded and compassionate view of humanity in general.

HG: The key thing is to look at what's in the text before you start to interpret, but I was overwhelmingly struck when doing research for the play by the events surrounding Roderigo Lopez. Lopez was hung, drawn and quartered, and let's remind ourselves that that is hanging somebody until they're not quite dead and then viscerally ripping them to bits and cutting out their belly, all in front of a shrieking, laughing crowd at Tyburn in Marble Arch. The Elizabethan love of watching these live events, even though there might be horror and distaste, was also there in the thrill of bear-baiting and cock-fighting, and, as we know only too well, is not that far from our own society. There's both the visceral impact of that and also the social and political events in London, in a country at war with Spain, having recently dealt with the Armada. It brought something out. And it's much too simplistic to say that it's just prejudice or hatred. Lopez was a man who wasn't a leader, but who was very close to the queen, who had permission to touch the royal fruitless private parts, he was one of only twenty-odd people given the Fellowship of the Royal College of Surgeons, he was at the highest level of court. He was a man whom the queen became very close to, but who was hated by the Earl of Essex and all these people; he was what they called a *marrano*, which means "pig," *converso*, somebody they thought was a secret Jew, although I suspect that he had given up his religion. All of these things bespeak in the court, and in society, a fear of the foreigner, especially in an island that was at war with Spain and frightened of the large numbers of exiled Portuguese (Spain had conquered it and the Portuguese king had fled to London)—Lopez being Portuguese and Jewish: a double alien! It is true, from research I found, that Lopez was trying to do deals and was acting as a fixer (not the same thing as a spy) for his patients, the queen and Lord Burleigh. There was fierce rivalry between Essex and Burleigh (Essex pro-war with Spain; Burleigh a peace-seeker). Essex basically tortured this seventy-year-old man [Lopez] until he got what he wanted out of him. Essex took him to his own private home to get outside of the city walls because Elizabeth didn't want him to be tortured, she believed in him. I think that all of that going on at court, where Shakespeare was already by then performing in various companies, inspired me as much as the detailed current events and specific textual events in the play. I personally find all that background really helpful and useful.

I found and read the papal bulls which from the Inquisition onward had been issuing orders to kill Jews. In Pisa and many different places they put them on bonfires and burned them. Venice didn't—why? Because Venice understood that they needed these people, because they spoke many languages so they could speak to the traders and pedlars and businessmen from all over the world. So there is built into the play that sense of mercantile life. Before I've even spoken a word, I find all that stuff really exciting. Context and history, personal and emotional. The signals and the clues are all from the text, never in spite of it, but they lead you back and then you can fill out what Shakespeare has done. I always find it fascinating how Shakespeare adapted and changed his sources, in this case *Il Pecorone*. The changes he made are very revealing: what did he keep, and what didn't he? The fact that he pushes the trial to go in a particular direction, and Antonio forces Shylock to become a Christian and pushes the events of the play away from the original story, tells us that Shakespeare is interested in certain things. All of those things are very important. A lot of people say, "This is all directors' stuff." Absolute nonsense. Any thinking, feeling, intelligent human being wants to understand the context, and I think that division between acting and directing is just ridiculous.

What was your take on the accusation that the representation of the part is anti-Semitic?

AS: I think it is as wrong to call *Merchant* anti-Semitic as it is to call *Othello* racist. The two plays examine these issues—anti-Semitism and racism—in a tough and uncomfortable way, but without ever condoning or promoting them. Yet *Merchant*'s flaw remains its silly Act 5, which seems to round off the dark and complex story in a totally trivial way. It's one of those rare occasions in Shakespeare where a modern audience—and specifically a post-Holocaust audience—has great difficulty accepting what he's written. A clear case, I think, of a play hijacked by history.

HG: In very simple language, I don't agree with it. I think it perpetuates an image to some degree, but is showing the Welsh and the Scotsmen in *Henry V* anti-Welsh or anti-Scot? No, it shows the rivalries, the clichés, the stereotypes, and the bitterness in the Elizabethan world, when everybody was about to go to war. I think what is, to me, overwhelming is that Shakespeare goes out of his way to show Shylock in a personal context, which doesn't explain or completely exonerate in any way his behavior, but it does contextualize it, and it does humanize it, and he gives him, like he gives Queen Katherine in *Henry VIII*, a public trial. If you think of the big trial scenes they usually give the foreigner a great voice actually. He doesn't allow us just to laugh at Shylock, although there is some of that, or to show him merely in his appalling behavior; he also says that this is a man with knowledge and insight and reason to think and feel and behave in the way that he does. There are certain key choices that you've got to make if you play this role. What's the learning curve? I think that he may be in very few scenes, but he has absolutely huge triggers before and during them. I believe he finds it not so easy to actually kill someone. Some people become so psychopathic in their hate that they can just stab a knife into somebody without even thinking about it. I don't believe he's become that, because all of his other self is justice, decency, control; and although he's got to a point of doing something appalling, I believe he has that moment of doubt. It might only be a millisecond, but he does.

Hamlet is not always played as peculiarly Danish, Macbeth does not always have a Scottish accent . . . could you imagine a production in which Shylock is not peculiarly Jewish?

AS: Shylock's Jewishness is far more critical than Macbeth's Scottishness or Hamlet's Danishness; one half of *Merchant*'s plot is fueled by the hatred between the Christians and the Jews. The question is, how Jewish to make him? I believe very Jewish—without, of course, spilling over into caricature. In Trevor Nunn's 1999 National Theatre production, set in 1930s Europe, Henry Goodman played a very Jewish Shylock with total authenticity, and the result was superb. You both believed in him as a three-dimensional man, yet also understood that when the Christians looked at him they saw one of those Nazi cartoons of verminous Jews. At the other extreme, there was Jonathan Miller's 1970 National Theatre production with Laurence Olivier. Backed by his Jewish director, Olivier chose to play a totally assimilated Jew, a sophisticated Disraeli-type figure (the setting was Victorian). I understood their point—the enemies of the real Disraeli (who wasn't just assimilated, but had actually converted to Christianity) often reverted to anti-Semitic abuse when they were on the attack—yet it was hard to believe that this particular Shylock had ever been spat upon. And it is this ugly, visceral little act which is, I believe, crucial to his side of the story. But how it relates to the other side, Portia's fairy-tale adventures, this simply mystifies me. When we began work on our RSC production in 1987, I was convinced that Bill Alexander, Deborah Findlay (Portia), and I would find a way of marrying the two halves, and yet when we finished two years later, after the Stratford and Barbican runs, I then felt it was impossible. I look forward to being proved wrong one day . . .

HG: Now I know it's a multilayered issue, but yes I can. See, there's a principle here. If you say no black person should ever play Shylock or no white person should ever play Othello, to me you can't do theater. What's the point of it? Being the other, undergoing their experience, that is the journey of theater. Now of course we live in an age where, thank heavens, black people can play kings of England and that's great, but we have to acknowledge that in the context of the time those prejudices did exist. It's wonderful that we're now growing as human beings and we can be color blind, but the plays do come from an era when people were not. It's as if Shakespeare could only have written about people living in Stratford-upon-Avon or London—it's a very far-reaching point, this. How could he write about all these different cultures? He can only *imagine* them. He might see some at court when he went to perform at Whitehall, he might have met some at Stratford Town Hall when his dad was hosting events. But then he captures those people and gives us characters. If he's got the right to *write* them, then we've got the right to *act* them. The problem is, does Shylock have to be the clichéd version of what a Jew is? Of course not. That's why I fully accepted the version of Olivier, even though it lacked certain things. Yes, the play does take on added (I'm not being naive) intensity and emotional authenticity and veracity if you feel in its context, as we did in Europe in the 1930s: that felt right. But if you imagine Jonathan Miller or Freddie Raphael or hundreds of modern Jewish writers or eminent lawyers or doctors or journalists, etc., etc., being Shylock, they might just speak like I'm speaking now. The issue is, do they have to have a funny accent, do they have to use their hands in a certain way . . . ?

That's the very dangerous thing with Shylock and people bend over backward to try and negotiate that. I went out of my way to show that he lives very religiously, he's devout. But anybody can do that research, you don't have to be Jewish to do that. If I'm playing Macbeth I'll look into understanding the things about his life, and his wife, and his society, and Scots, and the hatred of England, and lairds and lords. So yes I can. The question is the quality that it would bring to the work. And the trouble with Shylock is that he embraces and encourages—even tempts—extreme ways of playing him. Or you fall into the other trap of desperately trying not to be Jewish, make it absolutely, completely modern, just somebody who is wronged and is completely like all the other people in his community. It's a fascinating subject, and context and period is absolutely crucial in this play—more than in any other play, I think. We must remember that the Nazis did dozens and dozens of productions of this play during the era because they thought it was useful, but they cut out all things that were humane. Shakespeare didn't, he put them in.

SHAKESPEARE'S CAREER
IN THE THEATER

BEGINNINGS

William Shakespeare was an extraordinarily intelligent man who was born and died in an ordinary market town in the English Midlands. He lived an uneventful life in an eventful age. Born in April 1564, he was the eldest son of John Shakespeare, a glove maker who was prominent on the town council until he fell into financial difficulties. Young William was educated at the local grammar in Stratford-upon-Avon, Warwickshire, where he gained a thorough grounding in the Latin language, the art of rhetoric, and classical poetry. He married Ann Hathaway and had three children (Susanna, then the twins Hamnet and Judith) before his twenty-first birthday: an exceptionally young age for the period. We do not know how he supported his family in the mid-1580s.

Like many clever country boys, he moved to the city in order to make his way in the world. Like many creative people, he found a career in the entertainment business. Public playhouses and professional full-time acting companies reliant on the market for their income were born in Shakespeare's childhood. When he arrived in London as a man, sometime in the late 1580s, a new phenomenon was in the making: the actor who is so successful that he becomes a "star." The word did not exist in its modern sense, but the pattern is recognizable: audiences went to the theater not so much to see a particular show as to witness the comedian Richard Tarlton or the dramatic actor Edward Alleyn.

Shakespeare was an actor before he was a writer. It appears not to have been long before he realized that he was never going to grow into a great comedian like Tarlton or a great tragedian like Alleyn. Instead, he found a role within his company as the man who patched up old plays, breathing new life, new dramatic twists, into tired repertory pieces. He paid close attention to the work of the university-educated dramatists who were writing history plays and tragedies for the public stage in a style more ambitious, sweeping, and poetically grand than anything that had been seen before. But he may also have noted that what his friend and rival Ben Jonson would call "Marlowe's mighty line" sometimes faltered in the mode of comedy. Going to university, as Christopher Marlowe did, was all well and good for honing the arts of rhetorical elaboration and classical allusion, but it could lead to a loss of the common touch. To stay close to a large segment of the potential audience for public theater, it was necessary to write for clowns as well as kings and to intersperse the flights of poetry with the humor of the tavern, the privy, and the brothel: Shakespeare was the first to establish himself early in his career as an equal master of tragedy, comedy, and history. He realized that theater could be the medium to make the national past available to a wider audience than the elite who could afford to read large history books: his signature early works include not only the classical tragedy *Titus Andronicus* but also the sequence of English historical plays on the Wars of the Roses.

He also invented a new role for himself, that of in-house company dramatist. Where his peers and predecessors had to sell their plays to the theater managers on a poorly paid piecework basis, Shakespeare took a percentage of the box-office income. The Lord Chamberlain's Men constituted themselves in 1594 as a joint stock company, with the profits being distributed among the core actors who had invested as sharers. Shakespeare acted himself—he appears in the cast lists of some of Ben Jonson's plays as well as the list of actors' names at the beginning of his own collected works—but his principal duty was to write two or three plays a year for the company. By holding shares, he was effectively earning himself a royalty on his work, something no author had ever done before in England. When the Lord Chamberlain's Men collected their fee for performance at court in the Christmas season of 1594, three of them went along to the Treasurer of the Chamber: not just Richard Burbage the tragedian and Will Kempe the clown, but also Shakespeare the scriptwriter. That was something new.

The next four years were the golden period in Shakespeare's career, though overshadowed by the death of his only son Hamnet, aged eleven, in 1596. In his early thirties and in full command of both his poetic and his theatrical medium, he perfected his art of comedy, while also developing his tragic and historical writing in new ways. In 1598, Francis Meres, a Cambridge University graduate with his finger on the pulse of the London literary world, praised Shakespeare for his excellence across the genres:

> As Plautus and Seneca are accounted the best for comedy and tragedy among the Latins, so Shakespeare among the English is the most excellent in both kinds for the stage; for comedy, witness his *Gentlemen of Verona*, his *Errors*, his *Love Labours Lost*, his *Love Labours Won*, his *Midsummer Night Dream* and his *Merchant of Venice*: for tragedy his *Richard the 2*, *Richard the 3*, *Henry the 4*, *King John*, *Titus Andronicus* and his *Romeo and Juliet*.

For Meres, as for the many writers who praised the "honey-flowing vein" of *Venus and Adonis* and *Lucrece*, narrative poems written when the theaters were closed due to plague in 1593–94, Shakespeare was marked above all by his linguistic skill, by the gift of turning elegant poetic phrases.

PLAYHOUSES

Elizabethan playhouses were "thrust" or "one-room" theaters. To understand Shakespeare's original theatrical life, we have to forget about the indoor theater of later times, with its proscenium arch and curtain that would be opened at the beginning and closed at the end of each act. In the proscenium arch theater, stage and auditorium are effectively two separate rooms: the audience looks from one world into another as if through the imaginary "fourth wall" framed by the proscenium. The picture-frame stage, together with the elaborate scenic effects and backdrops beyond it, created the illusion of a self-contained world—especially once nineteenth-century developments in the control of artificial lighting meant that the auditorium could be darkened and the spectators made to focus on the lighted stage. Shakespeare, by contrast, wrote for a bare platform stage with a standing audience gathered around it in a courtyard in full daylight. The audience was always conscious of themselves and their fellow spectators, and they shared the same "room" as the actors. A sense of immediate presence and the creation of rapport with the audience were all-important. The actor could not afford to imagine he was in a closed world, with silent witnesses dutifully observing him from the darkness.

Shakespeare's theatrical career began at the Rose Theatre in Southwark. The stage was wide and shallow, trapezoid in shape, like a lozenge. This design had a great deal of potential for the theatrical equivalent of cinematic split-screen effects, whereby one group of characters would enter at the door at one end of the tiring-house wall at the back of the stage and another group through the door at the other end, thus creating two rival tableaux. Many of the battle-heavy and faction-filled plays that premiered at the Rose have scenes of just this sort.

At the rear of the Rose stage, there were three capacious exits, each over ten feet wide. Unfortunately, the very limited excavation of a fragmentary portion of the original Globe site, in 1989, revealed nothing about the stage. The first Globe was built in 1599 with similar proportions to those of another theater, the Fortune, albeit that the former was polygonal and looked circular, whereas the latter was rectangular. The building contract for the Fortune survives and allows us to infer that the stage of the Globe was probably substantially wider than it was deep (perhaps forty-three feet wide and twenty-seven feet deep). It may well have been tapered at the front, like that of the Rose.

The capacity of the Globe was said to have been enormous, perhaps in excess of three thousand. It has been conjectured that about eight hundred people may have stood in the yard, with two thousand or more in the three layers of covered galleries. The other "public" playhouses were also of large capacity, whereas the indoor Blackfriars theater that Shakespeare's company began using in 1608—the former refectory of a monastery—had overall internal dimensions of a mere forty-six by sixty feet. It would have made for a much more intimate theatrical experience and had a much smaller capacity, probably of about six hundred people. Since they paid at least sixpence a head, the Blackfriars attracted a more select or "private" audience. The atmosphere would have been closer to that of an indoor performance before the court in the Whitehall Palace or at Richmond. That Shakespeare always wrote for indoor production at court as well as outdoor performance in the public theater should make us cautious about inferring, as some scholars have, that the opportunity provided by the intimacy of the Blackfriars led to a significant change toward a "chamber" style in his last plays—which, besides, were performed at both the Globe and the Blackfriars. After the occupation of the Blackfriars a five-act structure seems to have become more important to Shakespeare. That was because of artificial lighting: there were musical interludes between the acts, while the candles were trimmed and replaced. Again, though, something similar must have been necessary for indoor court performances throughout his career.

Front of house there were the "gatherers" who collected the money from audience members: a penny to stand in the open-air yard, another penny for a place in the covered galleries, sixpence for the prominent "lord's rooms" to the side of the stage. In the indoor "private" theaters, gallants from the audience who fancied making themselves part of the spectacle sat on stools on the edge of the stage itself. Scholars debate as to how widespread this practice was in the public theaters such as the Globe. Once the audience was in place and the money counted, the gatherers were available to be extras on stage. That is one reason why battles and crowd scenes often come later rather than early in Shakespeare's plays. There was no formal prohibition upon performance by women, and there certainly were women among the gatherers, so it is not beyond the bounds of possibility that female crowd members were played by females.

The play began at two o'clock in the afternoon and the theater had to be cleared by five. After the main show, there would be a jig—which consisted not only of dancing, but also of knockabout comedy (it is the origin of the farcical "afterpiece" in the eighteenth-century theater). So the time available for a Shakespeare play was about two and a half hours, somewhere between the "two hours' traffic" mentioned in the prologue to Romeo and Juliet and the "three hours' spectacle" referred to in the preface to the 1647 Folio of Beaumont and Fletcher's plays.

The prologue to a play by Thomas Middleton refers to a thousand lines as "one hour's words," so the likelihood is that about two and a half thousand, or a maximum of three thousand lines, made up the performed text. This is indeed the length of most of Shakespeare's comedies, whereas many of his tragedies and histories are much longer, raising the possibility that he wrote full scripts, possibly with eventual publication in mind, in the full knowledge that the stage version would be heavily cut. The short Quarto texts published in his lifetime—they used to be called "Bad" Quartos—provide fascinating evidence as to the kind of cutting that probably took place. So, for instance, the First Quarto of *Hamlet* neatly merges two occasions when Hamlet is overheard, the "Fishmonger" and the "nunnery" scenes.

The social composition of the audience was mixed. The poet Sir John Davies wrote of "A thousand townsmen, gentlemen and whores, / Porters and servingmen" who would "together throng" at the public playhouses. Though moralists associated female playgoing with adultery and the sex trade, many perfectly respectable citizens' wives were regular attendees. Some, no doubt, resembled the modern groupie: a story attested in two different sources has one citizen's wife making a post-show assignation with Richard Burbage and ending up in bed with Shakespeare—supposedly eliciting from the latter the quip that William the Conqueror was before Richard III. Defenders of theater liked to say that by witnessing the comeuppance of villains on the stage, audience members would repent of their own wrongdoings, but the reality is that most people went to the theater then, as they do now, for entertainment more than moral edification. Besides, it would be foolish to suppose that audiences behaved in a homogeneous way: a pamphlet of the 1630s tells of how two men went to see *Pericles* and one of them laughed while the other wept. Bishop John Hall complained that people went to church for the same reasons that they went to the theater: "for company, for custom, for recreation . . . to feed his eyes or his ears . . . or perhaps for sleep."

Men-about-town and clever young lawyers went to be seen as much as to see. In the modern popular imagination, shaped not least by *Shakespeare in Love* and the opening sequence of Laurence Olivier's *Henry V* film, the penny-paying groundlings stand in the yard hurling abuse or encouragement and hazelnuts or orange peel

at the actors, while the sophisticates in the covered galleries appreciate Shakespeare's soaring poetry. The reality was probably the other
way around. A "groundling" was a kind of fish, so the nickname
suggests the penny audience standing below the level of the stage
and gazing in silent open-mouthed wonder at the spectacle unfold-
ing above them. The more difficult audience members, who kept up
a running commentary of clever remarks on the performance and
who occasionally got into quarrels with players, were the gallants.
Like Hollywood movies in modern times, Elizabethan and Jacobean
plays exercised a powerful influence on the fashion and behavior of
the young. John Marston mocks the lawyers who would open their
lips, perhaps to court a girl, and out would "flow / Naught but pure
Juliet and Romeo."

THE ENSEMBLE AT WORK

In the absence of typewriters and photocopying machines, reading
aloud would have been the means by which the company got to
know a new play. The tradition of the playwright reading his complete script to the assembled company endured for generations. A
copy would then have been taken to the Master of the Revels for
licensing. The theater book-holder or prompter would then have
copied the parts for distribution to the actors. A partbook consisted
of the character's lines, with each speech preceded by the last three
or four words of the speech before, the so-called "cue." These would
have been taken away and studied or "conned." During this period
of learning the parts, an actor might have had some one-to-one
instruction, perhaps from the dramatist, perhaps from a senior actor
who had played the same part before, and, in the case of an apprentice, from his master. A high percentage of Desdemona's lines occur
in dialogue with Othello, of Lady Macbeth's with Macbeth, Cleopatra's with Antony, and Volumnia's with Coriolanus. The roles would
almost certainly have been taken by the apprentice of the lead actor,
usually Burbage, who delivers the majority of the cues. Given that
apprentices lodged with their masters, there would have been ample
opportunity for personal instruction, which may be what made it
possible for young men to play such demanding parts.

9. Hypothetical reconstruction of the interior of an Elizabethan playhouse during a performance.

After the parts were learned, there may have been no more than a single rehearsal before the first performance. With six different plays to be put on every week, there was no time for more. Actors, then, would go into a show with a very limited sense of the whole. The notion of a collective rehearsal process that is itself a process of discovery for the actors is wholly modern and would have been incomprehensible to Shakespeare and his original ensemble. Given the number of parts an actor had to hold in his memory, the forgetting of lines was probably more frequent than in the modern theater. The book-holder was on hand to prompt.

Backstage personnel included the property man, the tire-man who oversaw the costumes, call boys, attendants, and the musicians, who might play at various times from the main stage, the rooms above, and within the tiring-house. Scriptwriters sometimes made a nuisance of themselves backstage. There was often tension between the acting companies and the freelance playwrights from whom they purchased scripts: it was a smart move on the part of Shakespeare and the Lord Chamberlain's Men to bring the writing process in-house.

Scenery was limited, though sometimes set pieces were brought on (a bank of flowers, a bed, the mouth of hell). The trapdoor from below, the gallery stage above, and the curtained discovery space at the back allowed for an array of special effects: the rising of ghosts and apparitions, the descent of gods, dialogue between a character at a window and another at ground level, the revelation of a statue or a pair of lovers playing at chess. Ingenious use could be made of props, as with the ass's head in *A Midsummer Night's Dream*. In a theater that does not clutter the stage with the material paraphernalia of everyday life, those objects that are deployed may take on powerful symbolic weight, as when Shylock bears his weighing scales in one hand and knife in the other, thus becoming a parody of the figure of Justice who traditionally bears a sword and a balance. Among the more significant items in the property cupboard of Shakespeare's company, there would have been a throne (the "chair of state"), joint stools, books, bottles, coins, purses, letters (which are brought on stage, read or referred to on about eighty occasions in the complete works), maps, gloves, a set of stocks (in which Kent is put in *King Lear*), rings, rapiers, daggers, broadswords, staves, pistols, masks and vizards, heads and skulls, torches and tapers and lanterns which served to signal night scenes on the daylit stage, a buck's head, an ass's head, animal costumes. Live animals also put in appearances, most notably the dog Crab in *The Two Gentlemen of Verona* and possibly a young polar bear in *The Winter's Tale*.

The costumes were the most important visual dimension of the play. Playwrights were paid between £2 and £6 per script, whereas Alleyn was not averse to paying £20 for "a black velvet cloak with sleeves embroidered all with silver and gold." No matter the period of the play, actors always wore contemporary costume. The excitement for the audience came not from any impression of historical accuracy, but from the richness of the attire and perhaps the transgressive thrill of the knowledge that here were commoners like themselves strutting in the costumes of courtiers in effective defiance of the strict sumptuary laws whereby in real life people had to wear the clothes that befitted their social station.

To an even greater degree than props, costumes could carry symbolic importance. Racial characteristics could be suggested: a breastplate and helmet for a Roman soldier, a turban for a Turk, long robes for exotic characters such as Moors, a gabardine for a Jew. The figure of Time, as in *The Winter's Tale*, would be equipped with hourglass, scythe, and wings; Rumour, who speaks the prologue of *2 Henry IV*, wore a costume adorned with a thousand tongues. The wardrobe in the tiring-house of the Globe would have contained much of the same stock as that of rival manager Philip Henslowe at the Rose: green gowns for outlaws and foresters, black for melancholy men such as Jaques and people in mourning such as the Countess in *All's Well That Ends Well* (at the beginning of *Hamlet*, the prince is still in mourning black when everyone else is in festive garb for the wedding of the new king), a gown and hood for a friar (or a feigned friar like the duke in *Measure for Measure*), blue coats and tawny to distinguish the followers of rival factions, a leather apron and ruler for a carpenter (as in the opening scene of *Julius Caesar*—and in *A Midsummer Night's Dream*, where this is the only sign that Peter Quince is a carpenter), a cockle hat with staff and a pair of sandals for a pilgrim or palmer (the disguise assumed by Helen in *All's Well*), bodices and kirtles with farthingales beneath for the boys who are to be dressed as girls. A gender switch such as that of Rosalind or Jessica seems to have taken between fifty and eighty lines of dialogue—Viola does not resume her "maiden weeds," but remains in her boy's costume to the end of *Twelfth Night* because a change would have slowed down the action at just the moment it was speeding to a climax. Henslowe's inventory also included "a robe for to go invisible": Oberon, Puck, and Ariel must have had something similar.

As the costumes appealed to the eyes, so there was music for the ears. Comedies included many songs. Desdemona's willow song, perhaps a late addition to the text, is a rare and thus exceptionally poignant example from tragedy. Trumpets and tuckets sounded for ceremonial entrances, drums denoted an army on the march. Background music could create atmosphere, as at the beginning of *Twelfth Night*, during the lovers' dialogue near the end of *The Merchant of Venice*, when the statue seemingly comes to life in *The Winter's Tale*, and for the revival of Pericles and of Lear (in the Quarto

text, but not the Folio). The haunting sound of the hautboy suggested a realm beyond the human, as when the god Hercules is imagined deserting Mark Antony. Dances symbolized the harmony of the
end of a comedy—though in Shakespeare's world of mingled joy
and sorrow, someone is usually left out of the circle.

The most important resource was, of course, the actors themselves.
They needed many skills: in the words of one contemporary com-
mentator, "dancing, activity, music, song, elocution, ability of body,
memory, skill of weapon, pregnancy of wit." Their bodies were as significant as their voices. Hamlet tells the player to "suit the action to the
word, the word to the action": moments of strong emotion, known
as "passions," relied on a repertoire of dramatic gestures as well as a
modulation of the voice. When Titus Andronicus has had his hand
chopped off, he asks "How can I grace my talk, / Wanting a hand to
give it action?" A pen portrait of "The Character of an Excellent Actor"
by the dramatist John Webster is almost certainly based on his impression of Shakespeare's leading man, Richard Burbage: "By a full and
significant action of body, he charms our attention: sit in a full theater,
and you will think you see so many lines drawn from the circumfer-
ence of so many ears, whiles the actor is the centre. . . ."

Though Burbage was admired above all others, praise was also
heaped upon the apprentice players whose alto voices fitted them for
the parts of women. A spectator at Oxford in 1610 records how the
audience was reduced to tears by the pathos of Desdemona's death.
The puritans who fumed about the biblical prohibition upon cross-
dressing and the encouragement to sodomy constituted by the sight
of an adult male kissing a teenage boy on stage were a small minority.
Little is known, however, about the characteristics of the leading
apprentices in Shakespeare's company. It may perhaps be inferred
that one was a lot taller than the other, since Shakespeare often wrote
for a pair of female friends, one tall and fair, the other short and dark
(Helena and Hermia, Rosalind and Celia, Beatrice and Hero).

We know little about Shakespeare's own acting roles—an early
allusion indicates that he often took royal parts, and a venerable tradition gives him old Adam in *As You Like It* and the ghost of old King
Hamlet. Save for Burbage's lead roles and the generic part of the
clown, all such castings are mere speculation. We do not even know

for sure whether the original Falstaff was Will Kempe or another actor who specialized in comic roles, Thomas Pope.

Kempe left the company in early 1599. Tradition has it that he fell out with Shakespeare over the matter of excessive improvisation. He was replaced by Robert Armin, who was less of a clown and more of a cerebral wit: this explains the difference between such parts as Lancelet Gobbo and Dogberry, which were written for Kempe, and the more verbally sophisticated Feste and Lear's Fool, which were written for Armin.

One thing that is clear from surviving "plots" or storyboards of plays from the period is that a degree of doubling was necessary. *2 Henry VI* has over sixty speaking parts, but more than half of the characters only appear in a single scene and most scenes have only six to eight speakers. At a stretch, the play could be performed by thirteen actors. When Thomas Platter saw *Julius Caesar* at the Globe in 1599, he noted that there were about fifteen. Why doesn't Paris go to the Capulet ball in *Romeo and Juliet?* Perhaps because he was doubled with Mercutio, who does. In *The Winter's Tale*, Mamillius might have come back as Perdita and Antigonus been doubled by Camillo, making the partnership with Paulina at the end a very neat touch. Titania and Oberon are often played by the same pair as Hippolyta and Theseus, suggesting a symbolic matching of the rulers of the worlds of night and day, but it is questionable whether there would have been time for the necessary costume changes. As so often, one is left in a realm of tantalizing speculation.

THE KING'S MAN

On Queen Elizabeth's death in 1603, the new king, James I, who had held the Scottish throne as James VI since he had been an infant, immediately took the Lord Chamberlain's Men under his direct patronage. Henceforth they would be the King's Men, and for the rest of Shakespeare's career they were favored with far more court performances than any of their rivals. There even seem to have been rumors early in the reign that Shakespeare and Burbage were being considered for knighthoods, an unprecedented honor for mere actors—and one that in the event was not accorded to a member of the profession for nearly three hundred years, when the title was bestowed upon Henry Irving, the leading Shakespearean actor of Queen Victoria's reign.

Shakespeare's productivity rate slowed in the Jacobean years, not because of age or some personal trauma, but because there were frequent outbreaks of plague, causing the theaters to be closed for long periods. The King's Men were forced to spend many months on the road. Between November 1603 and 1608, they were to be found at various towns in the south and Midlands, though Shakespeare probably did not tour with them by this time. He had bought a large house back home in Stratford and was accumulating other property. He may indeed have stopped acting soon after the new king took the throne. With the London theaters closed so much of the time and a large repertoire on the stocks, Shakespeare seems to have focused his energies on writing a few long and complex tragedies that could have been played on demand at court: *Othello*, *King Lear*, *Antony and Cleopatra*, *Coriolanus*, and *Cymbeline* are among his longest and poetically grandest plays. *Macbeth* only survives in a shorter text, which shows signs of adaptation after Shakespeare's death. The bitterly satirical *Timon of Athens*, apparently a collaboration with Thomas Middleton that may have failed on the stage, also belongs to this period. In comedy, too, he wrote longer and morally darker works than in the Elizabethan period, pushing at the very bounds of the form in *Measure for Measure* and *All's Well That Ends Well*.

From 1608 onward, when the King's Men began occupying the indoor Blackfriars playhouse (as a winter house, meaning that they only used the outdoor Globe in summer?), Shakespeare turned to a more romantic style. His company had a great success with a revived and altered version of an old pastoral play called *Mucedorus*. It even featured a bear. The younger dramatist John Fletcher, meanwhile, sometimes working in collaboration with Francis Beaumont, was pioneering a new style of tragicomedy, a mix of romance and royalism laced with intrigue and pastoral excursions. Shakespeare experimented with this idiom in *Cymbeline* and it was presumably with his blessing that Fletcher eventually took over as the King's Men's company dramatist. The two writers apparently collaborated on three plays in the years 1612–14: a lost romance called *Cardenio* (based on the love-madness of a character in Cervantes' *Don Quixote*), *Henry VIII* (originally staged with the title "All Is True"), and *The Two Noble Kinsmen*, a dramatization of Chaucer's "Knight's Tale." These were written after Shakespeare's two final solo-authored plays, *The Winter's Tale*, a self-consciously old-fashioned work dramatizing the pastoral romance of his old enemy Robert Greene, and *The Tempest*, which at one and the same time drew together multiple theatrical traditions, diverse reading, and contemporary interest in the fate of a ship that had been wrecked on the way to the New World.

The collaborations with Fletcher suggest that Shakespeare's career ended with a slow fade rather than the sudden retirement supposed by the nineteenth-century Romantic critics who read Prospero's epilogue to *The Tempest* as Shakespeare's personal farewell to his art. In the last few years of his life Shakespeare certainly spent more of his time in Stratford-upon-Avon, where he became further involved in property dealing and litigation. But his London life also continued. In 1613 he made his first major London property purchase: a freehold house in the Blackfriars district, close to his company's indoor theater. *The Two Noble Kinsmen* may have been written as late as 1614, and Shakespeare was in London on business a little over a year before he died of an unknown cause at home in Stratford-upon-Avon in 1616, probably on his fifty-second birthday.

About half the sum of his works were published in his lifetime, in texts of variable quality. A few years after his death, his fellow actors began putting together an authorized edition of his complete *Comedies, Histories and Tragedies*. It appeared in 1623, in large "Folio" format. This collection of thirty-six plays gave Shakespeare his immortality. In the words of his fellow dramatist Ben Jonson, who contributed two poems of praise at the start of the Folio, the body of his work made him "a monument without a tomb":

And art alive still while thy book doth live
And we have wits to read and praise to give . . .
He was not of an age, but for all time!

SHAKESPEARE'S WORKS:
A CHRONOLOGY

1595–97	*Love's Labour's Won* (a lost play, unless the original title for another comedy)
1595–96	*A Midsummer Night's Dream*
1595–96	*The Tragedy of Romeo and Juliet*
1595–96	*King Richard the Second*
1595–97	*The Life and Death of King John* (possibly earlier)
1596–97	*The Merchant of Venice*
1596–97	*The First Part of Henry the Fourth*
1597–98	*The Second Part of Henry the Fourth*
1598	*Much Ado About Nothing*
1598–99	*The Passionate Pilgrim* (20 poems, some not by Shakespeare)
1599	*The Life of Henry the Fifth*
1599	"To the Queen" (epilogue for a court performance)
1599	*As You Like It*
1599	*The Tragedy of Julius Caesar*
1600–01	*The Tragedy of Hamlet, Prince of Denmark* (perhaps revising an earlier version)
1600–01	*The Merry Wives of Windsor* (perhaps revising version of 1597–99)
1601	"Let the Bird of Loudest Lay" (poem, known since 1807 as "The Phoenix and Turtle" [turtledove])
1601	*Twelfth Night, or What You Will*
1601–02	*The Tragedy of Troilus and Cressida*
1604	*The Tragedy of Othello, the Moor of Venice*
1604	*Measure for Measure*
1605	*All's Well That Ends Well*
1605	*The Life of Timon of Athens*, with Thomas Middleton
1605–06	*The Tragedy of King Lear*
1605–08	? contribution to *The Four Plays in One* (lost, except for *A Yorkshire Tragedy*, mostly by Thomas Middleton)

1606	*The Tragedy of Macbeth* (surviving text has additional scenes by Thomas Middleton)
1606–07	*The Tragedy of Antony and Cleopatra*
1608	*The Tragedy of Coriolanus*
1608	*Pericles, Prince of Tyre*, with George Wilkins
1610	*The Tragedy of Cymbeline*
1611	*The Winter's Tale*
1611	*The Tempest*
1612–13	*Cardenio*, with John Fletcher (survives only in later adaptation called *Double Falsehood* by Lewis Theobald)
1613	*Henry VIII (All Is True)*, with John Fletcher
1613–14	*The Two Noble Kinsmen*, with John Fletcher

CRITICAL APPROACHES

Adelman, Janet, *Blood Relations: Christian and Jew in The Merchant of Venice* (2008). Fascinating psycho-theological analysis.

Auden, W. H., "Brothers and Others," in *The Dyer's Hand* (1962). Pioneering account of the homoerotic element.

Chernaik, Warren, *William Shakespeare: The Merchant of Venice*, Writers and Their Work Series (2005). Useful introduction to text in conjunction with performance issues.

Coyle, Martin, ed., *The Merchant of Venice: William Shakespeare*, New Casebooks Series (1998). Diverse collection of influential, theoretically informed essays.

Edelman, Charles, "Which Is the Jew That Shakespeare Knew? Shylock on the Elizabethan Stage," *Shakespeare Survey*, 52 (1999), pp. 99–106. Excellent correction of many misapprehensions about the representation of Jews on the Shakespearean stage.

Gross, Kenneth, *Shakespeare Is Shylock* (2006). Challenging, provocative, sometimes personal account of Shylock's outsider status making him a kind of double for Shakespeare himself.

Holmer, Joan Ozark, *The Merchant of Venice: Choice, Hazard and Consequence* (1995). Focuses on play's genre, structure, and language.

Janik, Vicki K., *The Merchant of Venice: A Guide to the Play* (2003). Useful introductory guide with a wide range of material.

Kaplan, M. Lindsay, ed., *The Merchant of Venice: Texts and Contexts* (2002). Useful introductory guide.

Mahon, John W., and Ellen Macleod Mahon, eds., *The Merchant of Venice: New Critical Essays* (2002). Useful collection of essays covering a wide range of approaches from text to theory and performance.

McCullough, Christopher, *The Merchant of Venice: A Guide to the Text and Its Theatrical Life*, Shakespeare Handbooks Series (2005). Useful study guide covering text, history, and performance.

Nuttall, A. D., "*The Merchant of Venice*," in his *A New Mimesis: Shakespeare and the Representation of Reality* (1983). Has a brilliant feel for the realized texture of the world of the play.

Shapiro, James, *Shakespeare and the Jews* (1996). Fascinating, detailed historical account.

Wheeler, Thomas, ed., *The Merchant of Venice: Critical Essays* (1991). Useful collection of essays from Granville-Barker on text, to Hazlitt on Shylock, up to contemporary productions of the play.

Wilders, John, ed., *Shakespeare: The Merchant of Venice*, Casebook Series (1969). Useful selection of early criticism and significant twentieth-century essays up to 1960s.

Yaffe, Martin D., *Shylock and the Jewish Question* (1997). Jewish religious scholar, generally sympathetic to Shylock, reads play as a work of political philosophy.

THE PLAY IN PERFORMANCE

Barton, John, *Playing Shakespeare* (1984). Chapter 10, "Playing Shylock," in which David Suchet and Patrick Stewart explore their different approaches to the role.

Bonnell, Andrew G., *Shylock in Germany: Antisemitism and the German Theatre from the Enlightenment to the Nazis* (2008). Scrupulously detailed study.

Brockbank, Philip, ed., *Players of Shakespeare* (1985). Actors discuss their roles: Chapter 2, Patrick Stewart discusses Shylock; Chapter 3, Sinead Cusack on Portia.

Brooke, Michael, "The Merchant of Venice on Screen," www.screenonline.org.uk/tv/id/564652/index.html. Summary overview of film and television versions, with links to clips.

Bulman, James C., ed., *The Merchant of Venice*, Shakespeare in Performance (1991). Excellent detailed overview of stage history.

Edelman, Charles, ed., *The Merchant of Venice*, Shakespeare in Production (2002). Detailed historical overview and annotated text with stage directions from important historical productions.

Gilbert, Miriam, *The Merchant of Venice*, Shakespeare at Stratford (2002). Detailed account of RSC productions.

Gross, John, *Shylock: Four Hundred Years in the Life of a Legend* (1992). Exemplary detailed account of Shakespeare's Shylock, dramatic interpretations and the character's afterlife.

Jackson, Russell, and Robert Smallwood, eds., *Players of Shakespeare 2* (1988). Ian McDiarmid on playing Shylock.

Jackson, Russell, and Robert Smallwood, eds., *Players of Shakespeare 3*
(1993). Deborah Findlay on playing Portia; Gregory Doran on Solanio.

Jones, Maria, *Shakespeare's Culture in Modern Performance* (2003). Chapter 3
on *Merchant of Venice*, pp. 57–100: detailed discussion of the "alien" in
Merchant in Shakespeare's time and today in relation to historical and
modern performance.

Kennedy, Dennis, ed., *Foreign Shakespeares: Contemporary Performance* (1993).
With Avraham Oz's influential essay, "Transformations of Authenticity:
The Merchant of Venice in Israel," pp. 56–75, which discusses perfor-
mance and the play's legitimacy.

Lelyveld, Toby, *Shylock on the Stage* (1960). Useful historical overview with
chapter on theatrical greats such as Kean and Irving.

O'Connor, John, *Shakespearean Afterlives: Ten Characters with a Life of Their
Own* (2003). Chapter 4, "Shylock," pp. 95–148, detailed stage history
and discussion of place of play in contemporary culture.

Overton, Bill, *The Merchant of Venice: Text and Performance* (1987). Part 1 has
a useful introduction to play; Part 2 discusses play in performance from
1970 to 1984.

Parsons, Keith, and Pamela Mason, eds., *Shakespeare in Performance* (1995).
Useful introduction to play, pp. 136–142; lavishly illustrated.

Smallwood, Robert, ed., *Players of Shakespeare 4* (1998). Christopher Luscombe on playing Lancelet Gobbo in *Merchant* (and Moth in *Love's
Labour's Lost*), pp. 18–29.

AVAILABLE ON DVD

The Merchant of Venice, directed by John Sichel for television (1973, DVD
2007). Stars Laurence Olivier as Shylock; with its Edwardian setting
and middle-aged cast, the production seems pervaded by *fin de siècle*
languor.

The Merchant of Venice, directed by Jack Gold for BBC Shakespeare (1980,
DVD 2005). Warren Mitchell as Shylock is compelling.

The Merchant of Venice, directed by Trevor Nunn for BBC films (2001, DVD
2003). Royal National Theatre staging with Henry Goodman as Shylock (the production discussed in his interview, above).

The Merchant of Venice, directed by Michael Radford (2004, DVD 2005).
Filmed in Venice, starring Al Pacino as Shylock, Jeremy Irons as Antonio, Joseph Fiennes as Bassanio, and Lynn Collins as Portia.

REFERENCES

1. William Poel, *Shakespeare in the Theatre* (1913, reprinted 1968), p. 77.
2. John Doran, *Their Majesties' Servants*, Vol. II (1865), p. 187.
3. Quoted by Francis Gentleman, *Dramatic Censor* (1770, reprinted 1969), p. 292.
4. Toby Lelyveld, *Shylock on the Stage* (1961), p. 41.
5. *Chronicle*, 6 March 1816.
6. *Spectator*, 8 November 1879.
7. *Daily Herald*, 29 July 1932.
8. *The Times*, London, 13 December 1932.
9. Avraham Oz, "*The Merchant of Venice* in Israel," in *Foreign Shakespeare* (1993), p. 63.
10. Oz, "*The Merchant of Venice* in Israel," p. 69.
11. *National Review*, 15 September 1989.
12. *News Chronicle*, 16 March 1953.
13. *Evening Standard*, 13 April 1960.
14. *Evening News*, 13 April 1960.
15. Robert Speaight, *Shakespeare Quarterly*, 12, p. 428.
16. Jonathan Miller, *Subsequent Performances* (1986), pp. 155.
17. James C. Bulman, *The Merchant of Venice*, Shakespeare in Performance (1991), p. 96.
18. *Shakespeare Survey*, 53, p. 268.
19. Charles Edelman, ed., *The Merchant of Venice*, Shakespeare in Production (2002), p. 86.
20. David Calder, interviewed by Liz Gibly, *Plays International*, June 1993.
21. David Nathan, *Jewish Chronicle*, 26 December 1997.
22. Arnold Wesker, *Sunday Times*, 6 May 1993.
23. Tracey R. Rich, "Love and Brotherhood," *Judaism 101*, www.jewfaq.org/brother.htm (accessed 4 September 2006).
24. John O'Connor, *Shakespearean Afterlives* (2003).
25. Benedict Nightingale, *New Statesman*, 97, 2511, 4 May 1979.
26. Peter Holland, *English Shakespeares*, 1997.
27. O'Connor, *Shakespearean Afterlives*.

28. Heather Neill, interview with David Calder, *The Times*, London, 1 June 1993.
29. Patrick Stewart, "Shylock in *The Merchant of Venice*," in Philip Brockbank, ed., *Players of Shakespeare* (1985).
30. Nightingale, *New Statesman*, 97, 2511, 4 May 1979.
31. Bulman, *The Merchant of Venice*.
32. Raymond, *Theatre Week*, 5 September 1988.
33. Michael Billington, *Country Life*, 14 May 1987.
34. Christopher Edwards, *Spectator*, 9 May 1987.
35. Billington, *Country Life*, 14 May 1987.
36. Christopher Edwards, *Spectator*, 9 May 1987.
37. Deborah Findlay, "Portia," in Russell Jackson and Robert Smallwood, eds., *Players of Shakespeare 3* (1993).
38. Michael Coveney, *Financial Times*, 30 April 1987.
39. John Pitcher, *Times Literary Supplement*, 15 May 1987.
40. Penny Gay, "Portia Performs: Playing the Role in the Twentieth-Century English Theatre," in John W. Mahon and Ellen Macleod Mahon, eds., *The Merchant of Venice: New Critical Essays* (2002).
41. David Suchet on playing Shylock, in Judith Cook, *Shakespeare's Players* (1983).
42. Patrick Stewart on Playing Shylock, in John Barton, *Playing Shakespeare* (1984).
43. O'Connor, *Shakespearean Afterlives*.
44. O'Connor, *Shakespearean Afterlives*.
45. O'Connor, *Shakespearean Afterlives*.
46. David Calder on playing Shylock, *The Merchant of Venice*, RSC Education Pack, 1993.
47. Alastair Macaulay, *Financial Times*, 5 June 1993.
48. Charles Spencer, *Daily Telegraph*, 7 May 1993.
49. Sinead Cusack, "Portia in *The Merchant of Venice*," in Philip Brockbank, ed., *Players of Shakespeare* (1985).
50. Michael Coveney, *Financial Times*, 22 April 1981.
51. B. A. Young, *Financial Times*, 17 April 1965.
52. James Shaw, "The Merchant of Venice," in Keith Parsons and Pamela Mason, eds., *Shakespeare in Performance* (1995).
53. Michael Billington, *Guardian*, 1 May 1987.
54. Irving Wardle, *The Times*, London, 1 April 1971.
55. Shaw, "The Merchant of Venice."
56. Findlay, "Portia."

57. Pitcher, *Times Literary Supplement*, 15 May 1987.
58. Sinead Cusack, "Portia in *The Merchant of Venice*."
59. Irving Wardle, *The Times*, 22 April 1981.
60. Michael Billington, *Guardian*, 5 June 1993.
61. John Peter, *Sunday Times*, 13 June 1993.
62. David Thacker, *The Merchant of Venice*, RSC Education Pack, 1993.
63. Thacker, *The Merchant of Venice*.

ACKNOWLEDGMENTS AND PICTURE CREDITS

Preparation of "*The Merchant of Venice* in Performance" was assisted by a generous grant from the CAPITAL Centre (Creativity and Performance in Teaching and Learning) of the University of Warwick for research in the RSC archive at the Shakespeare Birthplace Trust. The Arts and Humanities Research Council (AHRC) funded a term's research leave that enabled Jonathan Bate to work on "The Director's Cut."

Picture research by Michelle Morton. Grateful acknowledgment is made to the Shakespeare Birthplace Trust for assistance with reproduction fees and picture research (special thanks to Helen Hargest).

Images of RSC productions are supplied by the Shakespeare Centre Library and Archive, Stratford-upon-Avon. This library, maintained by the Shakespeare Birthplace Trust, holds the most important collection of Shakespeare material in the UK, including the Royal Shakespeare Company's official archive. It is open to the public free of charge.

For more information see www.shakespeare.org.uk.

1. Drinkwater Meadows as Old Gobbo (1858). Reproduced by kind permission of the Shakespeare Birthplace Trust
2. Directed by Denis Carey (1953). Angus McBean © Royal Shakespeare Company
3. Directed by John Barton (1978). Joe Cocks Studio Collection © Shakespeare Birthplace Trust
4. Directed by Gregory Doran (1997). Malcolm Davies © Shakespeare Birthplace Trust
5. Directed by David Thacker (1993). Malcolm Davies © Shakespeare Birthplace Trust
6. Directed by Darko Tresnjak (2007). © Donald Cooper/photostage.co.uk

MODERN LIBRARY IS ONLINE AT WWW.MODERNLIBRARY.COM

MODERN LIBRARY ONLINE IS YOUR GUIDE
TO CLASSIC LITERATURE ON THE WEB

THE MODERN LIBRARY E-NEWSLETTER

Our free e-mail newsletter is sent to subscribers, and features sample chapters, interviews with and essays by our authors, upcoming books, special promotions, announcements, and news. To subscribe to the Modern Library e-newsletter, visit **www.modernlibrary.com**

THE MODERN LIBRARY WEBSITE

Check out the Modern Library website at
www.modernlibrary.com for:

- The Modern Library e-newsletter
- A list of our current and upcoming titles and series
- Reading Group Guides and exclusive author spotlights
- Special features with information on the classics and other paperback series
- Excerpts from new releases and other titles
- A list of our e-books and information on where to buy them
- The Modern Library Editorial Board's 100 Best Novels and 100 Best Nonfiction Books of the Twentieth Century written in the English language
- News and announcements

Questions? E-mail us at **modernlibrary@randomhouse.com**.
For questions about examination or desk copies, please visit
the Random House Academic Resources site at
www.randomhouse.com/academic